Cooking with Bernard

Cooking with Bernard

BY BERNARD
with Patricia Linden

Grosset & Dunlap
A Filmways Company
Publishers New York

Published simultaneously in Canada
Library of Congress catalog card number: 74-27947
ISBN: 0-448-11927-7

First printing
Printed in the United States of America

Contents

Editor's Note

Bernard is the dynamic, young, Paris-born master chef whose displays of culinary prowess on TV and radio, in newspapers, cooking schools and restaurants have won the applause of professionals and the addictive devotion of home cooks. Everyone, particularly women, responds to his enthusiasm and charm. And he exudes a confidence that is contagious.

But it is experience and expertise that count in a cookbook. Bernard's training in classic French cuisine and his roster of other credentials, including that of professional restaurant chef, make his intriguing gastronomic prose a book of undeniable value to kitchen novices and old pros alike.

Bernard began training as a chef's apprentice in Paris, during his teen years; then went to college and majored in economics. This two-edged education in creativity and pragmatism provided an approach to cooking that is both thoroughly realistic and inventive. Based on their supply and demand, their chemistry and interactions, the beguiling and varied uses of foods are presented here in singularly clear and authoritative fashion.

After serving three years in Algeria as a Lieutenant in France's army, Bernard trained additionally as *sous-chef* in Paris, Vienna and Berlin. Before long, his earthy capitalistic drive brought him to the United States, where he hit New York like Charles Boyer in a three-hankie movie: with little money in his pocket and not a speck of English on his tongue. He made friends and professional contacts quickly, soon became intimately involved with the restaurant scene, and accepted a position as chef in Boston. Ambitious, keenly intelligent, intensely motivated, and impatient with less than perfection, Bernard then opened his own restaurant, Le Ticoz, in Rhode Island, where no French restaurant had ever before existed. Laudatory reviews by *The New York Times, Ladies' Home Journal,*

Redbook and other publications cascaded in. The gastronomic snowball grew. Cooking schools, newspaper columns, and television series followed; and Bernard's distinctive flair and engaging style blossomed. Audiences recognized instantly that behind the casual, larky approach was the firmness of a meticulous man who could imbue the facts of cooking with the excitement of fireworks.

What stuns viewers of his TV show, *Cooking with Bernard,* is his utter organization. "But that is what makes cooking easy," he explains. "The way to enjoy cooking is to start by putting everything out that you are going to use, so you don't have to keep stopping and starting and rethinking what you are doing. And to keep everything neat and clean as you go along. Orderliness not only makes the kitchen more pleasant while you are preparing a meal, it reduces the business of cleaning up afterward to nearly nothing."

The other most frequently received response to the TV series has to do with Bernard's obvious enjoyment of what he is doing. "I love to eat and I'm sure of what I am doing. Who wouldn't enjoy such a situation? Things go wrong, sure. But I fix the disasters as I go along, just the way I do — anyone does — in the kitchen at home. On one show the bottom fell off a cake just as I was about to serve it. Everybody who watched me that day learned how to patch together a Schwarzwald torte. Some other time, I might open a jar whose contents turn out to be rancid. Quickly, I'd have to make a substitution, and the audience would learn that, if you relax and are not tense about cooking, you will not fail."

Lifesaving tricks and informally delivered information are bonuses Bernard lavishes on his viewers, and on readers of this book. At the heart of everything, though, is the philosophy that underlies all of Bernard's cooking. It revolves around these three basics: economy, availability, and practicality. Throughout the book you will see these elements translated into how to avoid waste, how to take advantage of everyday ingredients, and how to make cooking a simple, pleasant experience. In other words, how to live high off the hog — economically.

So, welcome to sybaritic heaven. Most of the recipes in this book have been demonstrated on television. Many are classic French recipes simplified for today's world. Others are the original creations of a professional chef whose zest for life, people and gastronomy is matched by his solid understanding of everyday foods — and of you.

Preface

I hate to see a person suffer.

That is why I made this book for you. So you won't be intimidated about cooking. Or spend hours in the kitchen. Or waste money at being a failure. Confidence in your own ability as a cook will increase when you make use of the recipes and advice that will let you relax and enjoy yourself. And be a success.

I am a professional chef and I cook for a living. Whether you cook three meals a day, every day, for a family, or cook dinners just for yourself, you share the same concerns. If you are clever, you run your kitchen just like a business, according to the three things all my recipes are based on: economy, practicality, and availability. Boiled down, that means using and making the most of the everyday ingredients that are in your nearby store, in a way that makes every meal memorable but not extravagant.

As with everything tasteful in life — art, clothing, food — it is simplicity that makes for excellence. So it is fortunate that gastronomy, one of life's grand passions, has an enormous advantage over other passions: it can be made simple and logical. With culinary common sense as your guide, there is nothing at all complicated about creating superb meals.

Practice is all it takes to develop your talent and confidence as a cook. After you have mastered a few basic techniques, which are simpler than you think, you will be able to experiment, take a chance, be inventive. You'll know how to improvise and learn to make a variety of things from the same foods, instead of eating the same dish over and over. No more boredom; only applause! Cook as I do, French but simple, and you'll soon be able to look at long recipes that have bewildering names and rigid instructions and say, "Oh *that.* I know how it should be. I'll just skip right along, using this recipe as an idea, not a blueprint. I'll leave out the pretentious, fancy ingredients that are really no improvement. I'll make this *boeuf bourguignon* with, say, tarragon instead of thyme because experience tells me I prefer it that way. And I don't need truffles; a bit of cognac will do the trick." You see how easy it is to create your own recipes just by combining what you learn here with other ideas that you read or dream up?

Follow me, and I promise you a marriage with cooking that is all bliss and pleasure. And fun, besides.

Bernard

Cooking with Bernard

1
Hors d'Oeuvres

IF YOU STOP to think about it, certain American eating habits are really slightly crazy. You invite guests to dinner; then, before they can sit down to enjoy the feast you've so carefully prepared, you fill their stomachs with cheese curls, crackers, potato chips, clam dips, livers curled inside bacon, and pigs wrapped in blankets. To complete the onslaught, you drown their brains in torrents of strong liquor. Before they can get to the table, you have utterly ruined their ability to appreciate and remember your meal. Madness!

Here is the routine I prefer when I invite guests to dinner. First, I never serve hors d'oeuvres. In my opinion, hors d'oeuvres belong at hors d'oeuvres-and-drink parties, period. In this chapter, I will give you some of my best recipes for hors d'oeuvres that are beguilingly delicious, ravishingly attractive, easily prepared, and memorable. But please, use them *instead of*, not before, a magnificent dinner.

Now you ask, what do I serve before a dinner? The answer lies in simplicity and logic. Say my guests arrive at seven o'clock, hungry for an evening of food and pleasure. While dinner is reaching its ultimate splendor, I like to give them a half-hour or so to relax, to exchange conversations, and intensify their passions for the main event. So I serve them an apéritif — usually a fortified wine like Campari, Dubonnet or Raphaël, something like that — with a lemon twist or ice cubes if they wish. I do not ask, "What do you want to drink?" I simply offer a lightly alcoholic apéritif and with it some artfully arranged *crudités*, and possibly a very, very light dip. *Crudités* are enticingly crisp, alluringly colorful raw vegetables, such as zucchini strips, green beans, green or red pepper rings, cauliflowerets, celery or carrot sticks. Now I have given my hungry guests just enough to hold them till dinner, and a little condiment for the imagination besides. But not such a drenching that they cannot revel in the meal I have so enthusiastically prepared for them.

Hors d'oeuvres are one unit of a menu, the little flag that signifies the nature of the main course to follow. So you must be careful that what you plan is not so heavy that it will overfill your guests' stomachs, that it is harmonious with the main course, and that it is presented so as to tantalize the appetite. This is no time to try to impress people with copious quantities; you'll only daunt them. Put just enough food on their plates so they *could* have one more bite . . . but that bite is not there. Tease, don't stagger; that is my philosophy. Good things, when brief, are twice as good!

PÂTÉS

You know what a pâté is: a paste of ground meat mixed with fat, seasonings, and perhaps brandy or wine. And you know its relatives. A *pâté en croûte* is pâté in a crust. A *terrine* is a pâté served cold in its own baking dish, whence cometh the name, *terrine.* A *galantine* is meat or fish that has been poached in stock and is served chilled in its own jelly. A *ballotine* is pâté combined with vegetables and herbs, then tied in the shape of a bundle and cooked in stock. (The word *ballotine* means "little bundle.") Some of these epicurean gems are served hot, some cold; all are superbly flavorsome, intriguing and — perhaps this will surprise you — remarkably practical and economical. Especially when you compile them yourself instead of overpaying for the so-called prepared appetizers and hors d'oeuvres that you buy in tins or frozen-food packages.

Some people think pâté is made only from liver. This is not true, although many non-liver pâtés do contain some amount of liver as a blender, because it creates a silken-smooth paste. To be sure, liver all by itself makes a wantonly rich concoction. But you can also use it as the emollient for chicken, duck, pork, or practically anything. You can buy the cheaper cuts of meat that are not so good for roasting — maybe they have too much bone or fat — and make *rillettes,* for example. That is cooked pork blended afterward with some of the fat, seasoned, and refrigerated — and the tastiest thing you can imagine. When you are hungry you just take a piece of good French bread, slap on the *rillettes,* and there you have a delectable treat, for only a few cents.

A good, imaginative, homemade pâté of any type is a rhapsodic thing to have on hand, for lunch, or snacks, or midnight dazzlement. I advise you to always make a lot at one time, because it keeps for a whole month in the refrigerator and you can have it ready to provide instant joy.

Be Spanish: pronounce the "e" on the end: Gwah-kah-*moe*-lay. Be hospitable: serve the guacamole as hors d'oeuvres, with tiny tacos, crackers, or slices of cucumber. Be modest: say your thank you's quietly when everybody raves about the disarming, unprosaic, somewhat flashy dish you have presented. *You* know you deserve the applause!

GUACAMOLE

2 ripe avocados
2 tomatoes, peeled and chopped
1 small green tomato, peeled and chopped
1 onion, minced
Juice of 3 lemons
Juice of 3 limes
⅛ teaspoon chili powder
⅛ teaspoon nutmeg
1 teaspoon salt
⅛ teaspoon pepper

Cut the avocadoes in half, remove the pits, peel the fruit and mash the pulp thoroughly in a bowl. Add all the remaining ingredients and mix them very thoroughly. Chill the dip for about 2 hours. Serve it in a glass bowl or on a bed of lettuce, together with crackers for dipping.

"Stuffed mushrooms" sounds to me like vegetables that have gorged themselves. But Champignons Farcis are hors d'oeuvres that could have been invented only by the French. Just read the ingredients and you will know what makes them beautiful, delectable, and inspired.

CHAMPIGNONS FARCIS
(Stuffed Mushrooms)

2 dozen large mushrooms
Juice of 1 lemon
½ pound sausage meat
1 tablespoon chopped parsley
2 cloves garlic, minced
⅛ teaspoon monosodium glutamate
⅛ teaspoon thyme
1 ounce brandy
¼ cup fine, dry bread crumbs
½ teaspoon salt
2 tablespoons grated Parmesan cheese

Wipe off the mushrooms with a damp cloth and remove the stems. (Refrigerate the stems until you need them for soup or another dish.) Arrange the mushroom caps in a large, shallow buttered pan. Sprinkle them with lemon juice and set them aside.

In a skillet, cook the sausage meat slowly, stirring it often. Add the parsley, garlic, monosodium glutamate, thyme and brandy. Stir and continue cooking for another 15 minutes. Remove the skillet from the heat; stir in the bread crumbs and salt.

Stuff each mushroom cap with the sausage mixture and sprinkle the tops with grated cheese. Bake the stuffed mushrooms in a 375°F. oven for about 20 minutes, or until they are thoroughly hot and lightly browned.

This is a bit of Oriental intrigue. Very light, very interesting, very mysterious. Everybody always savors it, smacks their lips a little, smiles scrutably, and asks, "What's in it?" I never tell; who would believe that anything so excellent could be so simple?

PEKING MARINATED MUSHROOMS

1 pound small mushrooms
½ cup minced onion
1 tablespoon sugar
2 tablespoons soy sauce
3 tablespoons dry sherry
4 tablespoons wine vinegar
½ teaspoon salt
⅛ teaspoon monosodium glutamate
½ teaspoon grated ginger root

Wipe off the mushrooms well with a damp cloth and remove the stems. (Refrigerate the stems until you need them for soup or another dish.)

Combine all the remaining ingredients in a saucepan and bring them to a boil. Let the mixture simmer a few minutes. Put the mushroom caps into a bowl, pour the simmered marinade over the mushrooms and mix gently. Refrigerate for several hours. Drain off the marinade and serve the mushrooms (garnished with scallion tops, if desired).

Here's a lyrical prelude to dinner: bite-size morsels of chicken livers cloaked in a rich, velvety sauce that is flecked with zesty bits of bacon. All you need is a fork and a discerning appetite.

CHICKEN LIVERS NAPOLÉON

FOR DREDGING:
½ cup flour
1 teaspoon salt
½ teaspoon monosodium glutamate
½ teaspoon pepper
1 tablespoon chopped parsley
½ teaspoon garlic powder
⅛ teaspoon thyme

MAIN INGREDIENTS:
1 pound chicken livers
4 strips bacon
2 shallots, minced
¼ cup cognac
½ pound mushrooms, sliced
2 teaspoons flour
½ cup heavy cream
1 tablespoon ketchup
¼ cup port wine

Combine the flour, salt, monosodium glutamate, pepper, parsley, garlic powder, and thyme. Blend well. Wash and dry the chicken livers and cut them into bite-size pieces. Dredge the livers thoroughly in the flour mixture.

Cook the bacon in a skillet until it is golden and crisp. Remove the bacon to paper toweling. Reserve about 3 tablespoons of the bacon fat in the pan; discard the rest. Sauté the chicken livers in the bacon fat until they are nicely browned on all sides. Add the shallots and stir; then pour in the cognac and ignite it. When the flame dies down, remove the chicken livers to a dish and keep them warm in a low oven.

Add the mushrooms to the pan and sauté them quickly until they are just tender. Sprinkle in the 2 teaspoons of flour and stir until smooth. Stir in the cream and cook over low heat until the resulting sauce is smooth and thickened. Return the chicken livers to the pan; crumble and add the bacon; add the ketchup, wine and parsley. Stir a few minutes over heat, then serve in small individual dishes.

CHICKEN LIVERS ANANAS

12 chicken-liver halves
Salt and pepper to taste
12 half-strips of bacon
6 water chestnuts, cut in half
12 pineapple chunks
Polynesian Marinade (page 9)

Place a chicken liver half, sprinkled with salt and pepper, on a piece of bacon. Place half a water chestnut on the liver. Wrap the bacon around firmly and secure it with a small skewer or wooden pick. Spear a pineapple chunk on the skewer. Marinate for 2 or 3 hours.

Remove the skewered livers from the marinade and put them in a shallow pan. Bake in a 350°F. oven for 20 minutes, brushing the liver once or twice with the remaining marinade. Put the skewers under the broiler for a minute or two to crisp the bacon. Serve with Plum Brandy Sauce for dipping (page 212).

POLYNESIAN MARINADE

- ½ *cup soy sauce*
- ½ *cup crushed pineapple, undrained*
- ¼ *cup honey*
- ¼ *cup sherry*
- 4 *tablespoons brown sugar*
- 2 *tablespoons grated ginger root*
- 2 *tablespoons sesame oil*
- 1 *teaspoon monosodium glutamate*
- 1 *teaspoon dry mustard*
- 2 *tablespoons wine vinegar*
- 1 *tablespoon lemon juice*
- 1 *tablespoon minced garlic*

Mix all the ingredients together in a glass or ceramic bowl. Place the food to be marinated in the same bowl; or place the food in a shallow, glass dish and pour the marinade over it. Baste or turn the food in the marinade from time to time.

In Eastern Europe, this dish is served as an appetizer. You may, at times, see fit to serve it as a salad. In fact, it is robust enough to be admirable as an entrée.

HERRING À LA RUSSE

(Estonian Vinaigrette)
with Herring and Beets)

DRESSING:

- *3 tablespoons dry mustard*
- *1½ teaspoons sugar*
- *2 tablespoons warm water*
- *1 cup sour cream*

Mix the mustard and sugar with the warm water. Then add the mixture to the sour cream. Refrigerate the dressing until you are ready to use it for the salad.

SALAD:

- *1 hard-cooked egg, chopped fine*
- *1 small can diced beets*
- *1 pound boiled potatoes, peeled and diced*
- *½ pound dill pickles, cut lengthwise, then crosswise into bits*
- *1 filet of pickled herring, drained and cut into ¼-inch pieces*
- *½ pound of boiled ham, cut in ½-inch dices*
- *1 large, red apple, cored, peeled and cut into ¼-inch dices*
- *2 hard-cooked eggs, quartered*
- *8 lettuce leaves for decoration*

In a large bowl, combine all the salad ingredients. Add the sour cream dressing and toss lightly but thoroughly until all the salad ingredients are moistened with the dressing. Decorate with the lettuce leaves and the quartered, hard-boiled eggs.

This recipe will produce about four and one-half pounds of a terrine that is the essence of opulence, but will cost very little. As if that weren't wonderful enough, the terrine will keep in the refrigerator for a couple of weeks after it is cooked — providing you with a spectacular stream of appetizers, cold-cuts and sandwich makings, and perhaps establishing your reputation as an epicurean cook!

TERRINE DE CAMPAGNE

(Country-Style Terrine)

2½ pounds trimmed, lean pork, cut in ¼-inch pieces
½ pound veal, cut in ¼-inch strips
¼ pound chicken livers
1 celery stalk, sliced
1 carrot, sliced
1 onion, quartered
2 bay leaves
¼ teaspoon thyme
½ teaspoon salt
¼ teaspoon pepper
¼ cup white wine
½ pound salt pork, thin sliced (for lining the mold)

Combine all the ingredients except the salt pork, mixing them very well. Pack the mixture into a 3-inch high dish or mold, cover the dish with plastic wrap, and refrigerate it for 2 days. Mix once each day.

On the second day, take out the vegetables and veal strips; reserve them. Grind the pork and chicken livers (as for hamburger); then mix the ground meat with the following:

1 egg, raw
1 teaspoon salt
2 teaspoons flour
⅛ teaspoon allspice
¼ teaspoon white pepper
¼ teaspoon monosodium glutamate

Line a mold with the salt pork slices. Fill about one-quarter of the mold with the ground meat; then add half the reserved veal strips. Add another layer of ground meat, cover with the remaining veal strips, finish with the remainder of the ground meat. Cover the top with a few strips of salt pork. Set the mold into a larger pan;

then pour enough water into the outside pan so it surrounds the mold to a depth of about 2 inches. Place the pans in a 350°F oven for 2 hours.

While the pâté is in the oven, use the reserved vegetables to make a stock. Place them in the pan with:

1 quart water
2 envelopes plain gelatin

Bring the liquid to a boil, and let the stock cook until the volume is reduced to half.

When the pâté is baked, pour off the juices and fat from the mold. Replace this with the vegetable stock. After the mold has cooled for 15 or 20 minutes, put a piece of parchment paper on top and weight it down just enough to compress the pâté slightly. Remove the weight and refrigerate the terrine for 24 hours before using.

PÂTÉ

1½ pounds pork shoulder
¾ pound pork fat
¼ pound of pork liver
1 teaspoon pepper
⅛ teaspoon allspice
1 teaspoon sugar
½ teaspoon potassium nitrate
⅛ teaspoon nutmeg
1 tablespoon gelatin
1 onion, finely chopped
4 shallots, finely chopped
2 oz. Pernod
2 teaspoons salt
2 eggs
½ cup milk

First poach the pork fat in scalding water for about 4 minutes; drain and let cool for about 5 minutes. Then put the coarse blade of the meat grinder on and grind the pork fat through. Change blade to medium and grind the pork shoulder and pork liver. Put the fat and the meat in a large bowl with all the spices and gelatin; mix well together. Add milk and eggs. Blend again and place mixture in a terrine. Place the terrine in a baking pan with water in the bottom of it. Bake at 350°F for about 2 hours. When done, remove the terrine from the baking pan and place a half-pound weight on top of the paté until cold.

Imagine that you are in Russia in the days when royalty reigned. Outside, a whirling snowstorm swathes your country estate in blankets of white. Inside, the leaping flames in the huge fireplace and an ermine-trimmed wrap keep you warm. A footman knocks discreetly at your salon door and announces: "Dinner is served." You move languidly to the table and permit the servants to lay before you piping-hot, redolent portions of Pirozhki. Suddenly your aristocratic grace and dignity are forgotten as you lustily indulge your appetite for this robust, Rabelaisian dish.

If, like me, you do not happen to be Russian royalty and must make your own Pirozhki, I advise you to prepare two dozen or more of these little, meat-filled pastries at a time. That way, you can pop some, unbaked, into the freezer, all ready to whip out and bake for another meal. The pastries make superbly savory hors d'oeuvres and are a companionably rousing appetizer when served before an entrée such as Hungarian goulash, Beef Stroganoff (page 58), or German sauerkraut. They are also maddeningly inviting alongside a bowl of rich, steaming soup.

PIROZHKI

(Small Pastries Filled with Meat)

MAKES 2 DOZEN

- 4 *tablespoons butter*
- 3 *cups finely chopped onions*
- 1½ *pounds lean, ground beef*
- 3 *hard-cooked eggs, finely chopped*
- 2 *tablespoons finely cut dill leaves*
- 2 *teaspoons salt*
- ½ *teaspoon freshly ground pepper*
- 1 *8 oz. package frozen patty shells or Puff-pastry dough from supermarket freezer*

Over high heat, melt the butter in a heavy 10- to 12-inch skillet. Add the chopped onions. Stirring occasionally, cook them over moderate heat for 8 to 10 minutes or until they are soft but not brown. Stir in the beef, mashing the meat with a fork to break up any lumps. Cook until no trace of pink remains. Take the pan off the heat and add the chopped eggs and seasonings.

Preheat the oven to 400°F. On a lightly floured surface, roll the pastry dough into a large circle about ⅛-inch thick. From this large circle, cut out 2 dozen small circles of dough, each 3 to 3½ inches in diameter. Drop 2 tablespoons of the filling into the center of each round and flatten the filling slightly. Fold the dough around the filling. Place the pirozhkis side by side on a baking sheet. Bake them for 30 minutes or until they are golden brown.

You can use either quahogs or cherrystone clams for this exhilarating recipe, and the results will be equally tangy and succulent. Make as many as you need, to serve as hot hors d'oeuvres, an appetizer or a main dish.

BAKED STUFFED QUAHOGS

1 small onion, chopped fine
Juice of one lime
Salt and pepper to taste
½ clove garlic, mashed
1 pint shucked quahogs, chopped coarsely
About 12 clean quahog shells
Fine, dry bread crumbs
Butter

Mix together the onion, lime juice, salt, pepper, garlic and chopped quahogs. Spoon the mixture into the shells. Sprinkle the tops lightly with bread crumbs, then dot each stuffed shell with a sliver of butter. Set them over coals on a barbecue grill and let them bake for 10 to 12 minutes, until they are thoroughly hot and lightly browned. Or you may bake the stuffed shells in an oven at 400°F. until the tops are lightly browned.

CLAMS CASINO

2 dozen opened littleneck clams, on the half shell
2 tablespoons butter
1 small onion, finely chopped
½ green pepper, seeded and finely chopped
½ red pepper, seeded and finely chopped
2 shallots, finely minced
¼ teaspoon salt
4 slices bacon

Arrange the clams on a baking sheet. Melt the butter in a skillet. Add the onion, the green and red peppers, and sauté for 3 or 4 minutes. Remove the pan from the heat and stir in the shallots and salt. Divide the sautéed mixture, placing an equal amount on top of each clam. Cut the bacon strips in pieces about 1-inch square. Top each stuffed clam with a piece of bacon. Place the baking sheet under the broiler for 3 or 4 minutes, or until the bacon is crisp and the clams are thoroughly heated. Serve at once.

SCAMPI PORTOFINO

MAKES 4 SERVINGS

16 large shrimp
1 cup milk
Olive oil
½ cup flour
1 teaspoon salt
1 tablespoon butter
2 cloves garlic, chopped
1 shallot, chopped
1 cup dry white wine
4 tablespoons soft butter
2 tablespoons chopped parsley
4 lemon wedges

Shell the shrimp, leaving the tail portion of each shell intact. Cut each shrimp from the inside almost to the back, to butterfly them. Remove the veins. Put the shrimp in a bowl, cover them with milk and let them stand for 10 minutes.

In a deep skillet, heat about 1 inch of olive oil to 350°F. Remove the shrimp from the milk and drain them on paper toweling. Mix the flour with the salt and pepper and dredge the shrimp. Fry the shrimp (about four at a time) in the hot oil for about 2 minutes, or until they are nicely browned but not overcooked. Remove the shrimp as they are done and drain them on paper toweling. Keep them warm in a slow oven while the sauce is prepared.

In another skillet, melt the tablespoon of butter. Add the garlic and shallot and sauté until golden. Add the wine and bring the mixture to a boil. Let it simmer for about 2 minutes, then add all the shrimp and the soft butter. Stir carefully until the sauce turns just creamy. Remove it from the heat immediately. Divide the shrimp into equal portions and arrange them on individual, heated serving dishes. Divide the sauce equally and cloak the shrimp. Sprinkle with parsley and serve promptly, with lemon wedges as a garnish.

QUICHE

Here is one of those delectable gems that is ravishingly impressive whether it is served as a main course at lunch or supper, or (in smaller portions) as an appetizer before the entrée, or (baked in tiny individual shells) as party hors d'oeuvres. Basically, a quiche is a pastry shell filled with an egg-and-cream custard. The admirable quality is that you can create a variety of different quiches just by adding different things to the custard — such as morsels of seafood, piquant meat, vegetables, or any of the variations I give you here. Be blithe about your quiches; inventiveness only improves them. So does the accompaniment of a glass of white burgundy wine.

QUICHE DOUGH

2 cups flour
1½ sticks soft butter (6 ounces)
½ teaspoon salt
¼ cup ice water

This recipe will make enough dough for two 10-inch quiche shells. Measure the flour onto a board. With your hands, mix in the butter and salt very thoroughly. Work in the ice water, again mixing very well. Divide the dough into two portions and form each into a ball.

Sprinkle the board very well with flour. Roll out each ball of dough, separately, in a large circle about ⅛-inch thick. For ease in placing each circle of dough in its pie plate, roll it up on your rolling pin, lift and place it on the edge of the pie plate. Unroll carefully so the dough slips into the plate. Fit the dough in properly, trim any excess, and form pinched edges around the top. The shell is now ready for filling.

ONION FILLING FOR QUICHE

MAKES TWO 10-INCH PIES

1 cup thinly sliced onions
2 tablespoons butter
1 teaspoon dry mustard
Salt and pepper to taste
1 tablespoon flour
1 cup heavy cream
1 cup light cream
4 eggs, beaten
1 teaspoon salt
½ teaspoon nutmeg, freshly grated if possible
½ teaspoon white pepper
½ cup grated Swiss cheese (optional)

Preheat the oven to 375°F. Meanwhile, sauté the onions in the butter until tender. Add the dry mustard, the salt and pepper, the tablespoon of flour. Mix together well.

Heat both creams in a saucepan, but do not boil them. Take the liquid off the heat and mix in the beaten eggs. Add the rest of the seasonings to this custard mixture and blend together.

Mix together the sautéed onions and grated cheese and spread this over the bottom of the prepared pie shell. Pour the custard over all.

When the quiche is ready to bake, turn the oven down to 350°F. Bake for approximately 20 minutes, or until a knife inserted in the quiche comes out clean. Allow the quiche to cool slightly before cutting it into serving portions.

Here's a sneaky way to get a good green vegetable into those spinach-haters of yours, and make them love it! The sweet pungency of garlic gives spinach a *je ne sais quoi* that is irresistibly tasty.

SPINACH FILLING FOR QUICHE

MAKES TWO 10-INCH PIES

- *1 pound fresh spinach*
- *1 cup heavy cream*
- *1 cup light cream*
- *4 eggs, beaten*
- *1 teaspoon salt*
- *⅛ teaspoon nutmeg, freshly grated if possible*
- *½ teaspoon white pepper*
- *½ teaspoon cayenne pepper*
- *1 tablespoon flour*
- *½ cup grated Swiss cheese (optional)*
- *½ garlic clove, chopped fine*

Preheat oven to 375°F. Slightly cook the spinach by dropping it into boiling water and taking it right out. Drain the spinach, chop it coarsely and squeeze all the water out.

Heat both creams, but do not boil them. Mix in the beaten eggs. Add the salt, nutmeg, peppers, and flour and blend together for the custard.

Mix together the cooked spinach, the grated cheese, and the garlic, and spread the mix over the bottom of the prepared pie shell. Pour the custard over all.

Turn the oven down to 350°F. and bake the quiche for approximately 20 minutes, or until a knife inserted in the quiche comes out clean. Allow the quiche to cool slightly before cutting it into serving portions.

SEAFOOD FILLING FOR QUICHE

MAKES TWO 10-INCH PIES

- *1 shallot, chopped fine*
- *1 tablespoon butter*
- *½ cup grated Swiss cheese*
- *1 cup heavy cream*

½ cup cooked scallops
½ cup cooked shrimp
Salt and pepper to taste
¼ cup raw mushrooms, sliced
1 tablespoon dry white wine
⅛ teaspoon cayenne pepper
1 teaspoon finely chopped parsley
1 cup light cream
4 eggs, beaten
1 teaspoon salt
⅛ teaspoon nutmeg
½ teaspoon of white pepper
1 tablespoon flour (optional, used to make the custard firmer)

Preheat the oven to 375°F. Sauté the shallot in butter; then add the scallops and shrimp. Mix together; add salt and pepper to taste. Then add the mushrooms and wine and let cook for 2 minutes. Add the parsley and stir together well. Spread the mixture over the bottom of the quiche shell and sprinkle the grated cheese on top.

Heat both creams, but do not boil them. Beat the eggs thoroughly and mix them together with cream. Add the rest of the seasonings and the flour, and blend together. Pour the custard over the seafood mixture.

Turn the oven down to 350°F. and bake the quiche for approximately 20 minutes, or until a knife inserted in the quiche comes out clean. Allow the quiche to cool slightly before cutting it into portions.

When you're serving a light lunch or supper and you feel your entrée is not quite filling or quite dressy enough, trust this appetizer recipe to save the day. The ham, port wine, and peaches provide a masterly combination of flavors, and the dish is as pretty to see as it is heavenly to eat.

MOUSSE OF HAM GEORGIA

MAKES 6 SERVINGS

1 pound boiled ham
⅓ cup mayonnaise
⅛ teaspoon cayenne pepper
1 teaspoon salt
⅓ cup butter, softened
¼ cup imported port
6 ripe peaches

Cut the ham into pieces and put it through the fine blade of your meat grinder. In a mixing bowl, beat the mayonnaise, cayenne, salt, and softened butter. When this is well mixed, add the port very slowly; then fold the ham into the mixture. Chill for about 2 hours.

You may peel the peaches or not, as you prefer. Cut them in halves, remove the pits and stuff each peach half with the chilled mousse. Arrange on a nice platter and serve.

Vol-au-vent means windward flight — a fitting name for pastry shells so light they are like angels floating on a breeze, like clouds of butterfly wings in the sun. To keep the pastries from drifting upward from the table, fill them with this bewitching, creamed seafood mixture and serve as an appetizer.

VOL-AU-VENT WITH SEAFOOD

MAKES 6 SERVINGS

2 shallots, minced
½ cup mushrooms, sliced
2 tablespoons butter
2 tablespoons flour
1 tablespoon chopped parsley
½ cup chicken stock
1 cup heavy cream
1 beaten egg yolk
¼ cup sherry
1 pound shrimp, cleaned and cooked
⅛ teaspoon paprika
1 teaspoon salt
⅛ teaspoon pepper
6 baked pastry shells

Sauté the shallots and mushrooms in the butter until they are tender. Stir the flour in, mixing very well. Add the parsley and slowly stir in the chicken stock and cream. Quickly stir in the beaten egg yolk and cook until the sauce thickens, stirring continuously. When the sauce is thickened, stir in the sherry, shrimp, paprika, salt and pepper. Spoon the mixture into the pastry shells on serving plates, and serve promptly.

2 Soups

I HAPPEN to be a *connoisseur* of soups. The pity is that many restaurants and some homes serve nothing but canned soup, when making it yourself is the easiest thing in the world to do. I hate to say it, but there is not one canned soup that comes even close to a homemade one. Luckily, soup-making is simple, because you can cook a large batch and it will keep in the refrigerator for a week at a time; in fact, the soup will taste better a couple of days after you've made it.

As for the time and trouble involved, they are negligible. Say you spend 45 minutes to make a gallon of soup. That's good for four or five occasions. Divide the 45 minutes by four or five and you see you'll have spent about 10 minutes a meal to make the soup. That's French arithmetic!

The real trouble is that American cooks don't have the tradition of a constantly simmering soup kettle on the back burner, as they do in France. The reference point in America is not great-grandmother, but great big canning corporations instead. I prefer my own cooking to industry's. I like to use chicken backs and necks, or bones from beef, lamb or ham, genuinely fresh vegetables and personally selected, nonchemical seasonings — all simmered into a symphony of soup. Of course, I don't rush out and buy each of these ingredients whenever I feel like cooking soup; I have labeled containers in the freezer that hold soup-makings. In reality, they are savings from other meals I have cooked. It's a French habit I urge you to adopt.

The recipes in this chapter can serve four to eight people, depending on the meal. But don't be afraid of making a larger quantity than you can use right away. It's better to make an extra amount so you can have future portions ready to take from the freezer and melt down into pools of heavenly, homemade soup.

TYPES OF SOUPS

You say soup; I say *consommé* or *potage*. Consommé comes from the French word *consommer:* to accomplish, finish, boil down. It is a clear stock, made from meat or poultry, which you can use as is or as the basis for other soups or sauces.

Some people, when they think consommé, think of hospitals. But a true double consommé, properly made, is a vigorous, savory broth that has been simmered down so its force is concentrated. It makes a lovely introduction to a chicken or seafood dinner. You can make your consommé more emphatic, if you wish, by adding very thin pasta, by slicing a couple of crêpes into it, or by flecking it with chromatic frills of aromatic chervil. Consommé ungarnished makes a simple, inspiring beginning for a meal, a lyrical prelude to the appetizer or the bridge that leads firmly to your entrée.

Potage (pronounced poe-TAHJ) is a somewhat heavier soup. For me, it is one of the most fantastic things to savor before a dinner or lunch. When it is well-made, it is a marvelous thing for your system; it is so filled with vitamins. Some potages have enough gusto to be a whole meal by themselves, with perhaps a salad if you like.

What we in France call *potage* is a mixture of vegetables that have been ground up, or puréed, through a vegetable food mill; what we think of as "soup" has more grossly cut pieces of vegetables in it. Here's how you can produce both soup and potage at the same time, and add variety to your week's repertoire of menus. When you make a vegetable soup, reserve perhaps a half-gallon of it. Then, at the next meal, grind in some potatoes, to give the soup body, and — *voilà!* — you have potage.

You can make pea soup, chicken, beef-barley — so many kinds of soup. Here is a trick to get you started. Begin by sautéing a sliced or chopped onion in butter; then add some cubed, aromatic vegetables — such as carrots and celery — and stir so the flavors will come up in the heat. Add chicken or beef broth or bouillon, season, simmer — and there you are. A miracle of simplicity, is it not? As for the bouillon, you can use stock you have previously prepared and kept frozen, or you can use one of the good cubed or canned brands. Really, some of those cubes and cans aren't bad if you use them properly — that is, just a very little. And they are not expensive that way, either.

In my opinion, this clear soup with an Oriental flavor is a small gem — so sparkling and light that angels should bear it to the table. It is an intriguingly seasoned broth which you can make all the more intriguing by your epicurean choice of garnish.

CLEAR SOUP JAPONAISE

4 cups chicken stock
½ pound fresh spinach
2 tablespoons soy sauce
½ cup sliced mushrooms
½ cup chopped green onions (scallions)
Peel of one lemon
1 cup watercress, chopped
Salt and pepper to taste

Bring the chicken stock to a boil; then add the spinach. Keep the stock simmering and add all the remaining ingredients. Simmer for 10 minutes only. Remove the lemon peel and serve at once, without cooking the vegetables any longer.

This is one of the great classic French soups. Actually, it's chicken soup, elevated to regal status. Reducing the stock first is what makes it so enormously and distinctively tasty. Of course you'll serve it piping hot, and may I suggest that you present it in little earthenware pots rather than the usual soup bowls. The presentation adds a Gallic stylishness that is most appropriate.

SOUPE HENRI IV

3 quarts chicken stock
1 cup carrots, cut in half-inch cubes
1 cup celery, cut in half-inch cubes
½ cup white turnips, cubed
½ cup frozen baby onions
1 cup cooked, white chicken meat, cut up
1 teaspoon chopped parsley

Put one quart of the chicken stock in a sauce pan. Add the carrots, celery, turnips, and onions. Bring the stock to a boil, lower the heat and simmer until the vegetables are done. In another pan, simmer the remaining stock until it is reduced by half. Skim from time to time, if necessary. When this stock is reduced, add the simmered vegetables and the stock they were cooked in, along with the chicken. Stir together. Sprinkle with parsley and serve very hot.

It's midnight in Paris, and the streets are alive. *Après-théâtre* audiences mingle with cabaret revelers; intellectuals with café society. These are the night people of Paris, perpetually famished for warmth and gaiety. What they crave is the classic midnight food of France: hot, fragrant onion soup, meltingly capped with burnished-gold *croûtons gratinés.*

SOUPE À L'OIGNON MINUIT

(French Onion Soup)

4 tablespoons butter
10 medium onions, thinly sliced
3 tablespoons flour
3 quarts chicken stock
1 cup dry white wine
3 ounces cognac
½ teaspoon thyme
2 cloves garlic, minced
1 bay leaf
Salt and pepper to taste
Toasted slices of French bread
Grated Parmesan cheese

Melt the butter in a heavy kettle. Add the sliced onions and allow them to brown very well, doing half the onions at a time, if necessary, to be sure all the onion slices are well browned. When they are all nicely browned, sprinkle flour on the onions and mix in well. Gradually add the stock while continuing to stir. Add the wine, cognac, thyme, garlic, bay leaf, salt and pepper. Bring the soup to a boil, then lower the heat and simmer gently for 1 hour. Skim the top from time to time.

Place a slice of the toasted bread in each bowl, sprinkle the toast well with cheese, and then ladle the hot soup into the bowl. If desired, and if ovenproof bowls are used, place the bowls under the broiler until the cheese is melted and lightly browned before serving.

When Bernard makes pea soup laden with ham and bacon chunks, it is a luxury sybarites applaud. Follow my recipe — letting the potion simmer slowly, like a ballad — and you will win accolades, too.

BERNARD'S GREEN PEA SOUP LOUVIERS

1 pound green split peas
3 full slices bacon, diced
1 onion, chopped
½ cup carrots, diced
¼ cup celery, chopped fine
1 bay leaf
¼ teaspoon thyme
Pinch of allspice
2 quarts chicken stock or bouillon
½ cup dry white wine
Ham butt or hock, or thick slice of ham cut into large pieces

Wash and drain the split peas in a colander. In a heavy kettle, sauté the bacon gently until it is golden. Add the onion and cook over medium heat until the onion is tender but not browned. Add the carrots and celery and sauté 2 or 3 minutes; then stir in the drained split peas, the bay leaf, thyme, allspice, chicken stock and wine. Mix everything together very well and bring to a boil. Lower the heat to keep the soup at a gentle simmer. Add the ham; cover the kettle and simmer for 1 to 1½ hours, skimming occasionally and discarding the fat. Stir well from time to time, to keep the soup from sticking to the bottom of the pan.

When the soup is of the desired consistency, remove the ham butt or hock, cutting off and dicing the meat to be returned to the soup. Correct the seasoning, remove the bay leaf, and serve piping hot.

The happy thing about a soup supper is that it's so soothing, whenever you find an excuse to serve it — late at night, after the theater; early in the evening, to punctuate a brisk afternoon outdoors; or any time to halt a sniffle, impress a lover, or just to be good to yourself. Picture this: steaming-hot lentil soup, chunks of crisp French bread, a composed salad with character, and then some cheese and fruit.

LENTIL SOUP

6 strips bacon, diced
1 onion, chopped
1 clove garlic, minced
2 quarts water
1 pound lentils
1 bay leaf
⅛ teaspoon thyme
Salt and pepper to taste

In a large pan, cook the bacon until it is lightly browned, stirring occasionally. Add the onion and garlic and sauté until they are golden. Add the water, lentils, bay leaf and thyme. Let simmer for 1½ hours, stirring from time to time. Add salt and pepper to taste. Serve very hot.

FRESH TOMATO SOUP

3 tablespoons butter
1 onion, chopped
6 large tomatoes, peeled and chopped
4 cups chicken stock
1 teaspoon sugar
1 teaspoon salt
½ teaspoon pepper
2 potatoes, peeled and diced
1 bay leaf
⅛ teaspoon thyme
3 sprigs parsley

Melt the butter in a Dutch oven. Add the onion and sauté until it is golden. Add the tomatoes with the stock, sugar, salt and pepper. Bring this to a boil; then add the potatoes, bay leaf, thyme and parsley. Simmer for 30 to 40 minutes. Remove the bay leaf and parsley. Strain the soup or put it through a food mill. Correct the seasoning, if necessary. Serve piping hot.

MINESTRONE

¼ cup olive oil
2 cloves garlic, minced
1 onion, chopped
1 leek, sliced
½ teaspoon thyme
3 tomatoes, peeled and chopped
2 stalks celery, sliced
2 carrots, peeled and diced
2 potatoes, peeled and diced
½ pound green beans, cut up
2 quarts water
6 beef bouillon cubes
1 cup elbow macaroni
1 cup cooked kidney beans, drained
3 tablespoons grated Parmesan cheese
Salt and pepper to taste

Heat the olive oil in a large Dutch oven or saucepan. Add the garlic, onion, leek and thyme, and sauté until the onion is transparent. Add the tomatoes, celery, carrots, potatoes, green beans, water and bouillon cubes. Bring to a gentle simmer and let cook for about 45 minutes. Bring to a boil and stir in the macaroni. Lower the heat and again let the soup simmer, until the macaroni is about tender. Stir in the kidney beans and continue simmering for another 5 to 10 minutes. Stir in the cheese; taste, and add salt and pepper if needed. Serve with additional grated cheese, to be sprinkled on top of the soup, if desired.

Here you have garden vegetables heartened by ham hock or soup bones and immersed in a vigorous brown stock. Serve it before an entrée, or as lunch or supper all by itself — along with some good French bread, *naturellement.*

SOUPE MARAÎCHÈRE

Ham hock (or soup bones of any kind)
3 quarts water
2 tablespoons butter
1 cup coarsely chopped onions
1 cup diced celery
1 cup diced carrots
2 cups coarsely chopped cabbage
½ cup chopped green pepper
⅛ teaspoon thyme
1 bay leaf
2 whole cloves
2 cups cubed zucchini
1-pound can stewed tomatoes
½ cup sliced green onions (scallions)
¼ teaspoon pepper
Salt to taste

This soup may be made with whatever stock base you prefer, using ham, beef, or chicken soup bones, or any combination of these.

Place the ham hock or soup bones in a large kettle and cover with the water; bring to a boil over high heat. Lower the heat to keep a good simmering point and allow the liquid to cook, covered, for 2 hours or until the stock is well-flavored and the meat is tender. Add more water if the stock reduces too much.

When the stock is almost ready, melt the butter in a large pan. Add the onions, celery, carrots, cabbage and green pepper. Stir the vegetables with a wooden spoon and cook them over low heat until they start to steam and begin to look moist and shiny. Allow the vegetables to simmer over medium-low heat; be careful not to let them brown. Stir from time to time.

After the vegetables have cooked in this manner for 10 to 15 minutes, add them to the stock. Stir in the thyme, bay leaf and cloves. Allow the soup to continue simmering until the vegetables are almost done. (If you wish a heartier soup, you can add a cup or two of diced potatoes, also.)

Add the zucchini, tomatoes, and green onions, and allow the soup to simmer for another 5 to 10 minutes. Remove the ham hock or soup bones. Allow the bones to cool briefly; then cut off the meat. This meat may be returned to the soup or used in an omelet or sandwiches. Skim any excess fat from the top of the soup. Correct the seasoning. Serve piping hot.

Start with a whole fish or one that is cut into large pieces. The fish will flake in the cooking, and if you begin with small pieces they will be lost. To keep the large pieces from flaking into bits, move the fish around in the pan as little as possible. And as soon as the liquid comes up to a boil, shut off the heat under the pan; the fish will continue to cook in the hot water.

The potatoes in the recipe can be prepared in advance. Peeled potatoes will keep for as long as a week if you store them in freshly changed water and refrigerate them. When you cube and cook them, if you find you've been too generous in the amount of potatoes you've prepared, don't worry; you can always use them in something else. And remember to undercook them so they're still firm; you want a good-looking fish chowder, not a mealy potato soup.

The salt pork (or bacon, in a pinch) is a must. It is the backbone of every chowder.

Bring the chowder to the table in a healthy-sized tureen, or whatever you have that will provide the right atmosphere. When you ladle it out, provide large pieces of buttered country bread for everyone, and plenty of good dry white wine. An arrangement of deep-hued flowers on a dark tablecloth and a background of uncomplicated music will make everything taste better.

BERNARD'S FISH CHOWDER

¾ cup salt pork, finely diced
1 cup chopped onions
2 pounds firm, white fish
Water to cover
¼ cup dry white wine
1 bay leaf
1 sprig parsley
2 teaspoons salt
½ teaspoon white pepper
⅓ cup flour
1 chicken bouillon cube
1 teaspoon monosodium glutamate
3 teaspoons Worcestershire sauce
½ teaspoon celery salt
½ teaspoon thyme
1½ cups milk
3 cups cubed potatoes, cooked and drained
2 tablespoons butter

Put the salt pork into a heavy kettle over medium heat. Sauté for a few minutes; then add the onions and let them cook gently, stirring from time to time.

Meantime, put the fish into another pan, cover it with water (about 3 cups) and add the wine, bay leaf, parsley, salt and pepper. Bring to a boil, lower the heat, and let the liquid simmer for 5 minutes, or just until the fish flakes easily. Discard the parsley and bay leaf. Strain off the stock into a container and reserve it. Set the fish aside.

Add the flour to the salt pork and onions in the kettle, mixing it in very well. Add 3 cups of the reserved stock and continue stirring and cooking. Add the bouillon cube, monosodium glutamate, Worcestershire sauce, celery salt, thyme and milk. (Add more or less milk, according to whether you prefer a thinner or thicker chowder.) Add the potatoes and the fish, stirring them in carefully so that the fish pieces are broken up as little as possible. Heat thoroughly, but do not allow to boil. To serve, place butter in the tureen, or put a pat of butter in each bowl, and ladle the chowder over it.

Note: This may be made as a base by using all the ingredients except the milk. Refrigerate it until needed; then stir in the milk while heating.

I consider this recipe quite an accomplishment: it is my invention for ending the battle between the puritans of New England and the city slickers of Manhattan. You might call it New England Chowder Bernard Style, à la Français. Very cosmopolitan, *n'est-ce pas?* Also, very tasty, very simple to prepare, and very inexpensive. Here are a few tips to help you:

— Salt pork is a *must* for chowder, but if you haven't got any on hand, use bacon instead.
— Fresh clams are more flavorful than canned ones, which have already been cooked. If you use canned clams, add about one-half cup of bottled clam juice, for the extra flavor that's missing.
— Remember that you can peel your potatoes ahead of time and keep them refrigerated — for as long as a week — in freshly changed water. Take care not to overcook the potatoes; you want them firm and attractive.
— For a surprise, just to keep everybody on their toes, serve this chowder cold sometime, like vichyssoise, garnished with a scattering of chopped chives.

This is a chowder with body, one that talks to you. Serve it in simple pottery crocks, with brown bread or pieces of buttered country bread. To put everybody in the mood, add pleasant music and a bowlful of autumn-colored flowers.

NEW ENGLAND CLAM CHOWDER BERNARD

¼ cup diced salt pork
½ cup chopped onions
2 tablespoons flour
1 quart milk, heated
1 cup heavy cream
2 cups chopped clams
⅛ teaspoon thyme
1 tablespoon Worcestershire sauce
Salt and pepper to taste
1½ cups cubed, cooked potatoes
2 tablespoons butter

In a large saucepan, sauté the salt pork for 3 or 4 minutes. Add the chopped onions and sauté until transparent. Stir in the flour and blend until the mixture is smooth. While continuing to stir, gradually add the hot milk. Add the cream, chopped clams, thyme, Worcestershire sauce, salt and pepper. Bring just to a boil; then add the potatoes. Heat, but do not allow to boil. Add the butter and serve piping hot.

Foods with a Far East accent are delicate in appearance, consistency and flavor. You'll find this one quite substantial, however, and an excellent introduction to an Oriental feast.

MANDARIN CRABMEAT SOUP

2 tablespoons oil
2 scallions, chopped
1 tablespoon grated ginger root
1½ cups cooked, flaked crabmeat
2 tablespoons dry sherry
6 cups chicken or fish stock
¾ pound spinach, trimmed and chopped
1 teaspoon salt
⅛ teaspoon monosodium glutamate
1½ tablespoons cornstarch
½ cup cold water
Thinly sliced lemon
Chopped chives

Heat the oil in a large kettle. Add the scallions and ginger root and stir-fry quickly. Add the crabmeat and stir another 2 minutes. Stir in the sherry and stock, and bring to a boil. Add the spinach, salt and monosodium glutamate. Lower the heat so that the soup will just simmer for 10 to 15 minutes.

Mix the cornstarch and water to a smooth paste. Stir the paste into the soup and continue simmering, while stirring until thickened. Garnish with thin lemon slices and chives. Serve piping hot.

Like most of my recipes, this one is a basic plan from which you can create a bevy of wonderful delicacies. Substitute any other shellfish you like for the lobster, or use rabbit or squab. For a decidedly unprosaic and piquant switch on the soup routine, you can also whip up a garden bisque, using puréed vegetables in place of the lobster.

LOBSTER BISQUE

3 tablespoons olive oil
1 large onion, diced
¼ teaspoon cayenne pepper
2 or 3 lobster heads

3 carrots, diced
2 stalks celery, diced
2 cloves garlic, minced
4 shallots, chopped fine
4 sprigs parsley
2 bay leaves
½ teaspoon thyme
1 quart water
2 cups dry white wine
1 cup cooked rice
3 tablespoons tomato paste
Salt to taste
4 egg yolks, beaten
1 cup heavy cream
1 tablespoon arrowroot
½ pound cooked lobster meat, cut up

Heat the olive oil in a large kettle. Add the onion, carrots, celery, garlic, and shallots. Sauté until all are golden in color. Add the parsley, bay leaves, thyme, water, wine, cayenne pepper and lobster heads. Bring to a boil; then lower the heat and let simmer gently for a half-hour. Skim any froth from the top and discard. Continue simmering another half-hour.

Add the rice, tomato paste and salt, and simmer another 5 minutes. Then, using a colander to withhold the other ingredients, strain the stock into another pan. Discard vegetables and lobster heads. Return the stock to the heat and bring it to a simmer. Blend the egg yolks, cream and arrowroot together. Gradually stir them into the stock and bring the thickened liquid back to a simmer while stirring continually. Add the lobster meat and heat just a few minutes; then serve piping hot.

Note: Lobster heads can usually be obtained in any fish market where cooked lobster meat is sold.

This is the genuine article, the cream soup that is so extraordinarily fresh on the tongue and so stimulating to the soul. Made of potatoes and leeks that have been simmered in chicken stock, it is served chilled, its creamy-white surface flecked with snippets of fresh green chives.

THE CLASSIC VICHYSSOISE

MAKES 6 TO 8 SERVINGS

2 tablespoons butter
4 leeks (white parts only), chopped
2 onions, chopped
4 potatoes, peeled and sliced thin
1 quart chicken stock
1 teaspoon salt
½ teaspoon white pepper
1 quart light cream
1 tablespoon fresh, chopped chives

Melt the butter in a heavy saucepan. Add the leeks and onions and sauté them until they are soft. Add the potatoes, chicken stock, salt and pepper. Cook until the potatoes are very tender; then put the soup through a food mill. Adjust the seasonings if necessary. Allow the soup to cool; then stir in the cream and chill thoroughly. Serve the cold vichyssoise sprinkled with chopped chives.

This is a zesty soup, sweetened by the touch of carrot.

COLD CARROT SOUP

MAKES 8 TO 10 SERVINGS

1½ quarts chicken stock
4 potatoes, peeled and sliced thin
8 carrots, sliced thin
1 large leek, sliced thin
1 bay leaf
⅛ teaspoon thyme
1 teaspoon sugar
1 ham shank
1 teaspoon salt
½ teaspoon pepper
1 cup heavy cream
Pinch of ground cloves

Combine all the ingredients, except the heavy cream and cloves, in a large kettle. Bring the liquid to a boil; reduce the heat and let simmer for 1 hour. Remove the bay leaf and ham shank. Force the vegetables through a food mill and return the purée to the stock. Correct the seasoning, if necessary, and let cool. Place the soup in the refrigerator to chill thoroughly; then stir in the cream. Sprinkle with ground cloves and serve very cold.

CREAMY CAULIFLOWER SOUP

1 small cauliflower head
Water for parboiling
Salt
3 tablespoons butter
1 leek, minced
2 tablespoons flour
2 quarts chicken stock
1 teaspoon salt
½ teaspoon pepper
½ cup heavy cream
1 cup croutons (optional)

Wash the cauliflower. Separate the head into flowerets and put these into a pan with lightly salted water. Bring to a boil and simmer for about 5 minutes. Drain the cauliflowerets and cool them under cold, running water. Drain them again, and set aside.

Melt the butter in a heavy saucepan. Add the leek and sauté it for 2 or 3 minutes. Stir in the flour and cook for a few minutes; then add the chicken stock, salt, pepper and the cauliflower. Bring to a boil and lower the heat to a simmer, cooking for about 25 minutes. Put the soup through a food mill. Chill. Just before serving, stir in the heavy cream. Serve with croutons, if desired.

If you love lemon and eggs, you'll dote on this blithe and beguiling soup. Its light golden color reminds me of the sun-splashed Greek islands; its airy, refreshing flavor harmonizes perfectly with the insouciant moods of summer.

AVGOLEMONO SOUP

6 cups chicken stock
¼ cup raw rice
1 teaspoon salt
3 eggs
¼ cup lemon juice
1 lemon, sliced thin

Bring the chicken stock to a boil in a large saucepan; stir in the rice and salt. Lower the heat and simmer until the rice is tender.

Meanwhile, beat the eggs in a bowl until they are fluffy and pale yellow. Beat in the lemon juice. When the rice is cooked, ladle out about 2 cups of the stock. Slowly stir this into the beaten egg-and-lemon mixture with a whisk, stirring vigorously until all is blended. Then pour this mixture back into the saucepan, again stirring to keep the soup very smooth. Simmer briefly but do not boil or the soup will curdle. Cool the soup to room temperature; then chill it until it is very cold. The soup will thicken as it chills. Stir it carefully just before serving. Garnish with thin lemon slices.

There is something wanton about this soup's character that appeals to the Frenchman in me. It is creamy in texture, sweet and rich — surely a sinfully good beginning for an uncommonly provocative meal.

COLD SWEET POTATO SOUP

MAKES 6 TO 8 SERVINGS

1½ quarts chicken stock
2 pounds sweet potatoes, peeled and diced
1 pound white potatoes, peeled and diced
1 onion, chopped
2 stalks celery, diced
1 teaspoon salt
½ teaspoon pepper
1 cup heavy cream
⅛ teaspoon nutmeg

To the chicken stock, add all the potatoes, the onion and celery. Bring the stock to a boil, lower the heat, and simmer until the potatoes are tender. Force the soup through a food mill. Season it with salt and pepper. Cool the soup and then refrigerate it. When the soup is very cold, stir in the heavy cream and nutmeg. Serve very well chilled.

A delicate curry flavor is the leitmotif for Senegalese, a soup that is slightly theatrical and totally irresistible.

COLD SENEGALESE SOUP

6 tablespoons butter, divided
1 large onion, chopped
2 carrots, diced
2 stalks celery, diced
1 teaspoon curry powder
3 pieces cinnamon stick (each about 1-inch long)
2 bay leaves
1 teaspoon whole cloves
1 quart rich chicken stock
1 tablespoon tomato purée
¼ cup chopped almonds
1 tablespoon currant jelly
3 tablespoons flour
Salt and white pepper
2 cups heavy cream

Melt 2 tablespoons of the butter in a large saucepan. Add the onion, carrots and celery, and sauté them over moderate heat for 4 or 5 minutes. Stir in the curry powder and blend well. Add the cinnamon sticks, bay leaves, cloves, chicken stock, tomato purée, chopped almonds and currant jelly. Mix well and bring to a boil. Lower the heat and let the soup simmer gently for 45 minutes. Skim off any foam from the top.

Combine the remaining butter (4 tablespoons) with the flour and add this, a little at a time, to the soup. Add salt and white pepper. When the soup has thickened slightly, strain out the bay leaves, cloves and cinnamon sticks. Refrigerate. Just before serving, stir in the cream.

Gazpacho is a cold vegetable soup with panache. Its ingredients are fresh as dew, pert in flavor and radiant in color. Garnish each portion with gay confetti-flecks of any of the fresh vegetables it contains, and be sure to have plenty of crisp French bread alongside.

GAZPACHO

2 cucumbers, peeled
6 tomatoes, peeled
1 onion, peeled
1 dozen green olives
3 cloves garlic, peeled
1 shallot, peeled
4 or 5 sprigs parsley
6 anchovy fillets, mashed
3 tablespoons red wine vinegar
¼ cup olive oil
Juice of 1 lemon
4 cups tomato juice
Salt and pepper to taste

Chop all the vegetables quite fine; then mix them with all the remaining ingredients in a large bowl. Taste; add salt and pepper if needed. Refrigerate the soup until it is thoroughly chilled. Serve very cold.

3
Eggs

WE ARE lucky that hens are such busy little birds, because their eggs are about the most widely used food I can think of. You open your eyes in the morning and have an egg. You go to lunch and order an omelet, eggs Benedict, or something cloaked in an egg-laced sauce. It's the same at dinner: in one form or another you will almost surely eat an egg.

There is a provocative nostalgia about eggs, as there is about songs and scents you remember. Many an evening has been saved for me by the soothing qualities of eggs. When I come home from work tired and hungry, and there's nothing much in the house to prepare quickly, I am always comforted by a supper of eggs. It reminds me of how, when I was a child, I loved *l'oeuf à la coq* — soft-boiled eggs eaten with the long, finger-sized slices of buttered bread we call *baguettes*. The French always have to be elegant in some way, you know; so even on the farm we would eat our eggs from a *coquetier*, a flirtatious little egg cup, in which the boiled egg perches, shell and all. You lop off the egg top, add a touch of salt, gently mix the white and yolk, then dunk your buttered *baguette* pieces into the luscious golden bath. *Formidable!*

I think I've figured out the cure for people who have trouble poaching eggs. It's a simple operation, really, but there are a few quirks to master before you can make poached eggs pretty rather than shredded, messy things. First of all, to poach an egg (or anything else for that matter), the water should be only simmering, and not at a galloping boil, when it receives the egg. That's trick number one.

Trick number two is to have a few drops of vinegar in the water, to seal the egg white and prevent it from dispersing into pieces of rag. The third trick is to ease the egg into the simmering water slowly, with a rolling motion, so that it will stay whole. Another secret is to stir the water into an eddy as you are slipping the egg into it; the egg will nest in the whirlpool and cook in a nice shape. As for those miniature double boilers and other egg poaching contraptions — I don't care for them. They give the egg an unnatural, cookie-cutter shape rather than the free form a real poached-in-liquid egg should have. Use your poaching prowess to construct eggs Benedict, eggs Florentine, eggs Mornay and all the other poached-egg glories.

POACHED EGGS

4 eggs
1 quart water
¼ cup wine vinegar

Put the water and vinegar in a saucepan and bring it to a simmer. Break each egg into the water very carefully. Keep the water simmering until the egg white is cooked and the yolk done as desired. Remove the egg with a perforated or slotted spoon and place it on paper toweling to drain.

EGGS BENEDICT

MAKES 4 TO 6 SERVINGS

1 tablespoon butter
8 slices Canadian bacon
8 poached eggs
4 English muffins, split and toasted
1 cup warm Hollandaise sauce (page 209)

Melt the butter in a skillet. Add the Canadian bacon and sauté it just until it is golden brown on both sides. Place each slice of bacon on an English muffin half, and top each with a poached egg. Spoon Hollandaise sauce over each egg and serve immediately.

EGGS FLORENTINE

MAKES 4 SERVINGS

2 tablespoons butter
2 shallots, chopped
½ pound fresh spinach
½ teaspoon salt
3 tablespoons water
2 English muffins, split and toasted
4 poached eggs
1 cup warm white sauce (page 206)
2 tablespoons grated Parmesan cheese

Melt the butter in a skillet. Add the shallots and sauté them until golden. Add the spinach, salt and water; cover the skillet and cook the spinach for 3 minutes. Drain the spinach well and chop it coarsely.

Place the toasted muffin halves on a baking sheet. Top each one with some spinach, a poached egg and white sauce spooned over the top. Sprinkle with Parmesan cheese. Put the eggs Florentine in a 400°F. oven until the cheese is just melted and lightly browned.

SCRAMBLED EGGS

MAKES 4 SERVINGS

8 eggs
¼ cup heavy cream
Salt and pepper to taste
2 tablespoons butter

Beat the eggs with the cream, salt and pepper. Melt the butter in a large skillet. When butter is hot, pour in the eggs and cook them over medium low heat, stirring occasionally. Cook until the eggs are light and fluffy. Serve immediately.

For variety, you may add grated Swiss, Cheddar or other cheese when the eggs are almost cooked. For tarragon eggs, add 1 tablespoon of crushed tarragon leaves to the egg mixture before cooking.

There are two secrets to making an exquisite omelet. First, do not overbeat your eggs, because you must achieve a certain texture. Overbeating will give you a foamy nothing. Underbeating will result in ropy strings of white. The best method is to break the eggs into a mixing bowl and just flop them over a few times with your fork. That way the yolks and whites will be blended without being abused.

The second secret is to cook an omelet till just *baveuse* (runny). A well-done omelet is the same as a fried sponge. An undercooked egg is unspeakable.

OMELET

3 eggs
1 tablespoon water or milk
Salt and pepper to taste
1 tablespoon butter

Beat together the eggs, water or milk, salt and pepper. Melt the butter in a small skillet. When the butter is hot, add the egg mixture. Stir it quickly until a film forms on the bottom. Let the eggs cook gently; then fold half of the omelet over the other half. Turn the omelet carefully once more, and serve when the eggs are done as desired.

HAM AND CHEESE OMELET

MAKES 4 SERVINGS

12 large eggs
Salt and pepper to taste
½ cup light cream (optional)
8 ounces ham
4 ounces Swiss or American cheese
Butter

Break the eggs into a deep bowl and mix them well with a fork. Add the salt and pepper — and cream, if desired — stirring well. Dice the ham and cheese, so you have everything ready before you start cooking the omelet. Put a large skillet over high heat. Melt enough butter in the skillet, so that it covers the bottom of the pan. Pour in the beaten eggs and, as soon as a film starts to form on the bottom, stir them with a fork very quickly to cook bottom evenly. Put the ham and cheese in the center. Bring the edges into the center; then tip the pan so that the omelet will roll over double. Pour out onto a warmed serving platter and serve promptly.

Note: If the skillet is not big enough to do the omelet properly, it is better to divide the egg mixture and cook it in two or three lots. Omelets cook quickly, and the results will be better in smaller lots.

OMELET WITH CHICKEN LIVERS

MAKES 4 THREE-EGG OMELETS

½ pound chicken livers
¼ cup flour
2 teaspoons paprika
1 teaspoon salt
¼ teaspoon pepper
3 tablespoons butter
2 tablespoons chopped shallots
¼ cup port wine
1 dozen eggs

Wash the chicken livers and dry them thoroughly on paper toweling; cut each one in half. Dredge the livers well in a mixture of the flour, paprika, salt and pepper.

Melt the butter in a skillet over medium-high heat. Add the livers and sauté until they are nicely browned, stirring as necessary. Add the shallots, stir to mix; then add the wine. Remove from heat and divide the livers and shallots into four portions.

Prepare your omelets in the usual way. Place a portion of the chicken livers in the center of each omelet.

MUSHROOM OMELET

MAKES 4 THREE-EGG OMELETS

3 tablespoons butter
2 cups sliced mushrooms
2 tablespoons chopped shallots
½ teaspoon salt
¼ teaspoon pepper
2 tablespoons chopped parsley
1 dozen eggs

Melt the butter in a skillet. Add the mushrooms, shallots, salt and pepper. Sauté quickly over high heat for only 3 or 4 minutes. Remove the mushrooms from the heat and sprinkle them with parsley. Divide them into four portions.

Make your omelets as usual. Place one portion of the mushroom mixture in the center of each omelet.

OMELET PAYSANNE

MAKES 4 THREE-EGG OMELETS

8 slices bacon
½ cup cooked, diced potatoes
¼ teaspoon salt
2 tablespoons chopped parsley
1 dozen eggs

Cook the bacon in a skillet until it is crisp and golden. Remove it to paper toweling. Add the diced potatoes to the pan and fry them until they are nicely browned. Crumble the bacon and add it to the potatoes. Stir over the heat for a minute or two.

Pour the contents of the pan through a strainer, discarding the bacon fat. Sprinkle the potatoes and bacon with salt and parsley, and divide the mixture into four equal portions.

Prepare your omelets in the usual way. Use one portion of the potato-and-bacon mixture to stuff the center of each omelet.

EGGS CHASSEUR

MAKES 4 SERVINGS

6 tablespoons butter, divided
1 large tomato, cut in 4 thick slices
2 tablespoons chopped onions
¼ pound chicken livers, cut in large pieces
½ cup sliced mushrooms
½ teaspoon salt
¼ teaspoon oregano
4 large eggs
2 English muffins, split and toasted

Put 2 tablespoons of the butter in a skillet. Heat the butter; then add the tomato slices, turning each slice once when it is lightly browned. Remove the tomatoes from the pan and keep them warm. Add another tablespoon of the butter to the pan; then add the onions and livers and stir gently while cooking for 3 or 4 minutes. Add the mushrooms, salt and oregano and cook for another few minutes. Divide into four portions.

In a separate skillet, melt the remaining butter. Break the eggs gently into the pan when the butter is hot. Cook the eggs over low heat, spooning the butter over the eggs as they cook.

To serve, top each half a muffin with a portion of the liver mixture, a tomato slice, and an egg. Serve promptly.

EGGS BORGIA

MAKES 4 SERVINGS

4 tomatoes
Salt and pepper
8 eggs, poached
Béarnaise sauce (page 209)

Cut the tomatoes into halves and sprinkle them lightly with salt and pepper. Place them in a lightly buttered, shallow baking pan and put into a 375°F. oven for 8 to 10 minutes. Arrange two tomato halves on each warm serving plate, and top each with a poached egg. Spoon the sauce over the tops. Serve promptly.

4
Beef

CITIZENS, the time has passed for steaks and roasts to be a major part of our diet. To be sure, we still have huge ranges in the United States and plenty of cattle. But now we have a shortage of money, and beef is no longer cheap enough to eat in large quantities. Besides, it's boring to always eat the same food. You have to change your habits and learn fresh ways to use different cuts of beef. Experiment! Dare to arouse new gustatory passions in your home.

Take stew, for instance — that strange and unglamorous word — and alchemize it into ragoût, miroton, daube or Boeuf Bourguignon (page 60). You will know it's still stew, but by spiking it with new spices and ingredients you will have made it mysterious, sensuous, elegant. And that is the whole idea. When your family arrives home at dinner time asking, "What's for dinner?", you will bowl them over with a provocatively named dish. Next thing you know, they will be bragging to their friends about your stupendous epicurean skills. At any rate, you will advance their linguistic and gastronomic education, just by serving them such novel items as Beef Stroganoff, sautéed tidbits of beef with a cream-and-paprika sauce (page 58). In the bargain, you will become a more advanced cook, and they will barely be able to wait for your next culinary fireworks.

I will give you recipes that are tasty, tangy, zesty, exhilarating and superb. They are also sure-fire and simple to prepare. *Your* part of the deal is to shop with wisdom and cook with glee.

COOKING FROZEN MEATS

Keep in mind that the moisture, texture and tenderness of the meat will be more pleasing if you thaw it slowly in the refrigerator than if you try to thaw it quickly. Try to plan ahead, to allow the proper time. It takes a large roast about 4 or 5 hours per pound to defrost in the refrigerator; a small roast requires about 3 hours per pound.

When roasting meat that is still frozen, preheat the oven to 300°F. (that is, about 25°F. lower than usual roasting temperature) and increase the roasting time by one-half.

To broil frozen meat, keep it at least 5 or 6 inches from the broiler, and increase the broiling time by one-half.

This is one of the most popular of all the recipes I've demonstrated on my television show, perhaps because it veers your palate away from the traditional. One thing I recommend: sauté the steaks only until they are rare. That way, the flavor will remain brilliant and bold. Serve them with fresh, tender-crisp green beans, broccoli, or carrots; boiled, parsley-tossed potatoes; and an assertive white burgundy wine. Lavish the table with chrysanthemums, play your favorite symphony record, and enjoy a simple, yet classic meal.

AUTUMN STEAKS

4 small steaks or 1 large steak cut into small portions
3 tablespoons cracked peppercorns (ground pepper cannot be used)
½ teaspoon salt
4 tablespoons corn oil
¼ cup melted butter
¼ pound mushrooms, sliced
¼ cup cognac, warm
¾ cup sour cream
1 tablespoon prepared Dijon mustard
¼ cup white wine
Salt and pepper to taste
Parsley garnish

Press the hand-cracked pepper into the steaks with the heel of your hand. Season the meat with a dash of salt. Sauté the steaks in hot oil until they are brown on both sides and done to your taste. Remove the steaks and oil from the pan.

Place the melted butter in the same skillet, add the mushrooms and sauté them. Add the mustard and stir. While the butter is very hot, return the steaks to the pan, add the warm cognac, and flame the steaks.

Remove the steaks and stir in the sour cream, wine and, if desired, brown sauce. Correct the seasoning of the mushroom sauce. Spoon the sauce over the peppered steaks and garnish.

Here's a little lesson in French cuisine. Any time you see *Niçoise* (meaning, as prepared in Nice) on the menu, you can expect to be served something made with tomatoes and probably with garlic as well. Steak *Niçoise* has both of those virtues, and a few besides. I recommend that you serve it with vegetables that are on the heavy side: cauliflower is an amiable companion, as are roasted or baked potatoes.

SIRLOIN STEAK NIÇOISE

MAKES 4 SERVINGS

4 tablespoons olive oil
4 sirloin steaks, 10 ounces each
Salt and pepper
¼ cup chopped onions
1 clove garlic, minced
4 tomatoes, peeled and chopped
12 anchovy filets
12 pitted black olives
1 teaspoon marjoram

Heat the oil in a large skillet. Sprinkle the steaks lightly with salt and pepper, and sauté them in the pan, about 5 minutes on each side. Remove the steaks from the pan and keep them warm. To the pan, add the onions and garlic and cook until light brown. Add the tomatoes and cook for 5 minutes. Add salt and pepper to the sauce to taste.

Arrange the steaks on a warmed serving platter. Pour the sauce over the steaks, and arrange the anchovy filets and olives over the steaks. Sprinkle the tops lightly with marjoram. Serve promptly.

Pepper steaks belong in your repertoire of things to cook for a tête-à-tête, an important occasion, a new romance, or a session of cajoling. It's a simple dish to make but looks like a big production. Even though you spend only about 15 minutes at it, the results are guaranteed magic. To complete your sorcerer's act, serve Carrots Vichy (page 178), Pommes de Terre Fondues (page 185), and a light claret or a slightly heavier Pommard.

PEPPER STEAKS

MAKES 4 SERVINGS

4 boneless steaks, 14 ounces each
4 tablespoons coarsely crushed pepper
1½ tablespoons oil
1 ounce cognac
¼ cup dry white wine
¼ cup brown sauce
1 cup heavy cream
Salt to taste

The steaks should be at least 1-inch thick and of uniform size. Pat the pepper onto both sides of the steaks. Heat the oil in a heavy skillet; add the steaks and sauté them on both sides without burning the pepper, but getting the meat nicely browned. Cook the steaks quickly to keep the meat rare. Transfer the steaks to a platter and keep them warm.

Discard all oil from the pan. Add the cognac, wine and brown sauce and stir well. Return the pan to the heat and as soon as the mixture begins to bubble, stir in the cream. Let the sauce simmer until it is reduced to the texture desired. Return the steaks to the pan with the juice from the platter, leaving them over the heat for only 30 to 40 seconds. Serve immediately with the sauce spooned over each steak and a sprinkle of salt on each to taste.

This is a mother-in-law dinner, something to impress very special people. It looks and tastes extravagant, even though it's simple to create. Yet it isn't extravagant at all. Here's why. Although it's true that tenderloin tips are expensive, the way the meat is prepared, you'll use only 4 or 5 ounces per person. So, you see, it's an economical way to serve beef majestically. As for the wine to use, I recommend a Bordeaux, or perhaps a California zinfandel — whatever type of wine you'll be drinking with the meal. Serve the Tenderloin Tips Bordelaise with Green Beans à la Crème (page 173), and Oven-Browned Potatoes (page 186).

TENDERLOIN TIPS BORDELAISE

MAKES 4 SERVINGS

2 tablespoons oil
2 pounds tenderloin tips
Salt and pepper to taste
½ cup dry red wine
3 shallots, chopped fine
½ cup chopped parsley
⅔ cup brown sauce (see page 201)

Heat the oil in a skillet. Cut the meat into slices about ½-inch thick. Sauté the meat in small quantities until all the pieces are well browned. As each batch is done, salt and pepper the sautéed slices lightly, remove them from the pan and place them on a heated platter. When all the meat is browned, pour off the fat and deglaze the pan with the wine, stirring quickly over high heat. Add the chopped shallots and parsley; then stir in the brown sauce and mix very well. Return the meat to the pan just long enough to heat it through.

The trick to this dish is to cook it quickly, just moments before serving it. Fettucine Alfredo is a sensational accompaniment.

BEEF STROGANOFF

MAKES 4 SERVINGS

- 4 *teaspoons paprika*
- 1 *pound sirloin tips, cut in strips*
- 3 *tablespoons oil*
- ¼ *cup dry white wine*
- ⅓ *cup heavy cream*
- 4 *tablespoons brown sauce (see page 201)*
- ⅛ *teaspoon pepper*
- ⅛ *teaspoon monosodium glutamate*

Put the paprika in a shallow dish and coat the meat strips thoroughly with the paprika. Heat the oil in a skillet, add the meat and sauté it to a good brown color, turning the strips as necessary. Cook the pieces quickly, to keep the meat rare. Strain the pieces into a colander or sieve, discarding the oil. Let the meat stay in the colander while you deglaze the pan with the white wine. Add the cream to the skillet; then stir in the brown sauce, pepper and monosodium glutamate. Keep the heat low, after the cream is added, to prevent curdling. Return the meat to the pan and maintain the heat just long enough to thoroughly rewarm the meat.

Feel free to improvise, as every good cook does. With the exception of pastries, I can't think of a single recipe that can't be transformed into a great, new gastronomic adventure by using a little more of this, a bit less of that, or a generous lacing of whatever happens to be in the refrigerator. Once you know how this, or any other basic recipe, ought to look and taste, it's down with strict rules and dull routine . . . onward and upward with lively, imaginative cooking and dazzled taste buds.

ROULADE DE BOEUF

MAKES 4 SERVINGS

4 small steaks, each about ½-inch thick
3 strips bacon
1 clove minced garlic
¼ cup minced celery
¼ cup minced shallots
6 mushrooms, chopped
6 slices cooked ham, chopped
2 tablespoons brandy
¼ cup dry white wine
Pinch thyme
Pinch tarragon
Salt and pepper to taste
¼ teaspoon monosodium glutamate
½ cup grated Swiss cheese
Chopped parsley

Trim the steaks of any excess fat, if necessary, and set them aside. Sauté the bacon in a heavy saucepan; remove the bacon, drain and crumble the pieces and set them aside. Pour off all but 2 tablespoons of the bacon drippings. Add the garlic, celery and shallots, and sauté them for a few minutes. Then add the mushrooms, the crumbled bacon, chopped ham, brandy and wine. Season with thyme, tarragon, salt, pepper and monosodium glutamate. Remove the roulade sauce from the heat and allow it to cool slightly.

Pound the steaks to make them a bit thinner and larger. Carefully spoon some of the roulade mixture onto each steak and sprinkle the top with grated cheese. Then roll each steak up to enclose its stuffing and secure each roll with wooden picks.

Broil the steaks, turning them from time to time, until they are done (about 7 to 10 minutes). Serve with Bordelaise sauce (page 205) and a garnish of chopped parsley.

I like to cook this ragoût a day in advance, to give the flavors time to marry. I admit that the waiting is not easy, because the aroma always arouses my instant ardor! Often I make an extra quantity and, after the marriage period, freeze the extra portions in plastic containers. To dramatize your boeuf bourguignon, bring it to the table in a tureen and serve it with parsley-sprinkled rice and Burgundy wine.

BOEUF BOURGUIGNON

MAKES 4 TO 6 SERVINGS

¼ cup oil
2 pounds lean beef, cut in cubes
½ cup diced bacon
1 cup chopped onions
¾ cup chopped celery
¾ cup diced carrots
2 cloves garlic, minced
2 bay leaves
¾ teaspoon thyme
3 tablespoons flour
2 cups dry red wine
1 cup beef stock
2 tablespoons tomato paste
1 cup chopped mushrooms
Salt and pepper to taste

Heat the oil in a large skillet or Dutch oven. Add the beef cubes and sauté them over medium-high heat until they are evenly browned, turning them as necessary. Remove the meat with a slotted spoon and set it aside in a bowl.

Pour off and discard all but 1 tablespoon of the oil from the pan. Add the bacon and chopped onion to the pan and cook over medium-low heat for 4 or 5 minutes, stirring often. Stir in the celery and carrots and continue cooking another 5 minutes, stirring occasionally. Add the garlic, bay leaves and thyme; simmer 5 minutes.

Stir in the flour until it is well mixed; then blend in 1 cup of the wine to make a smooth, thick mixture. Stir in the remaining wine. Return the meat and any juice left in the bowl to the pan of wine. Bring the mixture to a boil; then stir in the beef stock, tomato paste, mushrooms, salt and pepper. Cover the pan and allow the ragoût to simmer for about 1½ hours, or until the beef is tender. Correct the seasoning if necessary. Remove the bay leaves before serving.

All you need with this distinguished beef-and-vegetable dinner is crusty French bread and perhaps some tiny new potatoes cloaked in butter and chopped parsley. Serve this with either a red or white Burgundy wine, depending on which one you have used to create the dish.

BOEUF À LA MODE

(French Pot Roast)

MAKES 6 TO 8 SERVINGS

2 tablespoons oil
4 pounds top round beef
3 onions, chopped
2 cloves garlic, minced
1 pound carrots, cut in ¾-inch slices
4 stalks celery, diced
1½ teaspoons salt
½ teaspoon pepper
4 tablespoons flour
2 cups water
2 beef bouillon cubes
1-pound can tomatoes
1 cup dry red wine
2 bay leaves
2 teaspoons thyme
6 mushrooms, quartered

Heat the oil in a heavy Dutch oven; add the beef and brown it well on all sides. Add the onions and garlic and sauté them until golden, stirring occasionally. Add the carrots, celery, salt and pepper. Sprinkle flour over the vegetables and mix it in well with a wooden spoon. Let the vegetables cook for 3 or 4 minutes over medium heat; then add the water, bouillon cubes, tomatoes, wine, bay leaves and thyme. Stir well. Cover and let the mixture cook at a gentle simmer until the meat is tender, about 2½ hours. If the vegetables cook too quickly, remove them with a slotted spoon and allow the meat to continue cooking. When the meat is almost done, return the vegetables to the pan, add the mushrooms and let everything simmer 5 to 10 minutes longer.

You'll never be tempted to call *daube de boeuf* "beef stew" once you've made it this way. The special ingredients lend an artful piquancy that underscores the *daube*'s essential richness, and produces a lusty enthusiasm around the dinner table. Serve it with noodles, winter squash, and a robust Burgundy wine.

DAUBE DE BOEUF PROVENÇALE

MAKES 6 SERVINGS

- 3 *pounds beef shoulder*
- 4 *tablespoons olive oil*
- 3 *cups chopped green olives*
- ½ *cup orange juice*
- 12 *anchovy filets, minced fine*
- ½ *cup pimientos, chopped*
- 3 *cloves garlic, minced*
- 3 *shallots, chopped fine*
- 1 *cup tomato juice*
- 1½ *cups dry red wine*
- ½ *teaspoon coarse black pepper*
- ½ *teaspoon oregano*
- 1 *bay leaf*
- 2 *tablespoons chopped parsley*

Cut the beef into 1½-inch cubes. Heat the oil in a Dutch oven until it sizzles. Add the beef and brown it on all sides. While the beef is browning, mix together very well all the remaining ingredients, except the parsley. When the meat is browned, add the mixed ingredients to the pan. Cover and bake in a 375°F. oven for about 2 hours, or until the meat is tender. Skim the excess fat from the top of the sauce. Serve the *daube* with parsley sprinkled over the top.

BEEF-VEGETABLE PIE

MAKES 6 TO 8 SERVINGS

2 tablespoons butter
1 onion, chopped
1 clove garlic, minced
¼ teaspoon savory
Pinch nutmeg
2 tablespoons chopped parsley
1 teaspoon salt
½ teaspoon pepper
1½ pounds lean, ground beef
1 egg
2 tablespoons flour
¼ cup dry white wine
⅛ teaspoon monosodium glutamate
½ teaspoon Worcestershire sauce

Heat the butter in a skillet; add the onion and garlic and sauté gently. Add the savory, nutmeg, parsley, salt and pepper. Stir and cook until the onion is golden and tender. Put the ground meat into a bowl with the egg, flour and wine. Mix very thoroughly. To this, add the sautéed onion mixture, the monosodium glutamate and Worcestershire sauce. Mix well. Press this meat mixture into a glass baking dish or large, glass pie plate, forming a "crust" of the meat about ½-inch thick on the bottom and side of the dish. Refrigerate the crust while preparing the filling as follows:

4 carrots, sliced
4 stalks of celery, chopped
2 potatoes, peeled and sliced
½ envelope dry vegetable soup
1 cup water
2 tablespoons dry white wine
1 package (10 ounces) frozen peas, defrosted
Butter

Partially cook the carrots, celery and potatoes until they are crisp-tender; then drain them. Mix the dry soup with the water and wine, and cook it over low heat for 5 minutes.

Take the meat shell from the refrigerator. Put the peas in the bottom; then add the carrots and celery. Pour the soup over the vegetables. Arrange the potato slices over the top and dot with butter. Bake in a 350°F. oven for about 45 minutes, or until the potatoes are tender.

When you see the word *jardinière*, you know you will have a dish that is enhanced by vegetables. I think it's the nicest complement you can give to short ribs. This is another of those miraculous creations that benefit from an overnight stay in the refrigerator; the reheating next day brings out the blend of flavors. Serve it with scalloped potatoes or broad egg noodles, crisp-tender broccoli, and buttered carrots.

SHORT RIBS OF BEEF JARDINIÈRE

MAKES 4 SERVINGS

- *2 tablespoons oil*
- *2 pounds short ribs of beef (cut in serving-size pieces)*
- *3 small onions, chopped*
- *½ cup diced carrots*
- *½ cup diced celery*
- *½ teaspoon thyme*
- *2 bay leaves*
- *2 cloves garlic, minced*
- *1½ tablespoons flour*
- *1½ cups beef stock or bouillon*
- *½ cup dry white wine*
- *1-pound can tomatoes*
- *Salt and pepper to taste*
- *1 tablespoon tomato paste*
- *1 tablespoon chopped parsley*

Heat the oil in a heavy Dutch oven. Add the short ribs and brown them well on all sides. Remove the meat to a platter and set it aside. Add the onions to the oil and sauté them until they are translucent. Then add the carrots and celery and let them sauté for 2 or 3 minutes. Add the thyme, bay leaves and garlic. Mix well; then return the browned meat to the pan. Sprinkle flour over

everything; then add the stock while continuing to mix. Add the wine, tomatoes, salt, pepper, and tomato paste while continuing to stir. Cover the pan and let the contents simmer for 1½ to 2 hours, until the meat is firm-tender. Correct the seasoning, if necessary. Sprinkle with parsley just before serving.

Leave it to the French to find a way to ennoble something as simple as hash. I hate to use that word; Hachis Parmentier is so much more lyrical — to the ear, the eye and the tongue. It's also a simple and opulent-seeming way to use leftover meat, or lean, ground beef from the supermarket. All you need with it is a vegetable, lightly seasoned. Lima beans would be nice, for a change.

HACHIS PARMENTIER

MAKES 6 TO 8 SERVINGS

3 pounds potatoes
Salted water to cook
2 tablespoons olive oil
3 onions, chopped
2 garlic cloves, minced
1½ pounds lean, ground beef
¼ teaspoon monosodium glutamate
1 teaspoon salt
½ teaspoon pepper
½ teaspoon celery salt
½ cup chopped parsley
1 beef bouillon cube
1 tablespoon dry white wine
⅓ cup fine, dry bread crumbs
4 tablespoons butter
¼ cup light cream

Peel and cut the potatoes and put them on to cook in lightly salted water. While they are cooking, put the oil in a large skillet and heat it over medium heat. Add the onions and garlic and sauté until they are golden. Add the ground beef and stir while it is browning. Add the monosodium glutamate, salt, pepper, celery salt, beef bouillon cube and wine. Stir very well and cook over medium heat for about 10 to 12 minutes. Taste and correct the seasonings, if necessary. Stir in the bread crumbs. Remove the skillet from the heat and set it aside.

When the potatoes are tender, drain them thoroughly; then mash them until they are very smooth. Beat in the butter and cream very well.

Butter a large casserole dish. Spread a layer of the mashed potatoes, then a layer of the meat mixture. Continue layering, ending with mashed potatoes on the top. Spread the top layer smoothly; then make a criss-cross design with the tines of a fork. Place a few thin pats of butter on top. Bake in a 350°F. oven until lightly browned, about 40 to 45 minutes.

Note: This dish may be readied in advance, then refrigerated until it is time for baking. Allow it to come to room temperature, or extend the baking time a bit if the dish is not warm when put into oven.

I would like to be at your table when you present the first slice of Meat Loaf Roulade, just to see the astonishment and hear the applause. The way the meat loaf arcs around the stuffing makes a dish as pretty to look at as it is delicious to taste. If you wish, repeat one of the flavors by serving braised celery or Carrots Vichy (page 178) as a vegetable, along with baked, sliced tomatoes.

MEAT LOAF ROULADE

MAKES 6 TO 8 SERVINGS

STUFFING:

2 onions, finely chopped
1 cup chopped celery
1 tablespoon butter
⅓ cup dry white wine
1 cup bread crumbs
3 or 4 whole carrots, cooked

Sauté the onions and celery in butter until they are soft and translucent. Stir in the wine and simmer for 5 minutes. Remove from the heat and stir in the bread crumbs. Set this aside, along with the cooked carrots, while you mix the meat loaf:

2 pounds lean, ground beef
1 egg
1 onion, finely chopped
½ cup milk
½ cup fine, dry bread crumbs
½ teaspoon monosodium glutamate
1 tablespoon chopped parsley
2 teaspoons salt
½ teaspoon pepper
7 or 8 bacon strips

In a large bowl, combine all the ingredients except the bacon strips. Mix them very thoroughly.

On a large sheet of aluminum foil or waxed paper, spread the meat mixture out to a large oval, about 1-inch thick. Spread the prepared stuffing over the meat to about ½-inch of each edge. Place the whole, cooked carrots in a straight line down the center of the oval. Lifting the foil along one of the long edges of the oval, roll the meat up lengthwise to form a "roulade" (as you would for a jelly roll). Seal the meat mixture at both ends of the roll. Place strips of bacon over the top. Transfer the roulade carefully to a shallow baking pan. Bake it in a 350°F. oven for approximately 1 hour. Carefully pour off any excess fat; then with two wide spatulas, lift the roulade to a heated serving platter. Serve with Sauce Roulade (page 202).

This recipe looks as if it has a lot of steps, but there's really nothing to it. Especially when you're in a sunshine mood and want a sample of good living. This dish is made with olive oil, which is the basis of all Italian cookery. If you steal oil and pasta from the Italians, they're finished — the same as if you steal wine from the French. The use of carrots brings a little sweetness into the dish. Use ground chuck if you really want to economize.

All you need with Cannelloni is a robust red wine. Chianti if you like, but something with *pow*. If you want to add a side dish, try vegetables Italian style: lima beans with tomatoes and pepper, or stewed tomatoes with olives, or Ratatouille (page 187).

CANNELLONI

MAKES 6 TO 8 SERVINGS

1 tablespoon olive oil
1 large onion, finely chopped
2 carrots, finely diced
1 pound ground beef
½ pound ground veal
1 teaspoon salt
½ teaspoon pepper
2 cups Mornay Sauce (page 208)
3 egg yolks
2 tablespoons chopped parsley
Lasagna sheets
Grated Romano cheese
Tomato Sauce (page 203)

Heat the olive oil in a heavy skillet; add the onion and sauté it gently until it is golden. Add the carrots and beef; stir and cook

until the beef is browned. Add the veal; sprinkle it with the salt and pepper; cover the skillet and cook gently about 5 minutes.

Put about a third of the cooked meat mixture into a blender; process it for a few seconds until it is smooth. Put it into a bowl. Repeat with the remaining meat mixture until all of it is blended. Mix in 1 cup of the Mornay Sauce along with the egg yolks and parsley.

Meantime, cook the lasagna sheets according to the package directions. Drain them thoroughly, then cut the sheets into 3-inch squares. Working with four squares at a time, spread the prepared filling across the center of each square; then roll each square neatly and place the rolls in a large shallow baking pan, with the seam sides down. Put just one layer in the pan; use two pans if necessary.

Spread the remaining Mornay Sauce over the top of the cannelloni, sprinkle with grated cheese, and spread tomato sauce over the top. Sprinkle the top with more grated cheese; then bake the cannelloni in a 350°F. oven for about 20 minutes.

Sometimes, I make a batch of very small stuffed cabbages so I can serve them for appetizers. When I use them as an entrée, I like to serve them with boiled potatoes or broad noodles drenched in butter and dappled with parsley. For drinking, either full-bodied red Burgundy wine or a good, heavy German beer is magnificent.

STUFFED CABBAGE

MAKES 6 TO 8 SERVINGS

1 large head cabbage
Boiling, salted water
1 tablespoon butter
¼ cup finely chopped onions
1 pound lean, ground beef
2 cloves garlic, minced
½ teaspoon curry powder
½ teaspoon ground thyme
1 teaspoon salt
½ teaspoon pepper
⅛ teaspoon monosodium glutamate
1 large can (28 ounces) tomatoes
1 egg
¼ to ½ cup bread crumbs
½ cup cooked rice
2 tablespoons sugar
Juice of half a lemon
1 beef bouillon cube
1 stalk celery, diced
1 carrot, sliced
1 onion, sliced

Remove the core and the outer leaves of the cabbage and discard these pieces. Carefully remove about 15 large cabbage leaves. Drop these into boiling, salted water and cook them gently (parboil) for 10 minutes. Drain and set them aside to cool.

Put the butter into a skillet; add the chopped onions and sauté them until golden. Add the ground beef and stir it while browning. Add the garlic, curry, thyme, salt, pepper and monosodium glutamate. Cover and cook over medium heat for about 5 minutes.

Coarsely chop 3 or 4 tomatoes from the can; add them to the skillet and cook for another 5 minutes. Remove the skillet from the heat. Mix in the egg and enough bread crumbs to absorb the extra juice; then stir in the rice. Correct the seasoning if necessary and let the mixture cool slightly.

Divide the stuffing equally among the cabbage leaves, placing a portion in the center of each leaf and rolling up each one securely. Place the cabbage rolls seam sides down in a large Dutch oven or casserole. Add the remaining canned tomatoes with their juice, the sugar, lemon juice, bouillon cube, diced celery, carrot and onion slices. Cover the casserole and bake in a 350°F. oven for 1 hour, basting occasionally. Remove the cover, increase the heat to 375°F., and bake for another 15 minutes to brown the top.

5
Veal

I WISH that veal could be as popular in the United States as it is in France and Italy. There, they really use it a lot and cook it in many ways. In America, good veal is neither plentiful nor cheap. What is more — I mean, less — American veal has very little flavor because the calves are killed too young. And sometimes they're fed grass, which results in red meat and beefy-tasting veal. Watch out for "baby beef," for there's no such thing; what you want is either veal *or* beef. Some Italian markets have very decent veal, which they get from special growers, though the price is quite high. An economical way to indulge yourself in good veal is to create a dish, such as Wiener Schnitzel (page 77) or Veal Scaloppine Marsala, (page 74) that serves each guest amply on portions of 4 or 5 ounces apiece.

The cucumbers are for breezy freshness, the shallots and garlic for pungency; the mushrooms and cream anoint the chops in a soothing sauce. Serve with hot, buttered noodles or Rice Pilaf (page 188), Peasant Peas (page 183) and a light red wine or a white Burgundy.

BRAISED VEAL CHOPS WITH CUCUMBER

MAKES 4 SERVINGS

3 tablespoons butter
4 veal chops, each 1-inch thick
Salt and pepper
1 shallot, chopped fine
1 clove garlic, minced
2 cucumbers, peeled and seeded, cut in wedges
4 mushrooms, sliced
¾ cup heavy cream
½ teaspoon fines herbes
½ teaspoon marjoram
Watercress

Melt the butter in a heavy skillet; add the chops and sauté them until they are nicely browned on both sides. Sprinkle them with salt and pepper. Add the shallots, garlic, and cucumber wedges to the pan. Sauté over medium heat until the vegetables are crisp-tender. Add the mushrooms and cook for another minute or two. Add the cream, fines herbes and marjoram. Let the sauce and chops cook over low heat until the veal has a total cooking time, from start to finish, of about 25 to 30 minutes. Remove the chops to a heated platter, and pour the sauce over the top. Garnish with watercress.

VEAL SCALOPPINE MARSALA

MAKES 4 SERVINGS

1½ pounds veal cutlets
½ teaspoon salt
⅛ teaspoon pepper
¼ cup flour
4 tablespoons butter
½ cup Marsala wine
2 teaspoons chopped parsley

Flatten the veal cutlets between sheets of waxed paper with a mallet or rolling pin. Sprinkle them with salt, pepper and flour. Shake off any excess flour. Melt the butter in a large skillet and brown the veal on both sides. Remove the veal from the pan to a warm platter. Stir the wine into the pan juices quickly; then pour the sauce over the veal. Sprinkle with chopped parsley and serve immediately.

The dash and zest of this dish reminds me of one of those romantics who used to swashbuckle across the silver screen. It's like essence of Douglas Fairbanks, cloaked in hot bubbly cheese . . . masculine, yet sentimental.

VEAL SCALLOPS PIÉMONTESE

MAKES 4 SERVINGS

- 3 *tablespoons butter*
- 1½ *pounds veal cutlets, pounded thin*
- ½ *cup Chablis wine*
- ½ *teaspoon salt*
- ⅛ *teaspoon pepper*
- ¼ *teaspoon basil*
- 4 *thin slices Provolone cheese*

Melt the butter in a large skillet and sauté the veal cutlets until they are brown on both sides. Add the wine, salt, pepper and basil. Stir well. Then place the cutlets in a shallow baking dish and pour the wine sauce over them. Arrange the cheese slices over the veal. Bake in a 375°F. oven for 10 minutes. Serve promptly.

MEDALLIONS OF VEAL CLAMART

MAKES 4 TO 6 SERVINGS

8 artichokes
Salted, boiling water
½ cup frozen small French peas, defrosted
3 tablespoons butter, divided
1 shallot, chopped
1 lettuce leaf, chopped fine
4 tablespoons water
8 veal medallions
Salt and pepper
½ teaspoon marjoram
1 shallot (additional), chopped
1 teaspoon chopped chives
4 anchovy filets, chopped
½ cup brown sauce (page 201)
¼ cup dry white wine
Parsley for garnish

Cook the artichokes in lightly salted, boiling water until they are tender. Cool them, remove the leaves and choke from each, and reserve only the artichoke bottoms for use.

Using 1 tablespoon of the butter, sauté the defrosted peas, chopped shallot and lettuce for a minute or two. Add the 4 tablespoons of water; cover and let the vegetables simmer for about 2 minutes. Remove from the heat, but keep the pan covered and warm.

Sprinkle the veal lightly with salt and pepper. Melt the remaining butter in a large skillet. Sauté the meat over medium heat for about 3 minutes on each side, or until nicely browned. Add the marjoram, the additional chopped shallot, the chives, anchovies, brown sauce and wine. Stir and spoon the sauce over the veal in the skillet until all the medallions are nicely coated with a smooth sauce. Correct the seasoning, if necessary.

Carefully place the artichoke bottoms on top of the sautéed vegetable mixture, cover the pan again and return it to the heat, to warm all the vegetables. Arrange the veal and sauce in the center of a warmed serving platter. Place the artichoke bottoms around the meat and fill them with sautéed vegetables. Sprinkle with parsley, if desired, and serve.

The cost of good veal is staggering, but flattening the cutlets makes each portion so plate-filling that you need only about 5 ounces per person. Be sure to use enough butter in the pan, because the bread crumbs will absorb a lot of it and, if you've been stingy, you'll wind up with scorched veal. And sauté the meat only until it turns golden; dark brown *tastes* dark brown, and it means dried, overcooked veal, besides. Serve with hot, buttered egg noodles or Pommes de Terre au Gratin (page 185); spinach or another green vegetable; and white Burgundy wine.

PENNSYLVANIA DUTCH WIENER SCHNITZEL

MAKES 4 SERVINGS

1½ pounds thin veal cutlets
¾ cup fine, dry bread crumbs
½ cup flour
Salt and pepper to taste
1 egg
1 tablespoon water
4 tablespoons butter
Juice of half a lemon
Parsley
Thin lemon slices

Put the veal pieces between 2 sheets of doubled waxed paper and pound them with a mallet or rolling pin until they are very thin. Put the bread crumbs onto another piece of waxed paper. Combine the flour with the salt and pepper on a separate sheet of paper. Beat the egg with water in a shallow dish. Dip the veal pieces first in the flour mixture, then in the egg, and finally in the bread crumbs. Make sure all the pieces are evenly coated. Let them rest for 10 to 15 minutes so that the coating will stay intact during the cooking.

Melt the butter in a large skillet until it is very hot and bubbly. Add the veal pieces carefully and quickly sauté each for 2 or 3 minutes on one side; then turn each piece and sauté it on the other side for a few minutes. Remove the meat to a warm platter. Sprinkle the veal lightly with lemon juice and drizzle a little melted butter over each cutlet, if desired. Garnish with parsley and thin lemon slices and serve promptly.

VEAL MARENGO

MAKES 4 SERVINGS

- *1½ pounds veal shoulder or breast*
- *Salt and pepper*
- *4 tablespoons olive oil*
- *2 cloves garlic, minced*
- *2 shallots, chopped fine*
- *12 tiny white onions, peeled*
- *2 tablespoons flour*
- *1 cup dry white wine*
- *1-pound can tomatoes*
- *4 mushrooms, chopped*
- *1 bay leaf*
- *¼ teaspoon thyme*
- *Dash of cayenne pepper*
- *2 tablespoons chopped parsley*
- *⅓ cup drained, pitted black olives*

Cut the veal into cubes and sprinkle the cubes with salt and pepper. Heat the oil in a heavy Dutch oven; add the garlic and sauté it gently for 2 or 3 minutes. Add the veal and brown it lightly over medium-high heat for about 5 minutes, stirring to brown the meat on all sides. Add the shallots and onions and sauté another 3 to 4 minutes.

Stir in the flour, mixing thoroughly; then add the wine and tomatoes. Stir in the mushrooms, bay leaf, thyme, cayenne pepper, parsley and olives. Cover and let the Marengo simmer for about 1½ hours, or until the meat is tender.

This is one of the most famous, most elegant dishes in the culinary galaxy of France. It has all the *noblesse* and *finesse* necessary for a party, and makes an everyday dinner an experience to celebrate. Serve it with Rice Pilaf (page 188) or boiled parsley potatoes, and a white Burgundy wine.

BLANQUETTE DE VEAU

3 pounds stewing veal, cut into 1-inch cubes
Water to cover
2 carrots, sliced
3 or 4 sprigs parsley
½ teaspoon thyme
2 bay leaves
1 clove garlic, chopped
1 shallot, chopped
1 onion, studded with 3 whole cloves
1 leek (optional)
2 cups dry white wine
Salt and pepper to taste
2 dozen small, whole white onions
1 teaspoon sugar
½ pound mushrooms, sliced
½ cup butter, divided
Juice of 1 lemon, divided
½ cup flour
2 egg yolks
½ cup heavy cream

Put the veal into a heavy Dutch oven. Barely cover it with water, bring the water to a boil, and skim the froth from the top. Add the carrots, parsley, thyme, bay leaves, garlic, shallot, onion studded with cloves, leek, white wine, salt and pepper. Bring the liquid back to a boil, lower the heat, cover the pan and simmer until the veal is tender, about 1½ hours.

With a slotted spoon, remove the meat cubes from the pan and set them aside. Strain the stock through a colander, discarding the vegetables and returning the stock to the Dutch oven. Set the stock aside.

Put the small, whole onions into a small pan, barely cover them with water, and boil until the onions are tender. Drain them thoroughly. Sprinkle them with the sugar; then return them to the pan and let them simmer gently until all the water is cooked off and the onions are golden.

Meanwhile, sauté the mushrooms in 1 tablespoon of the butter until they are golden. Stir in half the lemon juice and set aside.

Melt the remaining butter in a large saucepan. Stir in the flour to make a very smooth paste. Cook the paste over low heat for 2 or 3 minutes; then stir in about 4 cups of the reserved stock from the Dutch oven. Bring the mixture to a boil and continue to stir until the sauce is smooth and thickened.

In a separate bowl, combine the egg yolks with the heavy cream and the remaining lemon juice. Stir in a few spoonfuls of the hot sauce and blend; then stir this egg mixture into the large pan of sauce, mixing rapidly. Taste the sauce and correct the seasoning, if necessary. Stir in the sautéed mushrooms, the small onions and the cubes of meat. Simmer 15 minutes, stirring from time to time.

Braised veal shanks are given a surprise snap by the addition of *gremolata:* a packet of flavors that explodes into sudden glory at the last moment of cooking. Serve Osso Buco in the traditional manner (on risotto Milanese) or with fettucine: noodles tossed with an opulence of melted butter and grated Parmesan cheese.

OSSO BUCO VELLA JULIETTA

MAKES 4 SERVINGS

3 tablespoons butter
Salt and pepper
3 veal shanks, cut into 2-inch pieces
Flour
½ cup chopped onions
½ cup chopped carrots
½ cup chopped celery
½ cup sliced mushrooms
1 cup canned tomatoes, well drained
1 cup dry white wine
½ teaspoon rosemary
½ teaspoon sage
½ teaspoon basil
1 bay leaf
Thin rind of half a lemon, chopped fine

GREMOLATA:
1 clove garlic, minced fine
2 tablespoons chopped parsley
5 anchovy filets

Melt the butter in a heavy Dutch oven. Salt and pepper the veal; then dredge it lightly with flour, covering all surfaces well. Carefully place the veal in the hot butter and brown it on all sides, turning the meat as necessary. Add the onions, carrots and celery.

Lower the heat slightly; then stir in the mushrooms, tomatoes and wine, and allow to simmer for about 5 minutes. Add the rosemary, sage, basil and bay leaf; cover and let simmer for 1 hour. Taste the sauce and add salt and pepper if necessary. Cover and continue simmering for another 30 to 40 minutes, or until the meat is tender.

Combine the lemon rind, garlic, parsley and anchovy filets, mixing them together very well. When the meat is just about done, stir in this *gremolata* mixture and allow everything to simmer for another 5 minutes.

JARRET DE VEAU BRAISÉ AVEC CÉLERI

(Veal Shanks Braised with Celery)

MAKES 4 SERVINGS

3 tablespoons vegetable oil
4 veal shanks
Salt and pepper
2 tablespoons butter
2 celery hearts, cut into quarters
6 small onions, cut into quarters
1 cup mushrooms, cut into quarters
¼ teaspoon thyme
1 bay leaf
¼ teaspoon marjoram
1 cup dry white wine
3 tablespoons flour
1 cup chicken stock
1 clove garlic, finely chopped

Heat the oil in a heavy Dutch oven. Carefully add the veal shanks and brown them nicely, turning them as necessary. Sprinkle them lightly with salt and pepper. When all the shanks are browned, remove them from the pan and set them aside. Add the butter to the pan. When it is hot, add the celery hearts and allow them to sauté to a golden brown. Stir carefully from time to time. Add the quartered onions and sauté them to a golden brown. Add the mushrooms, then the thyme, bay leaf, marjoram and white wine. Stir in the flour and chicken stock. Let the sauce come just to boiling point. Return the shanks to the pan, making sure each piece is covered with sauce. Cover the pan and let the contents simmer gently until the meat is tender. Halfway through the cooking time, sprinkle finely minced garlic over the meat. Total cooking time will be about 1½ hours.

Delicate in flavor and light on the budget, this recipe is a favorite in the wonderful lively region of Gascony. Be sure to buy a good breast of veal from your most trustworthy butcher, so you won't be stuck with tough meat. And get a good-sized breast, so there'll be more meat than skin!

STUFFED BREAST OF VEAL GASCOGNE

3-pound boned breast of veal
Juice of 1 lemon
¼ teaspoon salt
⅛ teaspoon pepper
¾ pound lean, ground pork
1 cup bread crumbs
2 eggs
3 tablespoons heavy cream
1 clove garlic, minced
2 tablespoons chopped parsley
1 teaspoon chopped chives
1 teaspoon marjoram
1 teaspoon salt (additional)
¼ teaspoon pepper (additional)
½ teaspoon thyme
1 carrot, cut up
1 onion, chopped
2 stalks celery, cut up
4 strips bacon
1 cup water
¼ cup dry white wine

Spread the veal out flat. Season it with lemon juice, ¼ teaspoon of salt and ⅛ teaspoon of pepper.

In a bowl, mix the pork, bread crumbs, eggs, cream, garlic, parsley, chives, marjoram, and the additional salt and pepper. Combine thoroughly; then spread the pork mixture over the flattened veal. Roll the veal up lengthwise and tie it together securely with string.

Place the veal roll in a roasting pan. Sprinkle it with thyme and surround it with the carrots, onions and celery. Cover the roast with bacon strips; then pour the water into the pan. Roast in a

350°F. oven for about 2 hours, or until the meat is tender. Baste the roast occasionally with pan juices.

Remove the roast to a warm platter. Remove the vegetables with a slotted spoon and discard. Add the wine to the pan juices and stir; strain this sauce and serve with the roast.

STUFFED VEAL SHOULDER COMO

MAKES 6 SERVINGS

4 ounces prosciutto
¾ pound lean sausage meat
1 teaspoon chopped garlic
1 tablespoon chopped shallots
1 cup chopped mushrooms
Salt and pepper
½ cup chopped parsley, divided
1 egg
2 tablespoons white wine
1 tablespoon flour
1 boneless veal shoulder, about 2½ pounds
2 tablespoons butter, softened
½ cup white wine (additional)

Cut the ham into julienne strips. Put the ham strips into a bowl with the sausage meat, garlic, shallots and mushrooms, and mix these ingredients thoroughly. Add salt and pepper to taste, but remember that there already is seasoning in the ham and sausage. Add all but 2 tablespoons of the chopped parsley; then add the egg and mix well. Stir in the 2 tablespoons of white wine and the tablespoon of flour to complete the stuffing mixture.

Spread the boned veal out flat. Sprinkle it with the remaining parsley; then spread the stuffing over the veal's surface to within about an inch of each edge. Bring the veal up around the sides, and roll and tie it securely.

Put softened butter in the bottom of a baking dish or pan and spread it around. Place the roast in the buttered dish and pour the additional wine over the roast. Bake in a 350°F. oven for 2 to 2½ hours, or until the meat is nicely tender. Baste it occasionally with the pan juices.

Remove the roast and juices to a warm platter and garnish the dish with sprigs of watercress and chilled crab apples.

6
Lamb

ALTHOUGH the custom in America is to cook lamb until it is well done, I hope you will try lamb the delectable European way: medium-rare, still pink and juicy. That is when it has the most flavor. When you cook lamb and its fat too much, the meat acquires a strong, smelly taste like mutton. I prefer the bewitching flavor of *lamb.*

To roast lamb, I recommend inserting a few slivers of garlic cloves into the meat here and there, surrounding it on the pan with a few cut-up vegetables, and using a moderate oven heat of 325°F. to 350°F.

Lamb steak, when you can find it or have it cut for you, is a sensational change from beef steak, and certainly more economical than lamb chops. Ground lamb is a stirring change from hamburger.

When you have leg of lamb left over, try serving cold slices enlivened with your own homemade mayonnaise, which you've made piquant with a fleck of mustard.

Shoulder chops or steaks are not, heaven knows, the most exquisite cuts of lamb. But they are inexpensive, and they do have the advantage of being distinctively flavorsome. So it's worth doing something with them that will take them out of the plebeian category and into the luscious. This recipe not only fulfills that goal admirably, it gives your battery of menu ideas another dimension. For crispness and color, add potatoes, rissoléed or sautéed, and a fresh spinach salad.

STUFFED BAKED LAMB CHOPS OR STEAKS

MAKES 4 SERVINGS

4 shoulder lamb chops or steaks
Salt and pepper to taste
1 tablespoon vegetable oil
¼ cup dry white wine
Butter
Stuffing (recipe below)

Trim all excess fat from the lamb. Salt and pepper the chops lightly on both sides. Heat the oil in a heavy skillet and sauté the chops on both sides until they are nicely browned. Transfer them in a single layer to a baking dish. Top each piece of meat with a good portion of the stuffing. Pour wine around the meat and dot the tops with butter. Bake the chops in a 375°F. oven until the stuffing is lightly browned and the meat is done. This will take from 20 to 30 minutes, depending upon how well-done you prefer the meat.

STUFFING:

1 tablespoon oil
1 onion, sliced
1 clove garlic, minced
1 cauliflower head, cooked and drained
½ cup heavy cream
2 egg yolks
Salt and pepper to taste
2 tablespoons grated Romano cheese

Heat the oil in a heavy saucepan; add the onion slices and sauté them until golden. Add the garlic and cook for another few minutes. Cool the mixture slightly; then put it into a blender along with part of the cooked cauliflower and a tablespoon or two of the cream. Blend until this new mixture is smooth. Transfer it to a bowl. Blend the remaining cauliflower with cream in the same manner and add it to the bowl. Beat in the egg yolks, season to taste, and then add the grated cheese. Stir to mix the ingredients thoroughly.

HERBED LAMB STEAKS

MAKES 4 SERVINGS

1 tablespoon olive oil
2 cloves garlic, minced
1 teaspoon rosemary
Salt and pepper to taste
4 lamb steaks
Juice of 1 lemon
2 tablespoons chopped parsley

Mix together thoroughly the olive oil, minced garlic, rosemary, salt and pepper. Rub the mixture on both sides of each lamb steak. Cover the steaks with plastic wrap and let them stand in the refrigerator for about 2 hours. Broil the steaks about 3 inches from the source of heat for 4 to 5 minutes on each side, depending upon the rareness desired. Before serving, drizzle lemon juice over the steaks and garnish with parsley.

As good as plain leg of lamb is, I like to change my tune every now and then and present it in a different way. There is another motive that you might also consider: a stuffed leg of lamb extends the number of servings per pound. With the onions, baked or oven-roasted potatoes and a green vegetable, you'll have an abundant feast that won't bankrupt your budget.

BONELESS STUFFED LEG OF LAMB

MAKES 8 TO 10 SERVINGS

5-pound leg of lamb, boned
3 tablespoons butter
¾ cup chopped onions
2 cloves garlic, minced
1 cup sliced mushrooms
½ teaspoon rosemary
¼ teaspoon tarragon
1 cup chopped Italian parsley
2 teaspoons plain gelatin
¼ cup dry white wine
¼ cup fine, dry bread crumbs
½ teaspoon salt
¼ teaspoon pepper
Olive oil
2 onions, quartered
1 cup chicken bouillon

Trim all fat from the meat. Spread it out flat on a board and set it aside.

Melt the butter in a skillet. Add the onions and garlic and sauté lightly until the onions are transparent, about 2 or 3 minutes. Add the mushrooms, rosemary, tarragon and parsley. Mix well and continue cooking gently.

Soften the gelatin in the wine; then stir both into the skillet of onions and mushrooms. Add the bread crumbs, salt and pepper and mix well. Remove the pan from the heat.

Cover the prepared meat with a layer of the stuffing; then sprinkle lightly with olive oil. Roll the meat up and tie it securely with string. Place the lamb in a roasting pan and sprinkle it lightly with salt and pepper (and some additional rosemary, if desired). Place the onion quarters around the meat and pour the chicken bouillon into the bottom of the pan. Roast in a 350°F. oven for 1½ hours, or to the desired degree of doneness. Preferably, the meat should be nice and pink when sliced.

Remove the strings before serving. Slice the lamb and serve it with onions and pan juices spooned over each portion.

March is a month I could do without. The weather is apt to be disagreeable, it's the tail end of a season which is becoming a bore, and the Ides bode no good for anyone. But it has a redeeming grace: March is when the price of lamb begins to drop and tender young vegetables start to sprout. Therefore, it always makes me think of Navarin Printanier — spring lamb stew — so wondrously fragrant, so blissfully delicious. Present it with a savory rice-and-spinach pilaf and a velvety red wine.

NAVARIN OF LAMB PRINTANIER

Ragoût of Lamb

MAKES 6 SERVINGS

- *3 pounds lamb shoulder*
- *1 tablespoon butter*
- *2 onions, diced*
- *4 carrots, cut into 2-inch lengths*
- *4 stalks celery, cut into 1-inch lengths*
- *¼ teaspoon thyme*
- *1 bay leaf*
- *4 cups chicken stock or bouillon*
- *Salt and pepper to taste*
- *2 potatoes, peeled and grated*
- *3 cloves garlic, finely chopped*
- *12 small whole onions, peeled*
- *¼ cup dry red wine*
- *3 potatoes, peeled and cubed*
- *4 slices bacon*
- *Chopped fresh parsley*

Bone the lamb if necessary, removing excess fat. Cut the meat into cubes. Melt the butter in a heavy Dutch oven. Add the diced onions and cook them gently, only until they are limp. Do not allow the onions to brown. Add the meat cubes and stir, letting the meat brown evenly. Add the carrot and celery pieces to the skillet, along with the thyme and bay leaf, and stir to mix. Add the chicken stock and bring it to a boil. Lower the heat, cover the pan, and let the contents simmer about ½ hour.

Taste the sauce for seasoning, adding salt and pepper as desired. Stir in the grated potatoes and chopped garlic. (The grated potatoes serve to thicken the stock, in place of flour or cornstarch). Again, cover the pan and simmer for another 15 minutes. Then add the whole onions, red wine, and cubed potatoes. Simmer until all the vegetables and the meat cubes are tender.

Cook the bacon in a skillet until it is crisp. Drain the strips well on paper toweling; then crumble them into bits. Transfer the ragoût to a large serving bowl or tureen; garnish it with crumbled bacon and fresh parsley.

RAGOÛT DE MOUTON MÉNAGÈRE

(French Lamb Stew)

MAKES 4 SERVINGS

- *3 tablespoons butter*
- *2 pounds boneless leg of lamb, cubed*
- *2 cloves garlic, crushed*
- *3 carrots, sliced*
- *2 white turnips, quartered*
- *1 onion, sliced*
- *1 small cabbage, quartered*
- *2½ cups water*
- *1 bay leaf*
- *⅛ teaspoon thyme*
- *Salt and pepper to taste*
- *4 potatoes, peeled and thinly sliced*

Melt the butter in a Dutch oven. Add the lamb cubes and sauté until they are nicely browned. Add the garlic, carrots, turnips and onion; sauté for 3 to 5 minutes. Add the cabbage, water, bay leaf, thyme, salt and pepper; bring the liquid to a boil. Lower the heat, cover the pan and let the contents simmer for 1½ hours. Add the potatoes and continue cooking for another 15 to 20 minutes, or until the vegetables and meat are tender.

English Mixed Grill is so expensive looking and noble tasting that it makes me think I'm in London — at dinner after the theater, in one of those splendid, impeccable private clubs. The joy is, the mixed grill is really very economical, and very easy to prepare. If you examine the recipe, you'll see that the other ingredients extend the one expensive item, the rib lamb chops, so that you need only one chop per person. Here are some clues to getting the best of the rest of the ingredients:

Buy slab bacon rather than presliced. It's less costly, and you can cut thick slices.

Give the bacon slices and sausages a quick boil to firm them before sautéing, so they won't vanish in the cooking.

Calf's liver is tenderer than beef liver, but the latter is acceptable for this dish. Dust it with flour before you sauté it, to keep the blood inside and prevent the mess of splashing.

English Mixed Grill is handsome at the table. Add portions of sliced potatoes and onions, sautéed to golden crunchiness, and a dry red wine — *et voilà!*

ENGLISH MIXED GRILL

MAKES 4 TO 6 SERVINGS

6 firm tomatoes
Salt and pepper
Butter
½ cup water
1 pound sweet Italian sausage
12 thick slices bacon
3 lamb kidneys
6 rib lamb chops
½ pound sliced calf's liver
½ pound mushroom caps (medium-size)
½ cup dry white wine

Score the tops of the tomatoes; sprinkle them with salt and pepper and dot them with butter. Put them in a shallow, buttered baking dish and bake in a 375°F. oven until tender.

Put the water in a large skillet. Add the sausage and bacon and cook over medium heat until all the water is evaporated; then allow the sausage and bacon to sauté slowly, until nicely browned.

Meantime, clean and trim the kidneys by cutting them in half and removing the white centers. Set the kidneys aside. When the sausage and bacon strips are done, take them out of the skillet and set them aside, but keep them warm. Add the lamb chops and liver slices to the skillet and sauté them quickly to the degree of doneness preferred. Remove them from the pan and place on a warm platter with the sausage and bacon. Next, sauté the kidneys and mushrooms very quickly, cooking them for just about 2 or 3 minutes. Then return all the cooked meats to the pan and bring them back to serving temperature.

Arrange the meat on a warm platter and place the tomatoes around the meat. Pour off any fat left in the skillet; add the wine and stir it quickly over low heat to deglaze the pan. Pour the juices over the meat and tomatoes. Serve promptly while piping hot.

There is nothing innocent about Moussaka. It is rich, aromatically perfumed, kissed with the genius of Greek cuisine. One other cheerfully colored vegetable, such as carrots, is all you need for a meal that inspires dancing in the aisles.

MOUSSAKA

(Stuffed Eggplant)

MAKES 6 SERVINGS

4 to 6 medium-small eggplants
4 tablespoons butter, divided
1 cup chopped onions
1 pound ground lamb or beef
Pinch of rosemary
1 teaspoon salt
½ teaspoon pepper
2 tomatoes, peeled and chopped
2 tablespoons olive oil
Juice of half a lemon
1 tablespoon chopped parsley
1 cup tomato purée
¼ pound Feta cheese
2 eggs
2 tablespoons seasoned bread crumbs
1½ cups Béchamel Sauce (page 206)

Slice the eggplants in half lengthwise and scoop out the pulp carefully, leaving each shell about ½-inch thick. Chop the pulp coarsely. Put 2 tablespoons of the butter into a skillet; add the chopped onions and sauté until they are golden. Add the ground meat and stir while browning it evenly. Add the rosemary, salt and pepper, along with the chopped pulp from the eggplants and continue sautéing until eggplant is cooked. Add the chopped tomatoes to meat. Stir carefully to mix, then cover the pan and let the mixture cook over medium-low heat for 15 minutes.

Meanwhile, in another skillet, heat the olive oil. When it is hot, place as many eggplant shells as will fit in the pan, cut-side down, in the oil and allow them to sauté gently over low heat. Repeat until all the shells have been sautéed. Remove each in turn and carefully drain off any excess oil. Place all the shells in a buttered baking dish, cut-side up.

When the meat mixture has finished cooking, stir in the lemon juice, parsley and tomato purée. Remove the pan from heat and stir in the Feta cheese. Mix one of the eggs with the bread crumbs and set aside. Beat the remaining egg and mix it into the Béchamel Sauce and reserve.

Stuff each eggplant shell with some of the meat mixture, spread 2 tablespoons of the Béchamel Sauce over each portion of meat, and top each shell with a share of the bread crumb–egg mixture. Dot with the remaining butter. Bake in a 300°F. oven for 35 minutes.

I like to use recipes that I can fix ahead of time and just heat or broil at the last minute, so I can be with my guests where the fun is, instead of being stuck in the kitchen. This one's a knockout: very impressive looking, stupendously tasty and disarmingly simple to do. You might concoct some marinated mushrooms to serve on lettuce beds as an appetizer beforehand. Add some peas mixed with rice for an artful accompaniment to the Shish Kebab, plus a good red claret. Follow up with a piquant green salad, then finish with some cheese and fruit to go with any wine that's left in the bottle.

SHISH KEBAB

MAKES 4 TO 6 SERVINGS

MARINADE:

½ cup olive oil
1 cup salad oil
2 bay leaves
1 lemon, sliced
1 teaspoon thyme
1 teaspoon oregano
½ teaspoon basil
3 cloves garlic, chopped
½ teaspoon monosodium glutamate
1 teaspoon salt
½ teaspoon pepper or 6 whole peppercorns

MEAT AND VEGETABLES:

4-pound leg of lamb, boned
3 green peppers, seeded and cut in square pieces
2 or 3 hot peppers, cut up
12 small white onions, peeled
12 cherry tomatoes

Combine all the marinade ingredients in a large measuring cup or bowl. Mix them very well and set the marinade aside.

Trim all fat from the lamb and cut the meat into cubes about 2 inches square. Put the lamb and vegetables into a glass baking dish and pour the marinade over them. Cover the dish and refrigerate it for 24 hours, stirring the ingredients carefully from time to time.

To prepare the kebabs, alternate the meat with the vegetables on skewers, preparing one complete skewer for each guest. Place the kebabs over a hot charcoal fire, turning them from time to time to cook evenly. They will be done in about 15 minutes.

Kebabs may also be broiled in an oven broiler. Place a foil-lined pan underneath to catch drippings. The meat and vegetables may be brushed with marinade during the cooking, if they should appear to be drying out.

Couscous is a North African mélange that simply begs for improvisation. In fact, I don't think I've ever made it exactly the same way twice, and it's always a marvel. As a further blessing, Couscous is a one-dish party. You don't need another thing with it, nor even an appetizer beforehand. A side dish of roasted peppers would harmonize nicely, though, and a glass of wine is *de rigueur* for me. I suggest a light, almost paper-dry rosé. Afterward, serve the sweetest dessert you can think of — baklava is utter ecstacy — together with green tea or strong coffee.

The proper pot for preparing Couscous is a *couscousière:* a double-boiler affair resembling a covered clam steamer, but with small steam-holes in the bottom and sides of the upper pan. Lacking a *couscousière*, you can use a deep saucepan with a strainer that fits into it, but does not fit so deeply that the couscous grains in the strainer will touch the stew beneath. The object is to let the stew's vapors *steam* the couscous, not steep or boil it.

ALGERIAN COUSCOUS

3 tablespoons olive oil
2 pounds lamb stew meat, cubed
1 chicken (about 3 pounds), cut up
2 onions, chopped
2 cloves garlic, minced
3 carrots, sliced
1 cup chickpeas, soaked overnight and drained
2 white turnips, quartered
1 marrow bone
Water to cover
2 teaspoons salt
½ teaspoon pepper
½ teaspoon saffron
1 pound couscous (fine semolina)
Water to moisten
¼ cup raisins
1 tablespoon olive oil (additional)
2 zucchini, sliced
¼ pound green beans
¼ pound lima beans
3 tomatoes, cut up
¼ pound mushrooms, sliced
2 tablespoons chopped parsley
½ cup broth from stew
½ teaspoon cayenne pepper
3 teaspoons paprika
2 tablespoons butter

Heat the first measure of olive oil in a heavy Dutch oven. Add the cubed lamb and chicken pieces and brown them thoroughly, turning them as necessary. Remove the meat and chicken from the pan and set them aside. Add the onions, garlic, carrots, drained chickpeas, turnips and marrow bone. Return the meat and chicken to the pan. Cover the assortment with water, enough to cover by about 2 inches all the ingredients. Add the salt, pepper, and saffron. Cover the pan and bring the contents to a boil. Lower the heat and allow the contents to simmer for about 30 minutes.

Moisten the couscous slightly with a little cold water, working the grain with your fingers to prevent lumps from forming. Add the raisins; turn the couscous and raisins into the strainer part of your improvised *couscousière* and rake the grain with your fingers to aerate it. Place the strainer of couscous over the simmering stew, cover with a lid, and let the grain steam for about 30 minutes. Remove the strainer, transfer the couscous to a large bowl, and sprinkle it with cold water. Stir it well with a wooden spoon to break up any lumps; then stir in the remaining tablespoon of oil.

Arrange the zucchini, green beans, lima beans, tomatoes and mushrooms on top of the stewing meats in the Dutch oven and sprinkle with parsley. Return the couscous to the strainer, place it over the simmering stew, cover with a lid, and cook for another 30 minutes.

Remove ½ cup of broth from the stew and place in a bowl; stir in the cayenne and paprika to make a peppery side sauce.

To serve the couscous, pile the steamed grain on a large dish, add the butter and work it into the grain with a spoon as it melts. Arrange the meat, chicken, vegetables and broth in another bowl. Serve at once with the spicy, hot sauce on the side.

7
Pork and Ham

IT'S AMAZING how versatile pork is. You can make pork roast, pork chops, pork pie; you can serve pork hot or cold; use it jellied or as cold cuts, or incorporate leftovers in a vivacious tomato sauce. It's very easy to create other dishes from this meat, which is even more adaptable than beef. But for some reason, people get into the habit of always eating pork cooked in the same predictable ways.

Another advantage of pork, its low cost, exists no more, alas. Pork used to be wonderfully inexpensive, and maybe that's why it never had much status here except at Christmas and Easter. In Europe, it's always been another story. There, the pig is utilized joyfully and 100 per cent. The stomach and intestines make *andouille,* or sausage; the head and ears make head cheese; the feet are roasted, braised or grilled; the blood is used for black pudding; and the cooked skin renders jelly. Here, I am afraid, we make waste rather than use.

I am amazed at the people who go into a supermarket and spend good money on precut and prepackaged, paper-thin, dry pork chops. If all you're looking for is pork chops, here's how you can beat the system. Go to the store in the morning, before the best parts are already gone, and ask the butcher to cut you some 1-inch thick chops from the center of the loin, where the best chop meat is. That way you'll have good meat, get your money's worth, and be able to savor the gorgeous, special flavor of pork chops pan-fried in their own fat. It's one of my own special temptations.

While it is true that pork should not be served as rare as beef or lamb, that does not mean it should be cooked till it's like a shoe. Cook it well, until there is no blood or pink, but let it remain juicy and not dried-out.

Normandy is the country of sweet, meadow-fresh butter and cream, and of Calvados, a cider brandy. Calvados is a bit drier than the American applejack, but by all means — if there's no Calvados on hand — use applejack or other brandy. Drink a good hard cider with the chops, or else a robust white wine. Buttered carrots strewn with chopped parsley, and baked, stuffed apples mate companionably with the whole. Then you might as well go all the way and extend your wicked pleasures with a rich, creamy dessert.

CÔTELETTES DE PORC NORMANDE

(Pork Chops Normandy)

MAKES 6 SERVINGS

6 center-cut pork chops, each about 1 to 1½ inches thick
Salt and pepper
1 teaspoon oil
2 shallots, finely chopped
1 clove garlic, finely minced
½ cup Calvados
6-ounce can frozen orange juice concentrate (undiluted)
2 tablespoons Dijon mustard
1 cup heavy cream
1 tablespoon cornstarch
6 mushrooms, sliced

Sprinkle the chops on both sides with salt and pepper. Heat the oil in a heavy skillet; add the chops and brown them nicely on both sides. Drain off the excess fat. Add the chopped shallots and garlic; sauté them quickly.

Remove the pan from heat. Stir in the Calvados; then return the pan to the heat. Add the orange juice concentrate and the mustard, blending well. Cover the pan and simmer the contents gently for about 1 hour, or until the chops are done and tender. Check occasionally to see if a little water is needed.

When the chops are done, remove them to a warm platter. Mix a tablespoon or two of the cream in a cup with the cornstarch to make a smooth paste. Add the remaining cream to the paste and then stir it into the pan liquids. Bring the liquids to a boil and simmer while stirring, until the sauce is thickened. Add the mushrooms and let them simmer for 3 or 4 minutes. Return the chops to the sauce for a few minutes, to warm them; then arrange them on a serving platter and spoon sauce over the top of each.

CÔTELETTES DE PORC AUX ABRICOTS

(Pork Chops with Apricots)

MAKES 4 SERVINGS

- 4 *center-cut pork chops, each 1-inch thick*
- ¼ *teaspoon ginger*
- 1 *teaspoon salt*
- ¼ *teaspoon pepper*
- 2 *tablespoons butter*
- ½ *cup chopped green onions (scallions)*
- 2 *bay leaves*
- ¾ *cup dry red wine*
- 1 *teaspoon tomato paste*
- 8 *canned apricot halves, drained*
- 4 *tablespoons fine bread crumbs*
- 4 *teaspoons butter (additional)*

Season the chops on both sides with ginger, salt and pepper. Put the 2 tablespoons of butter in a large skillet, heat it, and brown the chops on both sides. Transfer the chops to a baking dish; sprinkle them with green onions and bay leaves.

Discard the fat from the skillet; add the wine and the tomato paste and bring the mixture to a simmer while stirring. Remove the pan from the heat and pour the mixture over the chops in the baking dish. Cover the meat with apricot halves, sprinkle with bread crumbs, and put a teaspoon of butter on each chop. Bake in a 325°F. oven for about 45 minutes or until the chops are tender.

Succulent, moist, rich, provocative . . . these stuffed pork chops are a gift-wrapped adventure in superb dining. Yet, as you will see, they're neither expensive nor difficult to prepare. The bananas — an exceptional food that is too-often overlooked — add just the right richness and texture. Add Rice Pilaf (page 00), a dry white wine or a light-bodied claret. For further glory, you might start with a light *potage* or *consommé*, and add a salad of endives.

STUFFED PORK CHOPS WITH BAKED BANANAS

MAKES 4 SERVINGS

4 large pork chops, each 1½ inches thick
5 tablespoons butter, divided
½ cup chopped onions
4 mushrooms, sliced
Pinch of allspice
Pinch of marjoram
⅛ teaspoon nutmeg
Salt and pepper to taste
⅛ teaspoon coriander
Peanut oil
3 firm, green-tipped bananas, cut in half lengthwise
½ cup heavy cream
2 tablespoons light brown sugar

With the point of a sharp knife, make a diagonal slit in the top of each chop, cutting toward the bone. Make another slit toward the outer edge to form a pocket, leaving the meat intact on the edges so that it can be folded over the stuffing. Set aside.

Heat 2 tablespoons of the butter in a heavy skillet. Add the onions and cook them just until golden, about 3 or 4 minutes. Add the mushrooms and cook gently for another few minutes. Stir in the allspice, marjoram, nutmeg, salt, pepper and coriander. Let the mixture simmer for another 6 or 7 minutes, stirring it occasionally.

When the stuffing mixture is ready, spoon it into the prepared chops, dividing it equally. Bring the flaps of the chops back over the stuffing and pat them into place. Pour enough peanut oil into a large, heavy skillet to just cover the bottom. Heat the oil; then add the chops, placing them stuffing-side down to brown. When the first side is nicely browned, carefully turn each chop with a spatula and allow the other side to brown. Transfer the chops to a baking dish large enough to contain them all without any overlapping.

Put the remaining butter (3 tablespoons) into a skillet. Melt it; then add the peeled banana halves. Quickly sauté until all the bananas are lightly browned on one side; turn and brown each on the other side. Arrange the bananas around the chops in the baking dish. Pour the cream into the dish around the chops, and dot each chop with a little butter. Bake in 350°F. oven for 45 minutes. While the food is baking, stir the brown sugar into the skillet of melted butter remaining from the sautéed bananas; use this sauce to baste the bananas two or three times during the baking period. When the chops are tender, serve them on a platter with the baked bananas and the sauce from the baking pan.

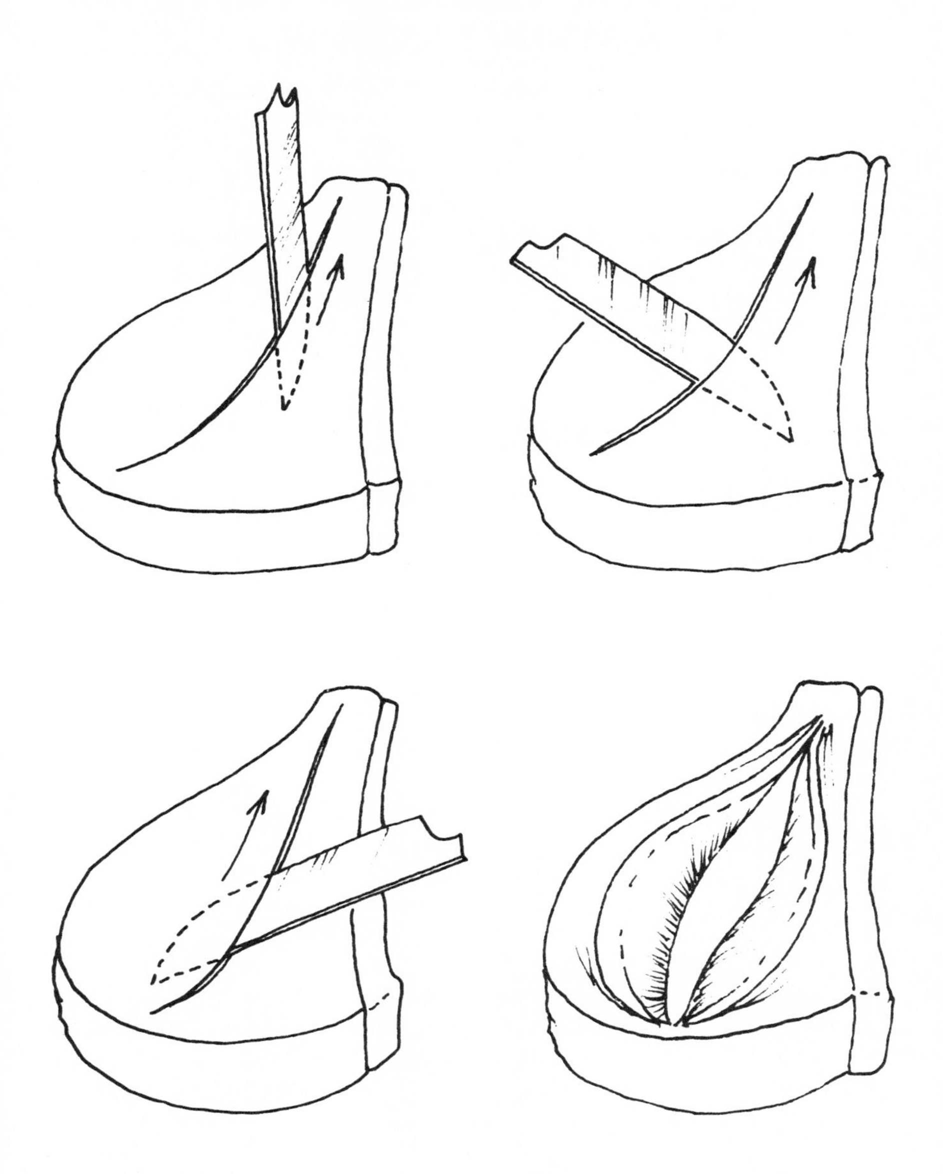

You only have to look at the ingredients to want to leap into the kitchen and start cooking. The flavor of the pork is enhanced by a zesty marinade. When you serve this exhilarating but simply made dish, stage it so that the vegetables it is cooked with become the accompaniment. Add bread or potatoes, or another starch, and a light red wine of the Bordeaux genre.

FILET DE PORC À LA PROVENÇALE

(Boneless Roast Pork, Provençal)

MAKES 6 SERVINGS

3-pound piece pork tenderloin
1 cup dry white wine
½ cup wine vinegar
1 teaspoon thyme
2 bay leaves
½ teaspoon tarragon
2 cloves garlic, minced
6 juniper berries, crushed
2 tablespoons olive oil
2 carrots, sliced
1 onion, sliced
1 stalk celery, sliced
1 green pepper, seeded and sliced
1 tablespoon chopped parsley
2 or 3 tomatoes, peeled and chopped
2 cloves garlic, minced
Salt and pepper to taste
2 tablespoons butter

Put the pork tenderloin into a deep glass dish. Combine the wine, vinegar, thyme, bay leaves, tarragon, garlic and juniper berries. Pour this marinade over the pork and refrigerate overnight.

The next day, heat the oil in a skillet. Add the carrots, onion, celery and green pepper and sauté them for about 5 minutes. Add the parsley, tomatoes, garlic, salt and pepper. Meanwhile, remove the meat from the marinade and dry it thoroughly on paper toweling. Strain the marinade and add it to the mixture in the skillet. Let it simmer for about 20 minutes.

Heat the butter in a Dutch oven. Add the dried pork and brown it on all sides. Then add the vegetable-marinade mixture and bring it to a simmer. Cover the pan and cook for 2 hours, or until the meat is tender. Transfer the contents to a heated platter, arranging sauce over and around the meat.

There are times, when the occasion is grand and ambition is not to be denied, that you need a recipe that is a non-stop extravagance of colors, flavors, textures and excellence. Here it is: a regally stuffed and majestically adorned pork roast — a sure-fire success that I guarantee will win raves of "*encore!*"

The roast itself is a very special piece of meat consisting of uncut rib chops arranged in a circle to form a crown shape. With the roast, serve Carrots Vichy (page 178) or fresh green beans . . . and French bread, of course. For the wine, a nice Beaujolais would be delightful. Afterward, offer a light, green salad, then some cheese to finish the wine: Camembert would do nicely. A fitting finale would be open-faced, French apple tarts.

CROWN ROAST OF PORK

1 crown roast of pork (about 4 pounds)
1 teaspoon each of savory, rosemary, salt, pepper, monosodium glutamate and minced garlic
¼ teaspoon ground cloves
Stuffing
2 carrots, cut up
2 stalks celery, cut up
1 onion, chopped
1 cup dry white wine, divided
1 cup rum
4 tablespoons flour
½ cup water
½ cup cider
½ cup veal or chicken stock
1 can apricots, drained
½ cup honey
1 jar kumquats (optional)

Wipe off the roast with a damp paper towel. Combine the herbs and seasonings and sprinkle them into incisions cut between the ribs and rub them generously into the outside fat. To maintain the crown shape, turn the roast rib-bones down, and fit it over an inverted Pyrex bowl, so the bowl supports the hollow area. Put the bowl in a roasting pan and place in a 450°F. oven for 15 minutes.

Prepare the stuffing (page 110). Remove the roast from the oven at the end of 15 minutes, and lower the oven heat to 300°F. Carefully remove the roast from the bowl; place the meat back in the pan, rib-bones up, and fill the center of the crown with the stuffing. Surround the roast with the carrots, celery and onion. Combine half the wine with the rum and pour this into the pan. Then return the roast to the oven and cook, allowing 30 minutes per pound.

When the meat is done, transfer it to a heated platter and keep it warm. Remove and discard the vegetables, and drain all but 4 tablespoons of the pan juices from the pan. Stir the flour into the reserved pan juices, mixing very well while cooking it over low heat for 3 or 4 minutes. Combine the remaining wine with the water, cider and stock, and slowly stir this into the pan juices. Continue to cook and stir until this gravy is thickened and smooth. Taste and correct the seasonings, if necessary.

In a small saucepan, cook the apricots in the honey until they are nicely glazed. Arrange them around the roast on the heated platter and place the kumquats on the rib-bone ends, if desired. Place the gravy in a warmed bowl and serve along with the roast.

CROWN ROAST STUFFING

2 strips bacon
1 clove garlic, minced
2 onions, chopped
1 stalk celery, chopped
1 apple, cored and chopped
½ teaspoon rosemary
1 pound ground beef
½ pound mushrooms, chopped
2 tablespoons chopped parsley
1½ cups cooked wild rice
¼ cup cognac
1 egg
⅛ teaspoon thyme
⅛ teaspoon vanilla
⅛ teaspoon ground cloves

Sauté the bacon in a skillet until it is crisp. Remove the bacon, drain it on paper toweling, and reserve. Add the garlic and onions to the pan. Sauté until they are translucent; then add the celery, apple and rosemary, and continue to cook until the apples and celery are tender.

Add the ground beef, stirring it about to break up chunks. Add the mushrooms and cook, while stirring, until the mushrooms are just barely tender. Crumble the bacon and return it to the pan; add all the remaining ingredients, stirring very well to mix thoroughly.

FRUITED STUFFED PORK CROWN

1 crown roast of pork (about 4 pounds)
¼ cup soy sauce
1 teaspoon garlic powder
3 tablespoons sugar
1 teaspoon salt
½ teaspoon pepper
1-pound can plums
Stuffing
1 jar kumquats (optional)
Plum sauce (page 212)

Invert the roast over a Pyrex bowl to keep the pork's shape during the first roasting, and place the bowl in a large roasting pan. Combine the soy sauce, garlic powder, sugar, salt and pepper. Add the juice drained from the can of plums and set the fruit aside for later use. Baste the outside of the roast very well with this soy sauce mixture. Place the supported roast in a 425°F. oven for 45 minutes, basting with the sauce two or three times during the cooking. Prepare the stuffing.

Take the pan out of the oven, carefully lift the roast off the bowl and place the roast back in the pan wide-side down. Fill the center of the crown with the stuffing, lower the oven heat to 350°F. and continue roasting the meat, allowing 25 minutes per pound.

Place the completed roast on a warm platter; arrange the reserved plums and the kumquats around the meat, and serve with warm plum sauce.

STUFFING FOR FRUITED STUFFED PORK CROWN

4 tablespoons oil
2 onions, chopped fine
1 cup finely chopped celery
¼ pound mushrooms, sliced
Salt and pepper to taste
1 clove garlic, minced
2 tablespoons soy sauce
2 ounces brandy
⅛ teaspoon monosodium glutamate
3 cups cooked wild rice
1 can (8 ounces) applesauce

Heat the oil in a skillet. Sauté the onions and celery until they are tender. Add the mushrooms and sauté another 3 or 4 minutes.

Stir in the salt, pepper, garlic, soy sauce, brandy and monosodium glutamate. Cook another few minutes; then remove from the heat. Stir in the wild rice and applesauce. Proceed to stuff the crown roast as directed.

Showcase the curried pork by wreathing it in a ring of fluffy rice.

STIR-FRIED CURRIED PORK

MAKES 4 SERVINGS

1 pound lean pork
1 green pepper
2 tablespoons oil
2 cloves garlic, minced
½ teaspoon salt
1 large onion, sliced thin
2 or 3 teaspoons curry powder
¼ pound mushrooms, sliced
½ cup sliced scallions (tops only)
1 tablespoon soy sauce
Juice of half a lemon
½ cup chicken stock
2 teaspoons cornstarch
2 tablespoons water

Cut the pork and the green pepper into thin strips. Heat the oil in a skillet or *wok*. Add the garlic and salt, then the pork. Stir-fry the meat until it loses its pinkness. Add the green pepper and onion slices; stir-fry just long enough to soften the vegetables. Add the curry powder and continue stirring 2 or 3 minutes longer. Add the mushrooms, scallions, soy sauce, lemon juice and chicken stock. Cook 5 minutes longer, over medium heat, stirring frequently.

Meantime, blend the cornstarch and water to make a paste. Stir the paste into the skillet, and cook just long enough to thicken the sauce. Serve promptly.

A tourtière is a pie for all seasons. I adore it hot and cherish it cold. It is perfect for a snack and, with a light salad, ideal for lunch or a simple supper. You can make it up in advance and freeze it. You can prepare a large pie or little individual pies, for when you're eating all alone. Furthermore, it's as simple to make as, well, pie.

Select ground pork that's not too fat, or it'll lie heavy on your ribs, and not too lean or it'll be dry as paper. The clue to the dish is the ground cloves, but don't abuse this ingredient and use too much, because it's a strong spice. You want just enough to give the tourtière snap. As for the crust, roll it out as thick or as thin as you like it. If you anoint it with egg before baking, it'll come out of the oven gleaming like gold.

TOURTIÈRE

(French-Canadian Pork Pie)

PASTRY:

4½ cups flour
2 teaspoons baking powder
2 teaspoons salt
1½ cups lard, divided
¾ cups warm water
4 teaspoons lemon juice or vinegar
1 egg, well beaten

Combine the dry ingredients. Add 1 cup of the lard, cutting it into the flour with a pastry blender or with two knives, until the mixture is mealy. Dissolve the remaining lard in the water, heating the water if necessary. Allow the solution to cool; then add it to the flour mixture. Add in the lemon juice and egg; mix the dough very well until it leaves the sides of the bowl and can be formed into a ball. Turn the dough onto a lightly floured board, and knead until it is well blended and smooth. Add more flour, if necessary. Wrap the dough in waxed paper and refrigerate it for several hours before using.

FILLING:

1½ pounds ground pork
1 onion, chopped
1 garlic clove, minced
1 teaspoon salt
½ teaspoon celery salt
¼ teaspoon pepper
¼ teaspoon ground cloves
½ cup water
1 tablespoon dry white wine
¼ to ½ cup fine bread crumbs

Combine all the ingredients for the filling, except the bread crumbs, in a large saucepan. Bring the contents to a boil; then lower the heat and simmer for 20 minutes, stirring occasionally. Remove the pan from the heat and stir in ¼ cup of bread crumbs. Let the mixture stand for 10 minutes. If the liquids are not sufficiently absorbed, add an additional ¼ cup of bread crumbs.

Divide the prepared and chilled dough into two equal parts. Roll out one portion of the dough for the bottom crust and line a 9-inch pie pan. Pour in the pork filling. Roll out the remaining dough, and place it over the filling. Seal the edges and cut slits in the top crust. Bake the pie in a 400°F. oven for 45 minutes, or until the crust is golden brown. May be served hot or cold.

HAM

The ham you buy is usually cured and precooked, not fresh, because fresh ham requires such a long cooking period. It's a tasty, tangy meat, with a kaleidoscope of uses. For instance, did you know that you can get four different kinds of ham meals from a shank-half of ham? Here is how:

1. Have your butcher saw off a generous-sized piece from the bone end and use it to make a boiled dinner, with carrots, onions, potatoes and cabbage.
2. Divide the center part of the shank into two portions. Use the larger section for baking.

3. Use the smaller section to make scalloped ham and potatoes, omelets, and other dishes.
4. Cut the large, boneless end-piece of the shank into thick slices and use those for broiling and frying.

Leftover baked ham can be used in a myriad of glories. Here are a few: Ham and beans, ham stew, ham soup with lentils, diced ham salad. Or grind the baked ham, combine it with cooked rice, diced onions and canned tomatoes. Stuff the mixture into parboiled green peppers and bake.

BACON

The secret of cooking bacon is to start it in a large, cool pan, and cook it slowly. If you use a large pan, the bacon won't drown in its own grease. If you cook it slowly, it won't shrink into nothing.

I have to admit that the bacon you buy today has too much fat. That's because the purveyors are taking too much meat out of the pork slab from which bacon is cut and using it for other purposes. You have to fry it to death, and what you have left is crispy fat. At two dollars a pound, that's an expensive way to buy fat. But you can turn even that to advantage, by saving the cooked fat in a covered can stored in the refrigerator. The rendered fat is marvelous for sautéing vegetables to be used in soup, for pan-frying, for anointing the skins of baking potatoes, and for many other dishes that benefit from the vigorous flavor of bacon.

People have sworn to me that they'd rather do logarithms or sweep stables than eat sauerkraut. Once they try it my way, they can't get enough of the stuff. The secret is, the sauerkraut must be cooked, as it is in this recipe. Add a side dish of boiled or steamed potatoes to your Choucroute Garnie, and you've the libretto for a hot buffet that's a banquet.

CHOUCROUTE GARNIE

(Garnished Sauerkraut)

2 1 lb. cans sauerkraut
¼ pound bacon, diced
2 onions, chopped
1 bay leaf
1 teaspoon thyme
2 cloves garlic, minced
1 cup dry, white Rhine wine or good light beer
Salt and pepper to taste
5 juniper berries (optional)
Water, if necessary
1 large apple, peeled, cored and quartered
Knockwurst, smoked ham hock, or fresh pork

Put the sauerkraut into a large colander. Run cold water through it; then squeeze all the excess water out.

Put the bacon into a heavy Dutch oven and cook over medium heat, stirring occasionally until the bacon begins to color. Add the onions, bay leaf, thyme and garlic. Mix well and continue cooking another 2 or 3 minutes. Mix in the sauerkraut; then stir in the wine or beer, salt, pepper and juniper berries (if desired). Press a spoon down on the sauerkraut; the level of the liquid should be almost to the top of the cabbage. If it is not, add a little water to bring it up. Put the quartered apple over the cabbage, cover the pan, and let the contents simmer over medium heat for about 1 hour.

If you are serving knockwurst with the sauerkraut, place it on top of the cabbage about halfway through the cooking time. If you are using a smoked ham hock or fresh pork, place it on top of the cabbage at the beginning of the cooking time. Serve with plain, boiled potatoes.

GLAZED BAKED HAM

1 pre-cooked ham half, shank or butt end, about 6 to 8 pounds
2 cups port wine
½ cup brown sugar
2 tablespoons Dijon mustard

Place the ham in a large roasting pan. Make crisscross cuts on the top with a sharp knife. Pour the wine over the top. Put the ham into a 350°F. oven for about 1 hour, basting it frequently with the wine. Meanwhile, mix the brown sugar and mustard together to a smooth paste. After 1 hour, take the ham from the oven and spread the mustard paste over the top. Return the ham to the oven and increase the temperature to 425°F. Roast for about 30 minutes longer, or until the ham is nicely glazed. Remove the ham to a warm serving platter, and let it stand for about 15 minutes before slicing.

The ingredients of this ham dish are not at all extraordinary, but the results most certainly are. The look is stunning, the textures and flavors a wow. The recipe takes a little doing, but not too much. Anyway, it's worth the bit of effort it takes. At least you will learn to make a good brioche dough and, after you've done it once, you won't be afraid to do it again. Think of all the delectable ways you can use your skill: tender breakfast rolls, crusty cloaks for beef Wellington, a stylish way to cap everyday leftovers.

JAMBON EN CROÛTE MADEIRA

(Ham Baked in a Crust with Madeira Sauce)

1 pre-cooked whole or half ham (about 8 lbs.)
Brioche Ordinaire (page 237, double the recipe if using whole ham)
Madeira Sauce (page 202)
1 egg, well beaten
1 egg yolk
1 tablespoon water or milk

Following the wrapper directions on the ham, cook it for half the recommended time, either by boiling or baking. Allow it to cool enough so that the excess fat can be trimmed easily, but do not let the ham cool completely. Partially slice the ham to the bone for easier serving, but do not cut the slices free.

Roll out the well-chilled brioche dough into a large sheet about ¼-inch thick. Place the ham in the center of the dough. Spread some of the Madeira sauce between the slices of ham. Brush the edges of dough surrounding the ham with the beaten egg. Bring the dough up and wrap it around the ham carefully, to completely seal the ham. Trim excess dough from the edges.

Flour a baking sheet, place the covered ham on it, and brush completely over the dough with egg wash (the egg yolk diluted with water or milk). Use strips of dough cut from the sheet to make a lattice top on the crust, or cut leaf-shaped pieces from the dough and use them to decorate the crust. Brush the decorations with egg wash after putting them in place.

With a knife, make two small holes in the top of the crust, to allow steam to escape; also mark where the first cut of ham is, to facilitate serving. Bake the ham in a 350° to 375°F. oven for 30 minutes, or until the dough is golden brown. Remove it to a serving platter and serve the sliced ham with warmed Madeira sauce.

8 Poultry

AN INCREDIBLE BIRD, the chicken. Its neutral flavor lends itself to a thousand sauces, to make a thousand different dishes. Because it is easy to raise and it reproduces prodigiously in a very short time, chicken has remained affordable even through depression years. And its versatility is without end. You can roast it, bake it, stew, poach, sauté or fry it . . . serve it hot, cold, for picnics or banquets . . . bathe it in red, white, brown or golden sauces . . . make it spicy or bland . . . feed it to invalids, dieters or hedonists. Nutritionally, chicken is a good source of protein. As for flavor and texture, however, the incredible bird has lost its former excellence. These days chickens are fed so that they will become full-grown 2½-pounders in a matter of months. "Tender" is no longer the word. Modern chickens have bones like marshmallows, and cook so quickly that if you try to make a proper stew, with long cooking to marry the flavors, they fall apart.

I can remember when I was a boy on my grandmother's farm in Normandy, whole families used to be fed from just one chicken. The birds were fed wheat and corn, not chemicals, and grew up to be big and healthy. By the time they were done in, each one made a terrific family dinner. But now we are in the age of chemistry, so we have to create new techniques to deal with our foods. Instead of the classic *coq au vin,* which simmered for hours, we have to reverse tradition and take care not to overdo. Otherwise there'll just be an uninviting collection of bare bones and fallen-off meat at the bottom of the pot.

Broiler-fryers are the youngest chickens, about 2½ pounds in size. Next come roasters, at 3 to 3½ pounds. They have a little more meat on them than broilers, and you pay more per pound. Hens for poaching are not such a good buy any more; they are old fowl which you have to cook for two or three hours. But they are good for soup, a use which is better than cooking them for the cold sliced meat. As for capons, they are no longer the sweet, juicy, meaty birds they once were. They are roosters that have been castrated, gotten fat, and cost you a lot of money.

DUCK is a magnificent bird, even though it is very expensive, pound for pound, and only serves two people apiece. Duck is easy to cook, but take care. It has a lot of fat, which is highly flammable when it reaches a certain temperature. A prudent cook removes some of the fat before cooking, and empties the melted fat into a separate container as the duck cooks.

GAME: I do not believe in hunting wild game and will not give you any recipes for cooking deer, bear or anything else that should be left to live its own life. As for domesticated game, pheasant has very little taste and I consider it hardly worth cooking. Domesticated rabbit is a fine dish, though, and I have included a recipe for it here.

Yesterday you poached a fowl and made a soup; today you're faced with serving what will look like leftovers if you don't do something to make the meal intriguing. Simple! Make a lovely Blanc de Volaille, using the white meat of chicken cradled in a sauce made from the stock you've already produced. Precede the entrée with bowls of the soup, and accompany your main dish with asparagus, Rice Pilaf and a tender white wine from the Loire or Bordeaux.

BLANC DE VOLAILLE

(Breast of Chicken)

MAKES 4 SERVINGS

3 tablespoons butter
3 shallots, finely chopped
3 cups cooked white meat of chicken, cut up

3 tablespoons flour
1½ cups chicken stock
1 cup heavy cream
Salt and pepper to taste
1 cup sliced mushrooms
1 egg yolk
3 tablespoons dry sherry
Parsley

Melt the butter in a heavy saucepan. Add the shallots and sauté them gently until golden. Stir in the flour, then the chicken stock; continue to stir and cook until the mixture thickens. Stir in the cream; then add the salt, pepper, cooked chicken, and mushrooms. Lower the heat and allow the chicken to warm. Beat the egg yolk lightly with a fork and mix in the sherry; then stir this into the chicken mixture. Reheat the sauce briefly and spoon it, with the chicken, onto hot toast points. Garnish with parsley and serve.

You might call this a white *coq au vin*, freshened by the inclusion of white wine and fruit. It's particularly engaging when served with *petits pois* and a starchy vegetable — potatoes, rice, or noodles. And, of course, serve a good, dry white wine.

POULET VALLÉE D'AUGE

MAKES 4 SERVINGS

1 broiler-fryer chicken, cut up
¼ cup oil
Salt and pepper to taste
1 tablespoon minced shallots
1 clove garlic, minced
⅛ teaspoon ground clove, or thyme or savory
½ cup applejack
2 apples, peeled and sliced
2 pears, peeled and sliced
½ pound mushrooms, sliced
2 cups dry white wine
2 cups chicken stock, divided
2 tablespoons flour
1 cup heavy cream

Wash and dry the chicken pieces. Heat the oil in a skillet and brown the chicken parts nicely on all sides, sautéing only a few pieces at a time. Season the chicken, while it is browning, with salt, pepper, shallots, garlic and the desired herb. As the pieces are browned, transfer them to another skillet set over a low flame and keep them warm. When all the chicken has been transferred, set aside the first skillet. Increase the heat under the second skillet and pour ¼ cup of the applejack over all the chicken pieces. Ignite and, when the flame dies down, put the chicken into a Dutch oven.

Add the sliced apples, pears and mushrooms to the pan used for flaming the chicken, and quickly sauté these ingredients for 2 or 3 minutes. Add them, along with all the juices in the pan, to the chicken in the Dutch oven. Pour in the wine, remaining applejack and 1 cup of the chicken stock. Bake the chicken and fruit, with the liquids in a 350°F. oven for about 1 hour.

Meanwhile, pour off all but 2 tablespoons of pan drippings from the first skillet, the one used for browning the chicken. Stir in the flour and cook over low heat, mixing well. Add the remaining cup of chicken stock slowly, and cook, while stirring, over medium heat until the sauce thickens. Correct the seasoning. Add the heavy cream and let the sauce cook gently until it is well heated and thickened nicely. Remove the baked chicken, fruits, and mushrooms at end of the cooking time and transfer them to a heated platter; pour the sauce over the chicken and serve.

I never met a person who didn't consider this dish a trip to gastronomic heaven. It's a golden sauté of moist and tender, white chicken meat, equally successful when you use veal instead. For enrichment, it's flecked with tangy ham and flourished with nutty Swiss cheese, then splashed with the sprightly perfume of white wine. Chicken Cordon Bleu has all the virtues cooks adore. It's inexpensive, hasn't a single esoteric ingredient, is simple and quick to make . . . and is what connoisseurs invent in their dreams. With your blue-ribbon chicken, serve zucchini or a Spinach Soufflé (page 188), and rice steamed in chicken broth.

CHICKEN CORDON BLEU

MAKES 4 TO 6 SERVINGS

4 skinless chicken breasts, boned and halved
1 tablespoon butter, melted
Fine bread crumbs (about ½ cup)
2 tablespoons butter, divided

4 thin slices Swiss cheese
4 thin slices boiled ham
2 eggs, beaten lightly
Flour (about ½ cup)
3 tablespoons oil
½ cup dry white wine
Juice of half a lemon
Parsley

Flatten the chicken breasts between two pieces of waxed paper with a mallet or rolling pin. Remove the paper. Place the chicken pieces flat and brush them with the melted butter. Cut the cheese and ham slices in half so there are 8 pieces of each. Place a piece of cheese on each half a chicken breast, then a piece of ham on each piece of cheese. Fold each piece of chicken over so the ham and cheese are doubled in the center.

Beat the eggs in a shallow dish. Put about ½ cup of flour on one sheet of waxed paper and the same amount of bread crumbs on another. Dip the prepared chicken in the flour, then in egg, then in the crumbs.

Melt 1 tablespoon of the butter in a skillet and add the oil. When the oil is hot, add the chicken pieces carefully. Sauté each piece on both sides, until the chicken is golden, about 5 minutes per side. When both sides are browned, and the cheese begins to melt, remove each piece of chicken to a buttered baking dish. Bake in a 350°F. oven 15 to 20 minutes, until the chicken tests done.

Add the remaining tablespoon of butter to the skillet and allow it to become foamy over medium heat. Pour the wine and lemon juice into the pan and stir rapidly to deglaze. Pour this sauce over the baked chicken, garnish with parsley, and serve.

This is rather a rich dish, which is appropriate, since Épernay lies in the champagne-making region of France. The recipe definitely calls for your loveliest china and linen, with long-stemmed crystal glasses for the champagne.

STUFFED BREAST OF CHICKEN ÉPERNAY

MAKES 4 SERVINGS

STUFFING:

2 chicken legs (with thighs)
1 small onion, chopped
2 shallots, chopped
2 tablespoons fine, dry bread crumbs
3 tablespoons chopped parsley
¼ teaspoon savory
1 egg
1 tablespoon heavy cream
1 tablespoon dry white wine
Salt and pepper to taste

MAIN RECIPE:

4 whole chicken breasts
Salt and pepper to taste
Juice of half a lemon
2 tablespoons butter, divided
1 small onion, sliced
½ cup dry white wine
2 stalks celery, chopped
1 carrot, chopped
1 small onion, chopped
Butter
½ cup Hollandaise Sauce (page 209)

Cut the meat off the chicken legs; discard the skin and bones. Put this meat through a grinder and into a bowl. Add the chopped onion, shallots, bread crumbs, parsley, savory, egg, cream, 1 tablespoon wine, salt and pepper. Mix together very well.

Bone the chicken breasts, removing excess fat but leaving the skin in place. Place the boned chicken breasts on a board, skin-side down, with the two halves of each one spread open. Lightly sprinkle the surfaces with salt, pepper and lemon juice. Divide the ground-chicken mixture equally, placing a portion in the center of each breast. Bring the edge of each breast half-up over the stuffing and tuck the skin in around the ends making neat packages.

Lightly butter a large baking pan. Place the stuffed breasts, seam-side down, in a single layer in the pan. Sprinkle each one lightly with salt and dot each with some of the butter. Place the onion slices around the chicken in the pan, add the ½ cup of wine, and place the pan in a 400°F. oven for 35 to 40 minutes, or until the chicken is nicely tender. Baste the chicken occasionally with the pan drippings and, halfway through the baking time, add the remaining chopped celery, carrot and onion.

To serve, transfer the baked breasts to a warm platter. Skim the fat from the baking-pan juices; then pour the remaining broth and cooked vegetables from the pan into a blender. Process this until the vegetables are puréed. To this mixture, add ½ cup Hollandaise Sauce, stir and then pour the enriched sauce over the chicken; serve promptly.

Here's another bit of sorcery that's quick and easy to make, looks beautiful and tastes absolutely terrific. It's nothing more complex than ribbons of raw chicken sautéed with a few mushrooms and wine. I like to serve it with two vegetables and no starch: carrots and green beans create a colorful palette. A delicate white wine does the rest. For a chaser, consider a salad of endive cloaked in a dressing made of light olive oil (or vegetable or walnut oil) and a flick of lemon juice, and spiked with just a touch of tingly, dry mustard.

BLANC DE POULET BIEN-AIMÉ

MAKES 4 SERVINGS

1½ pounds skinless chicken breasts, boned
2 tablespoons butter
2 shallots, finely minced
1 ounce brandy
3 ounces dry white wine
1 cup heavy cream
½ cup sliced mushrooms
Salt and pepper to taste

Cut the chicken breasts into strips about 4 inches long and 1 inch wide. Melt the butter in a heavy skillet until it is sizzling but not browned. Place the strips of chicken in the skillet and sauté until the meat is golden on all sides, about 6 to 8 minutes. Add the shallots and continue cooking for 2 or 3 minutes, while stirring carefully. Stir in the brandy, wine and cream. Bring to the simmering point, lower the heat and allow the food to simmer gently for about 5 minutes, or until the sauce is reduced to a smooth consistency. Stir in the mushrooms, salt and pepper to taste, and allow to cook another few minutes. Serve over hot rice.

Note: This dish may be prepared ahead, refrigerated, and then reheated carefully when needed.

When you're in the mood for fun, or when everybody's mad at you and you want to win them over, give them Chicken Papaya. It's so rich and rousing, nobody can resist it. Serve it with a Rice Pilaf (page 188) tossed with raisins, and a favorite green vegetable. A light, slightly sweet German wine from the Rhine or the Moselle region mates compatibly with the papaya.

BONELESS CHICKEN PAPAYA

MAKES 4 TO 6 SERVINGS

3 tablespoons butter
½ cup diced onions
2 cups raw chicken cut in small pieces, from boneless breasts
Salt and pepper to taste
⅛ teaspoon ground thyme
¼ teaspoon marjoram
⅓ cup heavy cream
½ cup fine bread crumbs
1 egg, beaten slightly
4 ripe papayas
3 tablespoons softened butter (additional)

Melt 3 tablespoons of butter in a skillet. Add the onions and sauté until they are lightly golden and tender. Add the chicken and cook while stirring lightly; cook the chicken only partially, as it will finish cooking in the oven. Stir in the salt, pepper, thyme and marjoram. Remove the pan from the heat; stir in the cream and then the bread crumbs, to thicken the sauce. Add the egg and mix well. Set the pan aside to cool.

To prepare the papayas, peel the fruit with a potato peeler; then cut a half-inch off the top of each one and gently scoop out the seeds in the center with a teaspoon. Be careful not to puncture the skinless shell. Sprinkle the inside of each papaya lightly with salt and pepper. Fill each with a portion of the chicken stuffing.

Arrange the stuffed papayas in a casserole, placing 1 teaspoon of softened butter under each one to prevent sticking. Cover the casserole and bake the papayas in a 350°F. oven for 45 minutes; then remove them. Melt the remaining butter (about 5 teaspoons) and drizzle a small amount over the top of each papaya. Return the fruit to the oven, without a cover, and continue baking for another 20 to 30 minutes, or until the fruit is tender and the stuffing is browned on top.

Note: The number of servings will depend upon the size of the papayas. If they are small, plan on one per serving. If large, each papaya will provide two servings. Also, the baking time will depend on the size and ripeness of the papayas, so adjust the time accordingly, allowing less for smaller and riper papayas.

Even professional chefs are stuck for an idea once in a while. Often, when it happens to me, I make Teriyaki using chicken, fish, pork or a combination of meats — whatever I have in the refrigerator. The other ingredients are always on the pantry shelf, so I don't have to do any special shopping. Sometimes I capitalize on the versatility of Teriyaki and serve it as an appetizer or hors d'oeuvre. When Teriyaki is the entrée, I like to accompany it with rice, broccoli, and an icy beer.

CHICKEN TERIYAKI

3 pounds chicken wings (or 2 pounds boneless chicken breasts, cut into bite-size pieces
Seasoned bread crumbs
Wooden skewers (for boneless chicken)

MARINADE:
¾ cup soy sauce
¼ cup dry sherry
3 cloves garlic, minced
⅛ teaspoon monosodium glutamate
1-pound can crushed pineapple
¼ cup honey
1 teaspoon ground ginger

Place the chicken wings or pieces in a glass bowl. Combine the marinade ingredients and pour the mixture over the chicken. Refrigerate for at least 2 or 3 hours, turning the chicken in the marinade often.

Drain the chicken and reserve the marinade. Dip the chicken pieces lightly in the seasoned bread crumbs. Place the breaded chicken on a buttered baking sheet, and bake in a 450°F. oven for 10 minutes. (If you are using boneless pieces, remove the chicken from the oven, at this point, allow it to cool just enough to be handled and spear the meat onto wooden skewers. Then return the chicken to the oven.) Reduce the oven to 350°F. and continue baking 20 minutes longer, or until the chicken is tender. Brush occasionally with the reserved marinade. If you want the pieces to be really crisp, put them under the broiler for a few minutes at the end of the cooking time.

Note: Other meat, or firm white fish, may be used in place of chicken.

Curry powder, as you know, is a blend of pungent spices. It adds nip and color to foods in proportion to the amount you use. The sauce recipe given here is mild; add more curry powder if you want a more vigorous dish. I've found that this curry of chicken improves with a little age. Refrigerate it for a day or two, then reheat *pour une surprise Parisienne.* Incidentally, the same sauce is sheer wizardry when used on eggs or fish.

CURRY OF CHICKEN PARISIENNE

MAKES 4 TO 5 SERVINGS

2 tablespoons oil
1 chicken, cut up
¾ cup chopped onions
2 slices bacon, diced
2 cloves garlic, minced
2 tablespoons flour
2 teaspoons curry powder
⅓ cup dry white wine
2 cups hot chicken stock
1 bay leaf
½ teaspoon thyme

Heat the oil in a heavy kettle or Dutch oven. Wash and dry the chicken pieces thoroughly; then brown them on all sides in oil, over medium-high heat. Reduce the heat, add the chopped onions, stir and cook gently for 2 or 3 minutes. Then add the diced bacon and garlic. Stir in the flour and curry powder, blending well and using a wooden spoon. Stir in the wine. Add the hot chicken stock, bay leaf and thyme. Bring the sauce up to a simmering point, lower the heat, cover the pan and let the contents cook gently for 30 minutes, or until the chicken tests done. Skim any excess fat from the surface of the sauce and remove the bay leaf before serving.

Chicken and red wine *do* go together, and this is the classic instance. Pour the wine generously: a total of two cups in the stew is good, as much as a bottle is magnificent; a second bottle to drink

with the meal is mandatory. Call it Coq au Vin and it's a party; tell yourself it's a casserole and it's an everyday but stylish family meal. Either way, I like to join it with Rice Pilaf (page 188) and green beans (or any other green vegetable that happens to appeal to me at the time).

COQ AU VIN

MAKES 4 TO 6 SERVINGS

3 to 4 pounds chicken, cut up
⅓ cup butter or oil
2 cups chopped onions
6 strips bacon, diced
3 stalks celery, diced
3 carrots, diced
2 bay leaves
1 teaspoon thyme
2 ounces brandy
6 tablespoons flour
2 cups dry red wine
2 cups hot beef stock or bouillon
6 mushrooms, sliced
4 cloves garlic, minced
1 teaspoon salt (or to taste)
½ teaspoon freshly ground pepper
1 tablespoon tomato paste (optional)

Wash and dry the chicken parts thoroughly, removing any excess fat. Heat the butter or oil in large Dutch oven, over medium heat. Place the chicken pieces, a few at a time, in the pan and brown them carefully, turning until they are golden brown on both sides. Remove the pieces to a platter as they are browned, adding more chicken pieces to the pan and sautéing them until all are nicely browned.

When all the chicken is done, add the onions, bacon, celery, carrots, bay leaves and thyme to the pan. Mix with a wooden spoon and allow to cook over low heat for 3 to 4 minutes. Return the chicken pieces to the pan and add the brandy; then sprinkle flour over all and mix well with a spoon. Let this cook 2 or 3 minutes; then add the wine. Stir and allow to simmer until the sauce comes to a boil. Add the hot beef stock, then the mushrooms and garlic. Season with salt and pepper to taste. Cover the pan and cook for about 45 minutes, or until the chicken tests done. Remove the bay leaves. Stir in tomato paste for color, if desired.

Note: Coq au Vin can be prepared a day in advance, refrigerated, and then reheated when needed. And the recipe can easily be doubled for larger servings.

Plan on serving a whole hen to each person. These are cherubic little birds — festive and flavorful — but they don't go a long way. They should be cooked only until just tender. This recipe will assure you of having Cornish game hen that is juicy and seasoned with exactly the right amount of gusto.

CORNISH GAME HENS

MAKES 4 SERVINGS

STUFFING:

1 cup wild rice
Boiling water
1 teaspoon salt
4 tablespoons butter
¼ pound prosciutto, chopped
½ pound mushrooms, chopped
4 shallots, minced
½ cup dry white wine
½ cup cooked and chopped chestnuts

MAIN RECIPE:

4 Cornish game hens
1 teaspoon paprika
4 teaspoons softened butter
Salt and pepper
Sage

To prepare the stuffing, wash the wild rice and put it in a saucepan. Cover it with boiling water, enough to reach about an inch over the top of the rice. Let it cool, and then drain the rice. Repeat this water-cool-drain process two more times. Then cover the rice with boiling water for a fourth time, add the salt, and simmer for about 10 minutes. Drain the rice well. Stir in the 4 tablespoons of butter, the prosciutto, mushrooms, shallots, wine and chestnuts.

Next, wash and dry the Cornish hens thoroughly. Divide the prepared rice mixture and stuff each bird with an equal portion. Mix the paprika and softened butter, and spread some over each bird. Then sprinkle the hens with salt, pepper and a little sage. Bake them in a 350°F. oven for about 1½ hours, or until the meat is tender. Serve the birds with Sauce Cassis (page 213).

ROAST SQUAB WITH HERBS

MAKES 4 SERVINGS

4 squabs (or Cornish hens)
Salt and pepper
1 teaspoon chives
1 teaspoon chervil
1 teaspoon parsley
1 teaspoon savory
2 cups fine bread crumbs
½ teaspoon salt
¼ teaspoon pepper
1 clove garlic, minced
2 eggs
½ cup milk
1 cup flour
¼ cup corn oil

Wash the birds under cold water. Dry them thoroughly inside and out with paper toweling. Sprinkle with salt and pepper.

In a shallow bowl or pan, combine all the herbs with the bread crumbs, and add the ½ teaspoon salt, ¼ teaspoon pepper and garlic. In a bowl, beat the eggs and milk together. Dredge the birds thoroughly with flour; next, coat them with the egg-and-milk mixture, and lastly, dredge them with the seasoned bread crumbs until they are well-coated. Let them stand for 15 minutes.

Heat the oil in a skillet and, one at a time, brown the birds thoroughly and evenly. Transfer them to a baking pan and place in a 375°F. oven for 35 to 40 minutes, until the birds are nicely done. They may be served hot or cold.

You won't believe how easy this opulent dish is to make; the results are audaciously luxuriant, drenched in theatrics, and utterly sublime. But read the recipe, then try it for yourself. To keep the meal superlative, I suggest a buttered vegetable — broccoli, cauliflower or asparagus, *pommes de terre frites* or steamed rice, and a dazzlingly dry white wine.

CHICKEN AND LOBSTER ROULADE

MAKES 4 SERVINGS

- *2 large, whole chicken breasts, boned and halved*
- *¼ pound lobster meat*
- *2 tablespoons butter*
- *3 shallots, finely chopped*
- *⅛ teaspoon cayenne pepper*
- *1 ounce cognac*
- *1½ cups heavy cream, divided*
- *Salt to taste*
- *1 cup flour*
- *3 cups fine bread crumbs*
- *2 eggs, beaten lightly*
- *2 tablespoons oil*
- *2 tablespoons butter*
- *1 can cream of shrimp soup*

Make each half a chicken breast into a butterfly shape by fileting it with a knife — dividing the single thickness into two thinner ones — but leaving it hinged at one end. Be careful not to cut all the way through at the hinged end. Spread the two sections apart on waxed paper and set them aside.

Cut up the lobster meat. Put the butter in a skillet, heat it to sizzling and add the lobster meat. Sauté gently for 2 to 3 minutes. Add the shallots, cayenne and cognac, continuing to stir carefully. Add 1 cup of the cream and salt to taste. Then lower the heat and allow the mixture to simmer about 10 minutes, reducing the sauce to a nice thickness. Set the pan aside to cool.

When the lobster mixture has cooled, divide it into equal amounts and place a portion on the flat surface of each half a chicken breast. Roll the chicken up around this stuffing and fasten the flaps with wooden tooth picks.

Place the flour and the bread crumbs on separate sheets of waxed paper. Coat each chicken roll with flour, dip it in the beaten eggs, and then coat it with the bread crumbs. Heat the oil and butter in a skillet. Add the chicken rolls carefully and brown them lightly on all sides. Transfer them to an ovenproof baking dish.

Heat the shrimp soup in a saucepan. Stir in the remaining ½ cup of cream; then spoon this sauce over the chicken in the baking dish. Bake the *roulades* in a 350°F. oven for 20 to 25 minutes. Remove the wooden picks before serving.

Antibes represents the glamor of the Riviera, the excitement of the gambling casinos . . . the fine effervescence of great champagne . . . and, long after midnight, a luxurious supper of exquisite crêpes. Perhaps your recreational tastes lean more toward a quiet game of backgammon in your own living room. Be glamorous in the food anyway — serve Crêpes Antibes, small portions as an appetizer, or in more sumptuous quantities for an entrée. Instead of champagne, sip an airy white wine.

CRÊPES ANTIBES

MAKES 6 SERVINGS

THE CRÊPES:

½ *cup milk*
¼ *cup chicken stock*
¼ *cup brandy*
1 *cup flour*
2 *eggs*
2 *egg yolks*
1 *tablespoon butter, melted*
⅛ *teaspoon each of parsley, thyme, chives, tarragon, and garlic powder*
Butter for greasing the pan

Combine the milk, chicken stock and brandy. Place the flour in a mixing bowl. Stir the liquids into the flour until there is a smooth batter. Beat the whole eggs and the yolks together and pour this into the batter, mixing well. Add the melted butter and the herbs. Whisk until very smooth. The batter should be the consistency of heavy cream.

To cook the crêpes, lightly butter a crêpe pan. (Use a shallow 6- or 7-inch skillet if you do not have a crêpe pan.) Heat the pan until the butter sizzles a bit, then pour in just enough batter to coat the pan's bottom. Pour off any excess batter that does not adhere.

When the bottom of the crêpe is lightly browned, turn it very carefully with a spatula or with your fingers, and cook the other side for about 30 seconds. Remove each crêpe from the pan as it is completed, stacking and keeping them warm while you continue to cook the remaining batter and proceed to make the filling. (Lightly butter the pan before making each new crêpe.)

FILLING:

6 boneless chicken cutlets
Salt and pepper
1 teaspoon tarragon
⅛ teaspoon thyme
2 tablespoons butter
¼ cup brandy
6 very thin slices prosciutto ham
1 small can pâté de fois gras

Season the cutlets with the salt, pepper and herbs. Heat the butter in a skillet. Add the cutlets and sauté them over moderate heat 4 to 6 minutes on each side, or until they are done. (The length of time will depend upon the thickness of the cutlets.) Add the brandy and flame it. Remove the chicken from the pan, and place it, along with the ham slices, in the oven to keep warm. Allow the pâté to remain at room temperature while you prepare the sauce.

SAUCE:

2 tablespoons butter
6 shallots, chopped
1 cup sliced mushrooms
2 cups Mornay Sauce (page 208), heated
½ cup heavy cream

In a small, heavy saucepan, melt the butter; then add the shallots and sauté until they are translucent. Add the mushrooms and cook for another minute or two. Stir in the Mornay Sauce until the mixture is smooth and creamy. Stir in the cream.

To assemble, place a crêpe on a plate; place a slice of the ham, then a piece of the chicken on the crêpe. Spread pâté on the chicken; then wrap the crêpe around the entire filling. Place the completed crêpe on an ovenproof platter. Continue until as many crêpes as desired are readied. Spoon the sauce over the crêpes. Put them under the broiler for 2 or 3 minutes, until they are lightly browned. Serve them immediately.

The sight and scent of a roast duckling inspire most people to rhapsody. Cooking a duckling is apt to be another matter; many people are afraid to undertake the task. Fear not. You need only puncture the skin on the thighs and breast before roasting, and the fat will drain out all by itself. Spoon it off if it gets too deep. Don't overdo the décor with orange salad or fantasy vegetables. Rice or a baked potato is all you need, along with a red wine.

DUCKLING ROASTED WITH HERBS

4-pound duckling
1 teaspoon salt
¼ teaspoon pepper
½ teaspoon rosemary
¼ teaspoon thyme
2 onions, coarsely chopped
1 orange, cut in eighths
2 stalks celery, coarsely chopped
2 carrots, cut up
1 tomato, quartered
Giblets, chopped
½ cup dry white wine

Trim excess fat from the duckling. Coat the inside and outside with salt, pepper, rosemary and thyme. Stuff the center cavity with chunks of onion, orange sections and a few pieces of the celery. (Stud one of the onion pieces with a whole clove, if desired.) Prick the skin on the thighs and breast to allow the fat to drain while roasting. Place the duckling on a rack in a roasting pan. Surround it with the remaining vegetables and the giblets. Add the wine to the pan. Roast in a 375°F. oven for 2 hours, or until nicely done.

Rabbit is essentially mild in flavor, and this recipe does not try to make it into something it is not. It merely seasons it so as to enhance the natural goodness. The cooking is very much the same as in making Coq au Vin, which leads me to share a secret with you. When I entertain guests who I suspect will not be overjoyed to learn they're eating rabbit, I announce the entrée as *viande au vin* — meat cooked with wine. I never hear a complaint.

LAPIN AU VIN BLANC

(Rabbit in White Wine)

MAKES 4 SERVINGS

1 fresh-frozen rabbit
Salt and pepper
3 tablespoons butter
12 small white onions
2 tablespoons flour
3 shallots, chopped
2 cups white wine, divided
1 ounce brandy
2 cloves garlic, minced
½ teaspoon thyme
1 bay leaf
8 mushrooms, quartered
2 cups strong chicken stock
3 tablespoons chopped parsley

Thaw the rabbit. Wash and dry the pieces; then sprinkle them lightly with salt and pepper. Melt the butter in a heavy Dutch oven. Add a few pieces of rabbit at a time to the pan and sauté the meat to a golden brown, turning the pieces as needed. Remove these pieces to a dish and continue with the remaining pieces until all are browned. (Include the liver, as this is a choice part.) When all the meat is browned, add the whole onions and allow them to brown lightly.

Return the meat to the pan, sprinkle it lightly with the flour and stir well. Add the shallots and 1 cup of the wine. Stir until the sauce thickens. Stir in the remaining wine and the brandy. Add the garlic, thyme, bay leaf, mushrooms and chicken stock. Stir well, then taste to see if additional salt and pepper are needed. Cover the pan and simmer for 1 to 1½ hours, until the rabbit is nicely tender. Remove the bay leaf. Sprinkle the meat with chopped parsley just before serving.

This is a rich and savory stuffing, which you can vary as you wish. The quantity will fill a 9- or 10-pound bird, though of course you can make more or less of it very readily, using this recipe merely as a guide. As a matter of fact, you don't even need a bird. I often bake stuffing all by itself in a greased casserole at 350°F. for about ½ hour.

CONTINENTAL STUFFING

1 tablespoon butter
2 small onions, chopped
½ clove garlic, chopped
1 pound ground pork
5 mushrooms, chopped
½ teaspoon monosodium glutamate
½ teaspoon thyme
1 cup chopped parsley
1 pound lean, ground beef
½ cup dry white wine, divided
1 teaspoon salt
1 chicken bouillon cube
½ teaspoon pepper
1 cup roasted, shelled chestnuts
¼ pound chicken livers, cut up
1 bay leaf
1 cup fine, dry bread crumbs
2 eggs

Melt the butter in a large skillet. Add the chopped onions and garlic, and sauté gently until the onion is translucent. Add the pork and mushrooms and stir while the cooking continues. Add the monosodium glutamate, thyme, parsley, ground beef, ¼ cup of the wine, salt, bouillon cube and pepper. Stir and cook for 7 or 8 minutes over medium heat without a cover. Reduce the heat, cover the pan and simmer for 10 minutes. Add the chestnuts, chicken livers and bay leaf. Cover the pan and simmer 20 minutes longer. Remove the pan from the heat to cool the contents slightly. Stir in the bread crumbs, the remaining ¼ cup of wine, and the eggs, and mix them together very well. This recipe makes enough to stuff a 10-pound bird.

9
Seafood

IF I HAD my way you couldn't buy fish filets. The markets would carry only whole fish, with the skin, bones and head intact. That way you could enjoy every iota of beautiful, moist seafood flavor. Furthermore, you would pay about half of what you pay for fileted fish, since the costs of fileting and packaging would be eliminated. Sometime, when you're on a vacation, try having a whole fish that comes sparkling-fresh from the lake or ocean. You'll discover the scintillating look and flavor of honest fish — as different from packaged, store fish as platinum is from plastic.

If you happen to be where the water is relatively free of pollution, treat yourself to the dazzle of just-caught shellfish. See how bright the color is, compared with the dulled tone of most shellfish nowadays. Study how the shell of even a prosaic clam is a piece of art: the perfect, poetic jewel case for the treasure within.

Many times I am asked my opinion of fish that's been frozen, fresh-shipped or canned. Here are the answers. Frozen, fileted fish tends to lose its moisture when it is cooked because the moisture freezes away from the tissues and runs out on defrosting, so the fish dries out quickly when you cook it. Fresh-shipped fish that is containerized so as to maintain a temperature of about 33°F. — just above freezing — keeps its freshness without losing its moisture, and is preferable to frozen fish. Canned fish is not my idea of a worthy food.

The trick to buying good, fresh fish is to sniff it. Really fresh fish never smells "fishy." If you are lucky and can buy whole fish, see that its eyes are bright, clear and bulging; that its gills are reddish pink and not slimy; that its scales are shiny; and that its flesh is firm and elastic, not separated into ridges. Don't buy fish ahead of time. Shop for your fish the same day you are going to serve it, so it will be as fresh as possible.

Cook fish with a light hand; you can devastate it by overcooking. You can tell fish is ready when the meat loses its translucency and becomes opaque and milky-looking, the first juice splutters out, and the meat flakes easily with a fork. If you cook it properly, you won't have a dried-out fish.

This is a basic, classic recipe which takes to embellishment as naturally as fish take to the sea. Here is an improvisation that will produce a seemingly elaborate entrée for practically no money . . . and one that requires very little extra preparation. Before rolling the filets, spread each one with a thin layer of breadcrumb stuffing, buttered and seasoned to your taste, leaving a one-inch border around the edges of the filet. Then spoon on a small amount of crabmeat, lobster pieces, or a combination of any shellfish. Roll the filets, proceed with the rest of the recipe and — *voilà* — status seafood!

FILET OF SOLE BONNE FEMME

MAKES 4 TO 6 SERVINGS

2 pounds filet of sole
Salt
1 teaspoon dry white wine per filet
2 tablespoons butter
2 tablespoons chopped shallots
1 bottle (8 ounces) clam juice
1 cup dry white wine
1 teaspoon lemon juice
4 mushrooms, sliced
White pepper

Sprinkle the filets with salt; then sprinkle one side of each filet with a teaspoonful of white wine. Roll the filets. Put them in a skillet, or another shallow pan, with the butter, shallots, clam juice, the cup of wine, and the lemon juice. Spread the sliced mushrooms over the filets and lightly sprinkle white pepper over everything. Cover the pan and bring the contents to a boil. Lower the heat and let simmer gently for 3 or 4 minutes. Remove the pan from the heat and, with a slotted spoon, remove the filets to a warm platter. Strain the cooking liquids, and reserve. Place the filets in a warm oven, while you prepare the sauce.

SAUCE:

2 tablespoons butter
1 teaspoon chopped shallots
2 tablespoons flour
1 ½ cups reserved fish stock, strained
1 teaspoon grated Romano cheese
Parsley sprigs and lemon wedges, for garnish

Melt the butter in a skillet. Add the shallots and cook them gently 2 or 3 minutes. Add the flour to the skillet and stir to make a smooth paste *(roux)*. Gradually add the reserved, strained stock, continuing to stir until the sauce is smooth and thickened. (If there is not enough stock, add more bottled clam juice.) When the sauce is thick and bubbling gently, taste it and correct the seasoning, if necessary. Stir in the cheese. Pour the sauce over the warmed fish and sprinkle it with a little more grated cheese. Put the fish under the broiler for a few minutes, until the tops are golden brown. Serve garnished with parsley and lemon wedges.

SOLE DEAUVILLOISE

(Filet of Sole in Cider Sauce)

MAKES 4 SERVINGS

¼ cup butter
½ cup finely chopped onions
½ cup heavy cream, divided
1 ½ pounds filet of sole
1 cup bottled clam juice
¾ cup cider
½ teaspoon salt
½ teaspoon pepper
1 strip lemon peel, about 2 inches long, minced
1 tablespoon butter, additional
1 tablespoon flour
⅛ teaspoon nutmeg
1 teaspoon dry mustard
3 tablespoons bread crumbs

Start the sauce preparation by heating the ¼ cup of butter in a small saucepan. Add the chopped onions and cook them until they are soft. Then purée the onions in a blender, with 2 tablespoons of the heavy cream. Set the purée and the remaining cream aside, while you poach the fish.

Fold each filet in half and place all the fish in a shallow, lightly buttered pan or flameproof serving dish. Pour the clam juice and cider over the fish; then sprinkle with salt, pepper, and lemon peel. Cover the pan or dish with a piece of foil and simmer the contents for 10 minutes. Strain off the poaching liquid and reserve it. Keep the filets warm in the oven, while you complete the sauce.

Melt the additional tablespoon of butter in a saucepan. Stir in the flour until it makes a smooth paste. Cook the butter and flour for a few minutes over medium heat. Add in 1¼ cups of the reserved poaching liquid, stirring constantly until the mixture is smooth. Add the onion purée and the remaining cream, the nutmeg and the mustard. Bring the sauce to a boil while stirring, and simmer it for 2 or 3 minutes. Pour the sauce over the warmed fish. Sprinkle with bread crumbs and dot with a little butter. Place under the broiler for a few minutes, until the tops of the filets are lightly browned. Serve at once.

The texture of the *quenelles* should be as light and soft as clouds. They may be shaped in ovals, discs or cones. Often one or two are served, hot, as an appetizer course. When you serve *quenelles* as a lunch or dinner entrée, plan on making four or five dumplings per person. My preference is to precede the quenelles with a consommé, and to accompany them with French bread and a light vegetable, such as asparagus, braised lettuce or celery, or *petits pois*. A subtly dry, white Bordeaux is the wine of choice.

SOLE QUENELLES

MAKES 6 SERVINGS

1½ pounds filet of sole
1 small head of lettuce
½ teaspoon salt
¼ teaspoon white pepper
½ teaspoon savory
¼ cup butter, melted
¼ cup heavy cream
1 teaspoon chopped chives
¼ teaspoon monosodium glutamate

1 egg
3 egg yolks
2 quarts boiling, salted water
Avocado Sauce (page 212)

Put the raw fish through a food grinder. Blanch the lettuce leaves for a minute or two in boiling water, drain them very well, and then put them through the food grinder. Put the ground fish and lettuce into a blender, with the salt, pepper, and savory; add the egg and the egg yolks, the melted butter, cream, chives, and monosodium glutamate. Cover and blend for 2 minutes, or until the mixture is perfectly smooth. Refrigerate the mixture for about an hour, or until it is well-chilled.

When you are ready to shape and poach the *quenelles*, bring about 2 quarts of lightly salted water to a full boil in a large kettle. Lower the heat so the water is simmering gently. Using two tablespoons, dip both into the hot water, then take up a large spoonful of the fish mixture, and form it into an oval shape. Use one of the spoons to carefully push the mixture off the other spoon and into the simmering water. Continue until all of the mixture is spooned into the kettle. Keep the water at a gentle simmer and cook the *quenelles* for 7 minutes, or until they float to the top of the water. Remove each *quenelle* with a slotted spoon and place on a dish lined with paper toweling for draining. Transfer the *quenelles* to a warm serving platter, spoon hot Avocado Sauce over the tops, and serve. Extra sauce may be served separately from a bowl.

This recipe is fun, unusual, and a delectable surprise. Individual helpings of fragrantly seasoned fish are sealed inside neat little envelopes of buttered paper *(papillote)*. Cover each *billet doux* with the creamy clam sauce, provide plenty of good fresh bread for mopping up the extra sauce, pour copious portions of white Burgundy wine, and you're bound to be loved in return. For vegetables, I suggest Rice Pilaf and baked acorn squash, or any other vegetable that pleases you.

FILET DE POISSON EN PAPILLOTE

MAKES 4 SERVINGS

1 can (8 oz.) minced or chopped clams
1 cup heavy cream
2 pounds white fish filets
Parchment paper
4 teaspoons butter
Salt and pepper
6 mushrooms, sliced
3 shallots, finely chopped
½ cup chopped parsley
1 small onion, sliced
4 tablespoons dry white wine
4 thin slices lemon

Put the clams and accompanying juice into a saucepan. Place this over medium-high heat and let it simmer until the liquid is reduced by half. Stir in the heavy cream and continue simmering until the liquids are reduced to a fairly thick consistency.

Meanwhile, divide the fish filets into 4 portions. Cut the parchment paper into 4 pieces, each measuring about 8 by 12 inches. Place a teaspoon of soft butter on each piece of paper and spread the butter over the area that the fish will cover. Arrange the fish on the buttered paper.

Sprinkle each fish portion with salt and pepper. Divide the mushrooms into 4 portions and place a portion on each piece of fish. Repeat with the shallots, parsley, and onions. Sprinkle each portion with 1 tablespoon of white wine. Place a thin slice of lemon on top of each portion, then sprinkle with more salt and pepper.

When the sauce is thickened, spoon 2 or 3 tablespoons onto each portion. Fold the paper over to meet at the edges and crimp it securely, sealing each portion within its packet. Place the packets on a cookie sheet, or in a shallow pan, and bake them in a 375°F. oven for 20 minutes.

Serve on individual dinner plates, each package to be torn open by the diner. Serve fresh French or Italian bread to absorb the sauce.

This is a mixed grill using two varieties of fish, and it is an excellent choice for an outdoor barbecue. Serve with roasted corn and baked potatoes, both cooked on the hot coals of the grill. Use unhusked corn wrapped in foil and allow ½ hour for roasting. The potatoes will take 1 hour to bake, and foil is optional for them.

The quantities needed will depend on how many guests you plan to serve. Plan on about ½ pound of fish per person. (One swordfish steak will serve two or more persons, depending upon its thickness, which may be anywhere from ½ to 2 inches.)

The marinated swordfish is just as luscious when you cook it indoors as when you cook it on the grill. Place it on a pan 4 to 5 inches from the broiler unit, and turn the fish just once during the cooking period.

FISH BROIL

MARINADE:

1 cup tomato juice
¼ cup soy sauce
⅛ teaspoon pepper
⅛ teaspoon monosodium glutamate
⅛ teaspoon garlic salt
Juice of 1 lime
Juice of half a lemon
½ teaspoon chervil

Swordfish steaks
Thick filets of white fish
Butter
Salt and pepper to taste
Fine, dry bread crumbs
Thin lemon slices
Paprika

Combine all the marinade ingredients in a bowl. Cut the swordfish into serving-size portions, place the pieces in a large, flat dish, and pour the marinade over them. Turn the pieces over once, to coat them thoroughly. Let the swordfish marinate while you prepare the other foods.

Place the fish filets on a large piece of heavy-duty foil. Dot them with butter; then sprinkle each of them with salt and pepper, about a tablespoon of bread crumbs, thin lemon slices, and paprika. Wrap the filets securely in the foil and place the package over a bed of hot coals to cook. Allow about 25 minutes of cooking time, depending upon the thickness of the filets.

Remove the swordfish from the marinade and drain the pieces well. Place the fish on a grill directly over the coals and cook each piece 6 to 7 minutes on one side; then turn and cook it the same length of time on the other side, or until the fish flakes easily when tested with a fork. Do not overcook.

PAN-FRIED TROUT

MAKES 2 TO 4 SERVINGS

2 trout
¾ cup milk
1 teaspoon salt
¼ teaspoon white pepper
¼ teaspoon monosodium glutamate
1 cup flour
Oil for frying

SAUCE:
4 tablespoons butter
½ teaspoon thyme
3 teaspoons capers
Juice of half a lemon
1 tablespoon chopped parsley
⅓ cup croutons

Wash the fish thoroughly and dry them. Pour the milk into a shallow, flat dish. Add the salt, pepper, and monosodium glutamate, stirring to dissolve. Put the flour on a large sheet of waxed paper. Dip the trout first in the seasoned milk (making sure the fish is well-coated, inside and out) and then in the flour, again coating the fish thoroughly, inside and out.

Pour oil in the bottom of a large skillet to a depth of about ½ inch, and heat thoroughly. Then carefully place the fish in the hot oil. Cook each trout over medium heat until it is nicely browned on one side; then turn it and cook the other side, until this too is nicely browned and the fish flakes easily with a fork. Be careful not to overcook, as this results in dry fish. Transfer the fish to a heated platter.

In a small skillet, melt the butter. Add the thyme, capers, lemon juice, parsley and croutons. Stir lightly with a fork over medium heat for 2 or 3 minutes. Spoon the sauce over the fish and serve promptly. This recipe serves 2 to 4 persons, depending upon the size of the fish. If the fish are small, plan on one for each; large fish can be split in two and each half will be an ample portion.

Skate is not the most common fish in the market, yet it is uncommonly good to eat and not at all exotic. When you see it, buy it! You'll find its texture is firm, its meat is white and very mild. Choose good-sized skate wings that are 1½ to 2 inches thick at the thickest part.

SKATE WINGS AU BEURRE NOIR

MAKES 4 TO 6 SERVINGS

6 large skate wings
Water to cover
2 bay leaves
Pinch thyme
1 teaspoon salt
½ teaspoon pepper
1 onion, cut in wedges
½ cup white wine
Beurre Noir (black butter — page 211)

Put the skate wings in a heavy pan. Cover them with water and add the bay leaves, thyme, salt, pepper, onion wedges, and wine. Bring the liquid to a boil and let it simmer for 10 to 12 minutes, or until the skate is tender. Drain the fish and let it cool for a few minutes; then remove the skin from both sides of each wing. Place the fish on a warmed serving platter; pour Beurre Noir over the fish evenly, and serve promptly.

Tender, tasty scallops — enriched by a modicum of shrimp and cloaked in a creamy, ambrosial sauce! Does that sound like too-heavy embroidery? It's not. For all its creamy richness, Coquilles

St. Jacques is a light-hearted and beguiling dish, one that is ideal to set before somebody you care to please. With Rice Pilaf, buttered asparagus, and a dry white wine, the pleasures of your table are assured.

COQUILLES ST. JACQUES À LA PARISIENNE

2 teaspoons shallots, minced
1 teaspoon butter
1 pound scallops
Water to cover
⅛ teaspoon thyme
1 bay leaf
1 teaspoon salt
½ teaspoon white pepper

Cook the shallots in butter until they are barely translucent. Remove the pan from the heat and add the scallops to the pan. Add just enough water to barely cover the scallops; then add the thyme, bay leaf, salt and pepper. Return the pan to the heat and bring the water to a boil; as soon as the water starts to boil, remove the pan from the heat and let the contents cool. Remove the scallops with a slotted spoon, place them in a bowl and set aside. Strain the cooking liquid and reserve it. Meanwhile, prepare the shrimp.

½ pound fresh shrimp, unshelled
Water to cover
½ teaspoon salt

Put the shrimp, water and salt into pan and bring the water to a boil. Promptly remove the pan from the heat and drain off the water. Plunge the shrimp into cold water to cool them quickly. Shell and devein the shrimp and set them aside, while you prepare the mushrooms.

1 teaspoon shallots, chopped
1 tablespoon butter
½ cup water
½ teaspoon salt
⅛ teaspoon pepper
1 cup sliced mushrooms

Combine the shallots, butter, water, salt, pepper and mushrooms in a saucepan. Put the pan over low heat and bring the water to a boil. Let the mushrooms simmer just a minute or two; then remove the pan from the heat and strain the cooking liquid into the reserved stock from the scallops. Set the drained mushrooms aside, while you proceed to make the sauce. (Note: There should be a total of 4 cups of stock at this point. If not, in the next step, add bottled clam juice to make up the measure.)

THE SAUCE:

½ *cup butter*	¾ *cup flour*
2 *teaspoons shallots, chopped*	4 *cups reserved stock*
	½ *cup grated Swiss cheese*

Melt the butter in a heavy saucepan over low heat. Add the shallots and cook, while stirring, 3 or 4 minutes. When the butter is foamy, add the flour in thirds, mixing well and keeping the *roux* very smooth. Do not allow it to brown. Cook for about 2 minutes after all the flour is added, keeping the *roux* light and foamy. Stir in about 1 cup of the stock, mixing the *roux* thoroughly to remove all lumps. Continue adding the stock in fourths, mixing very well after each addition. When the mixture comes to a boil, immediately lower the heat so the sauce is just simmering. When the sauce is fairly thick, stir in the cheese and continue mixing until the cheese is completely melted. Taste and correct the seasoning, if necessary.

To assemble the dish, cut the shrimp into pieces about the size of the scallops. Add all the seafood and the mushrooms to the prepared sauce. Stir carefully to mix. Spoon the mixture into individual seafood shells, small shell-shaped casseroles, or one large casserole. Bake in a 425°F. oven 5 to 10 minutes for shells or small

dishes, or 10 to 14 minutes for large ones — but only until bubbles start to appear. Do not over-bake, as this toughens fish.

Note: The sauce, seafood, and mushroon mixture may be used as a filling for crêpes (see directions for making crêpes, page 253).

Mussels may also be added to this recipe. Scrub the shells well; then steam the mussels in a small amount of water until the shells open. Remove the shells and reserve the meat until you are ready to combine all the seafood. Again, reserve the cooking stock and add it to the other reserved liquids.

There's a drama to these deviled scallops, a flair that makes a dish theatrical. The marvelous flavor, color and texture of the scallops are spellbinding, and the showy presentation is a sure-fire way to gain the rewarding applause all cooks crave. Keep it your secret how easy the dish is to make.

SCALLOPS DIABLO EN COQUILLES

MAKES 4 SERVINGS

1½ pounds scallops
Flour (about ¾ cup)
Salt and pepper
½ teaspoon monosodium glutamate, divided
6 tablespoons olive oil, divided
2 teaspoons finely chopped garlic
1 tablespoon chopped shallots
1-pound can tomatoes, drained
4 tablespoons chopped parsley
1 cup Marinara Sauce
¼ cup dry white wine
¼ teaspoon Tabasco
Grated Romano cheese
Lime wedges

If the scallops are large, cut them into halves. Combine the flour, salt, pepper and half of the monosodium glutamate. Use this mixture to coat the scallops lightly. Put the scallops into a sieve and shake them gently to remove excess flour.

Heat 4 tablespoons of the oil in a heavy skillet. When it is hot, add the scallops carefully and brown them evenly, turning them as necessary. Remove the browned scallops with a slotted spoon and drain them thoroughly on paper toweling. Continue sautéing until all the scallops are done, browned, and drained. Divide them equally and spoon into 4 baking shells. Discard the used oil remaining in the pan.

Add the 2 tablespoons of fresh oil to the pan, heat, and sauté the garlic and shallots quickly for 2 or 3 minutes. Add the well-drained tomatoes, parsley, Marinara Sauce, wine, the remaining monosodium glutamate, and Tabasco. Stir this sauce and correct the seasoning, if necessary. Dividing the sauce equally, spoon it over the scallops in the shells. Sprinkle the tops lightly with grated cheese, then put the shells into a 375°F. oven for about 15 minutes, or until the scallops are thoroughly heated and the sauce is lightly browned on top. Serve each shell with a lime wedge.

Inside the thin, blue-black shell of the mussel is nestled one of King Neptune's *pièces de résistance:* the tender, sweet meat that is so delicately delicious and so very useful, I would gladly be stranded on any desert island that happened to be surrounded by these treasures. If you're wondering what the best way to buy

sea-fresh mussels is, remember the old Dublin song about sweet Molly Malone, who was forever crying, "Cockles and mussels — *alive, alive,* oh!"

To enjoy mussels to the fullest, be sure to give them a little attention before you cook them. Always go through the batch first and discard any that are broken or have open shells. Then scrub them thoroughly, scraping off the beard; soak them in cold water and scrub again, so there'll be no grit. Six or eight mussels, made according to any of the following recipes, make a marvelous appetizer. A dozen or more mussels — attended by fresh, French bread and a light, green salad — will give you a lunch or supper entrée you will long remember.

MUSSELS À LA CRÈME

MAKES 4 SERVINGS

2 pounds mussels
1 cup heavy cream, divided
1 teaspoon salt
¼ teaspoon pepper
3 tablespoons chopped parsley
¼ cup port or Madeira wine
1 egg yolk

Pick over the mussels, discarding any with broken or open shells. Scrub them thoroughly under cold, running water. Soak them briefly; then scrub them again.

Put the cleaned mussels in a heavy kettle; add ¾ of the cup of cream, salt, pepper, parsley and wine. Cover and bring to a boil over high heat. Lower the heat and cook for 3 or 4 minutes, or until shells open.

In a small bowl, combine the egg yolk with the remaining ¼ cup of cream and beat lightly. As soon as the shells are open, stir the egg yolk mixture into the liquid. Remove from the heat and serve promptly, with some of the liquid broth accompanying each serving.

MUSSELS BAYOU

MAKES 4 SERVINGS

- *2 pounds mussels*
- *2 tablespoons butter*
- *½ onion, sliced*
- *3 cloves garlic, crushed*
- *1 cup stewed tomatoes*
- *2 tablespoons chopped parsley*
- *2 teaspoons Worcestershire sauce*
- *¼ teaspoon Tabasco*
- *½ cup dry red wine*
- *¼ teaspoon oregano*
- *½ teaspoon salt*
- *Pinch of pepper*

Pick over the mussels, discarding any with broken or open shells. Scrub them thoroughly under running cold water. Soak them briefly, then scrub them again.

Heat the butter in a heavy kettle until it is bubbly. Add the onion and sauté just until golden. Add the garlic and sauté a few minutes longer, then add the mussels and all the remaining ingredients. Cover the pot and bring the contents to a boil over high heat. Lower the heat and cook for 3 or 4 minutes, or until the mussel shells open. Serve promptly, with some of the broth accompanying each serving.

MUSSELS MARINIÈRE

MAKES 4 SERVINGS

- *2 pounds mussels*
- *1 teaspoon salt*
- *½ teaspoon pepper*
- *4 tablespoons chopped onion*
- *2 tablespoons butter*
- *4 tablespoons chopped parsley*
- *½ cup dry white wine*
- *2 cloves garlic, crushed*

Pick over the mussels, discarding any with broken or open shells. Scrub them thoroughly under running cold water. Soak them briefly, then scrub them again.

Put the cleaned mussels in a heavy kettle. Add all the remaining ingredients. Cover the pot and bring to a boil over high heat. Reduce the heat to keep the contents of the pot simmering. Cook until the mussel shells open, about 3 or 4 minutes. Serve promptly, with some of the broth accompanying each serving.

Fast, easy, guaranteed delicious — I say, without bragging, that is the Bernard trademark. And I point it out to you so that you'll never be hesitant to fix shrimp, or anything else you once thought complex and scary.

SHRIMP À LA BERNARD

MAKES 6 SERVINGS

2 pounds medium-sized shrimp
6 tablespoons oil
4 tablespoons butter
3 teaspoons chopped chives
1 teaspoon tarragon
1 teaspoon oregano
⅓ cup dry white wine
½ cup bottled clam juice
½ teaspoon salt
¼ teaspoon pepper
¼ teaspoon garlic powder
¼ teaspoon monosodium glutamate

Peel all the shrimp, leaving the tail section of each shell intact. With a sharp knife, remove the black vein along the outer curve of each shrimp; then cut through each one along the inner curve, splitting it lengthwise almost to the back. Heat the oil in a skillet. Place the shrimp carefully in the hot oil and sauté them quickly for only a minute or two; just to seal in their juices. Pour the shrimp into a colander, allowing them to drain well and discarding the oil.

Wipe out the skillet with a paper towel. Return the pan to the heat and add the butter. As soon as the butter starts to bubble, add the shrimp and stir them gently over low heat for a few minutes. Add the chives, tarragon, and oregano, and mix gently. Stir in the wine and clam juice; then add the remaining seasonings. Let the mixture come to a simmer, cover the pan, and cook for 3 to 4 minutes. Serve at once with Rice Pilaf.

Note: Crabmeat or lobster meat may be cooked in this same manner.

NARRAGANSETT BAKED STUFFED SHRIMP

MAKES 3 OR 4 SERVINGS

12 jumbo shrimp (8 or 10 to the pound)
¼ cup water
2 cups Narragansett Shellfish Stuffing
4 tablespoons melted butter

Peel all the shrimp, leaving the tail section of each shell intact. With a small, sharp knife, remove the black vein along the outer curve of each shrimp and cut through the inner curve of shrimp lengthwise, splitting it but not cutting it entirely in half. Wash thoroughly and dry them on paper toweling.

Hold the shrimp open in your left hand and put about a tablespoon or more of stuffing in each. Place the shrimp in a flat, buttered baking dish, arranging them so they fit snugly together. Pour about ¼ cup of water into the bottom of the dish. Bake in a 375°F. oven for 15 minutes. Pour the melted butter over the baked shrimp just before serving. If you prefer, serve the melted butter in small, individual dishes for dipping.

NARRAGANSETT SHELLFISH STUFFING

2 cups Ritz cracker crumbs
2 tablespoons finely chopped shallots
4 tablespoons chopped parsley
2 cloves garlic, finely minced
2 tablespoons paprika
½ teaspoon monosodium glutamate
½ teaspoon celery salt
¼ teaspoon seasoned salt
½ teaspoon coarsely ground pepper
½ cup butter, melted
2 tablespoons dry white wine

In a large bowl, mix thoroughly the cracker crumbs, shallots, parsley, garlic, paprika, monosodium glutamate, celery salt, seasoned salt, and pepper. Drizzle the melted butter over all and stir in well. Add the wine and again mix well.

This stuffing can be used with any shellfish — lobsters, clams, shrimp. You can prepare it in advance, put it into a plastic bag, and refrigerate it until you need it.

I won't tell you that lobster is cheap, but this recipe makes it economical and practical. Although lobster is the theme of your dinner, the preparation transforms just half of a small lobster per person into an ample portion. It's an extremely rich dish — and extremely good. So I advise you to forget about dieting until tomorrow, and enjoy yourself tonight.

Now, here's a menu for a complete and grand meal, all of which you can prepare in advance: First, Clams Casino (page 15). For the entrée, Stuffed Lobster Suprême, with a sturdy white wine. Next, a green salad. Finally, a bit of fresh fruit and some good, black coffee.

STUFFED LOBSTER SUPRÊME

MAKES 2 SERVINGS

1 lobster (about 2 pounds)
Boiling, salted water
2 tablespoons butter
2 shallots, chopped fine
6 mushrooms, chopped
2 tomatoes, peeled and chopped
1 ounce dry sherry
1 tablespoon Pernod (optional)
1 teaspoon dry mustard
½ teaspoon paprika
White Fish Sauce (page 208)
Salt and pepper to taste
1 avocado
1 cup heavy cream

Fill a large kettle with water, add a tablespoon of salt, and bring to a full, rolling boil. Plunge the lobster, head-first, into the boiling water. Cover the kettle and cook the lobster at a low boil for 15 minutes. When it is cooked, remove the lobster from the water with tongs, and set it in the sink to drain and cool.

When the lobster is cool enough to handle, remove the claws. Then place the lobster on its back and, with a large sharp knife, cut right down the center of the body, completely separating it into two pieces. Remove the tomalley (liver), reserving it for the sauce. Remove the meat from the body and cut it into large chunks, discarding the black vein. Remove the meat from the claws and cut it up. Set the meat aside.

Put the butter in a heavy saucepan over low heat. When it is hot, add the shallots and cook them gently for a minute or two; then add the mushrooms and continue cooking. Add the chopped tomatoes; stir and cook for another few minutes. Stir in the sherry, Pernod, dry mustard, paprika, the reserved tomalley, and half the White Fish Sauce. Add salt and pepper. Stir the sauce well, taste, and correct the seasoning, if necessary. Add the lobster meat, stirring it in carefully so as not to break up the pieces. Peel and stone the avocado, cut it into cubes and add it to the sauce.

Place the lobster-shell halves in a shallow baking pan. Spoon the filling into the shells, dividing it equally. Whip the cream and stir it into the remaining fish sauce. Spread this over the filled shells, covering them nicely to their edges. Put the shells in a 450°F. oven for 10 to 12 minutes, or until the filling is hot and is golden on top. Garnish with parsley sprigs and lemon wedges, if desired. Serve promptly.

This is a concoction to dazzle the eye and delight the palate. Half the fun is in the presentation; create an impressive mold and bring it forth on your fanciest platter. Serve the molded salad as an entrée, or as an appetizer when you're really going all out.

SHRIMP AND CURRY SALAD MOLD

1½ pounds shrimp, peeled, deveined and cooked
4 celery stalks, chopped fine
1 medium onion, chopped fine
3 tablespoons lemon juice
3 tablespoons ketchup
2 tablespoons horseradish
1 tablespoon wine vinegar
1 tablespoon Worcestershire sauce
2 tablespoons soy sauce
½ teaspoon sugar
Salt to taste
½ teaspoon monosodium glutamate
½ cup crushed pineapple
2 teaspoons curry powder
¼ cup of chopped green onions
Mayonnaise
1 envelope gelatin mixed with ¼ cup of water

Combine all but the last two ingredients together in a large bowl. Then add enough mayonnaise to bind everything together. Finally, add the gelatin mixed with water; this will help make the salad firmer.

Put the shrimp salad in a mold of your liking and refrigerate it for about 3 hours. Then unmold, decorate, and serve ice-cold.

SHRIMP TEMPURA

BATTER:
¾ cup flour
2 eggs
½ cup water
½ cup milk
⅛ teaspoon monosodium glutamate
½ teaspoon salt
¼ teaspoon curry powder
¼ teaspoon baking powder

1 pound medium-sized shrimp (15 to the pound)
2 cups salad oil

Combine the flour, eggs, water and milk. Make a smooth, thick liquid. If the batter is lumpy, pass it through a fine strainer. Add the monosodium glutamate, salt, curry powder and baking powder. Let the batter stand in the refrigerator while you prepare the shrimp.

Shell and devein the shrimp, leaving each tail intact. Cut each shrimp along the inner curve, to split it lengthwise without cutting entirely through. Spread each shrimp flat and score it lightly to prevent curling. Heat the salad oil to 350°F. Dip the shrimp into the ice-cold batter; then fry them until they are golden brown. Keep warm while you prepare the sauce.

GINGER SAUCE:

¼ *cup soy sauce*
¼ *cup sherry*
½ *teaspoon ground ginger*

Mix all the ingredients together and warm in a pan. Serve the sauce in small bowls suitable for dipping the shrimp.

The batter and a light touch with the cooking lend fragility to this filling appetizer.

The following two dishes are seafood mélanges: although it has a Portuguese influence, Cioppino is from California; Paella, of course, is from Spain. They share many advantages: they're robust and flavorful, are fun to eat, and can be prepared in advance. Serve them in wide, deep soup plates, with lots of bread for dunking. They need no other accompaniment, except perhaps a tangy spinach salad afterward.

CIOPPINO

MAKES 6 TO 8 SERVINGS

SAUCE:

- ½ *cup olive oil*
- 1 *cup chopped onion*
- ¼ *cup chopped green peppers*
- 4 *cloves garlic, minced*
- 1 *can (24 ounces) Italian tomatoes*
- 1 *can (3 ounces) tomato paste*
- 1½ *cups dry red wine*
- 1 *lemon, thinly sliced*
- ¾ *cup chopped parsley, divided*
- 1 *teaspoon basil*
- 1 *teaspoon oregano*
- 1 *teaspoon salt*
- ½ *teaspoon pepper*
- ¼ *teaspoon thyme*
- *Pinch cayenne pepper*
- 1 *bay leaf*

STEW:

- 1 *pound firm fish filets (cod, haddock, bass, turbot, etc.)*
- 12 *clams*
- 12 *mussels*
- 2 *chicken lobsters*
- ½ *pound shrimp, peeled*

Prepare the sauce first: Heat the oil in a large Dutch oven or heavy kettle. Add the onion, green peppers and garlic. Cook over medium heat for 10 minutes, stirring occasionally. Do not allow the ingredients to brown. Add the tomatoes, tomato paste, wine, lemon, half the chopped parsley and all the seasonings. Stir well with a wooden spoon. Bring the mixture to a boil; then reduce the heat and allow it to simmer for 20 to 25 minutes.

While the sauce is cooking, prepare the fish. Cut the filets into pieces about 2 inches square. Scrub the clams and mussels thoroughly under cold, running water, being sure to remove all the "beard" (vegetation) that may adhere to the mussel shells. Cut the lobsters in half, then cut each half into 3 or 4 pieces leaving shell on.

When the sauce has cooked for the indicated time, add the lobster, shrimp, clams and mussels to the kettle. Cover and cook them gently for 10 minutes. Add the fish pieces, again cover, and cook for another 10 minutes, or until the clams and mussels are open and the fish is done. If the sauce is too thick, add some clam juice. Remove the bay leaf. Sprinkle the remaining parsley over the top of the stew, and serve in large bowls, with garlic bread.

PAELLA

MAKES 6 TO 8 SERVINGS

Paella should correctly be cooked in a very large, shallow pan on top of the range, over direct heat. But as this takes considerable watching and care, you may prefer to layer the ingredients in a kettle and cook them in the oven.

4 tablespoons olive oil
4 chicken drumsticks or thighs
¾ cup chopped onions
2 cloves garlic, minced
1½ cups raw rice
2 cups chicken stock
Half a bay leaf
Pinch saffron (optional)
12 littleneck clams, scrubbed
12 mussels, scrubbed
8 to 10 small shrimp, unshelled
1 chicken lobster, unshelled but cut into pieces
1 pound chorizo (sausage), cut in ½-inch slices
1-pound can tomatoes, well-drained
1 jar (4 ounces) pimientos, drained
½ package (5 ounces) frozen green peas
Salt and pepper to taste

Heat the oil in a large Dutch oven. Add the chicken pieces and brown them nicely on all sides. When they are done, remove the browned chicken pieces and set them aside. Put the chopped onions and garlic in the pan, and sauté them until just limp but not browned, about 3 or 4 minutes. Add the rice, stir well and allow it to sauté over medium heat for 3 or 4 minutes. Then add the chicken stock, bay leaf and saffron. Bring the liquid to a boil, lower the heat and let the rice simmer for 10 minutes. Drain the rice in a colander, reserving the strained stock, and set both ingredients aside.

Arrange all the ingredients in layers in the Dutch oven, starting with the clams, mussels and shrimp at the bottom. Add a layer of the cooked rice, then a layer of cut-up lobster, followed by another layer of rice. Add the chorizo and the sautéed chicken pieces and cover with the remaining rice. Spoon the tomatoes over the top, along with the pimientos and peas. Sprinkle with salt and pepper, if desired. Cover the pan and place it in a 350°F. oven for 30 minutes. Remove the cover and check to see if the mixture appears too dry. If needed, add the reserved stock, which should be added hot. Continue baking, without a cover, for another 10 minutes, or until the rice is tender. Serve the paella very hot in large, flat soup plates, giving each person a selection of the various seafood, the chicken and sausage.

10 Vegetables

FRESH VEGETABLES make this earth celestial. I know of nothing more sublime than a vegetable that is freshly picked from the garden, pauses briefly in the kitchen to be cleaned and delicately prepared, and arrives on the table at the peak of its sparkling brilliance. That is perfection.

But perfection is rare. Most people don't have gardens, and so must do the next best thing: buy their vegetables from a store. Still, there are ways to elicit the best from even store-bought vegetables, so that they will be as close as possible to the garden-fresh ideal.

The first rule is to cook vegetables briefly, until they are just barely tender. Overcooking will make them watery, like atrocious steam-tabled or canned vegetables. Long cooking breaks down the tissues and produces the characteristics of a sponge.

It is important to have the right amount of moisture in the vegetables in the first place, so they won't take eons to cook and become tough, off-tasting, dreary-colored and de-vitaminized in the process. When you find that the vegetables you have bought are old and dry, follow this procedure. Before cutting the vegetables, soak them for an hour or two in water; to retain their crispness, refrigerate them while the water is being absorbed. Then drain the vegetables, cut or pare them, and plunge them into salted water that is already boiling (so they won't be immersed a minute longer than necessary). The vegetables will cook from the inside out, rather than from the outside in, and in their own liquor, so they won't taste like water. Cook them as briefly as possible until tender — the pre-soaking will cut the usual time in half; and do not cover the pan, so the color will stay bright. Drain the vegetables, quickly cool them under running water, and sauté them lightly in a pan with butter or olive oil and seasonings; then serve. If you wait to butter and season them at the table, you will just be applying a veneer of seasoning, not marrying it with the food.

Use as little water as you can get away with for the boiling process. Peas, for example, have quite a high water content and need very little water in the pan.

You can prepare vegetables in advance by undercooking them. Drain them in a colander, place under cool water to prevent further cooking, and leave them in the colander at room temperature until you are ready to proceed. To finish: melt butter down to the warm, foamy stage, add the vegetables, and stir or toss them over low heat until they begin to soften slightly and the colors are bright.

When you have leftover cooked vegetables, refrigerate them overnight and add them to soup the next day. Or reheat them in butter, or in a sauce, with sautéed onions, or another compatible seasoning.

When you're chopping or mincing onions, parsley or chives, prepare an extra amount and freeze it in plastic bags or cartons; the vegetables will be all ready to use next time you need them.

If you are marooned on the steppes of Siberia and cannot get fresh vegetables, you can use commercially frozen ones. Though certainly not all frozen vegetables are bearable, they do have an advantage over canned vegetables in that you can control their cooking somewhat by using stock instead of water.

Don't be a slave to habit. There are many different things you can do with every vegetable there is. That goes for vegetables you usually serve raw, as well as those you are accustomed to cooking. Lettuce, cucumber and celery are heavenly when braised, while spinach served raw is the soul of a pungent salad. Make combinations, make sauces, make an Eden of the garden of vegetables. And don't overlook such flavorful items as celery leaves, onion tops and parsley and mushroom stems. If you use your imagination and are adventurous, you'll find it's easy to delight and astonish everybody . . . including yourself.

Once you've cut an artichoke, it turns black from contact with the air. So, immediately after cutting each vegetable, plunge it into boiling water to which lemon juice has been added. The lemon will prevent them from blackening. In case, for some reason, you have to wait between cutting and boiling the artichokes, save them from disaster by instantly sprinkling the leaves with lemon juice.

ARTICHOKES À LA LYONNAISE

MAKES 4 SERVINGS

4 large artichokes
Boiling water to cover
Juice of 2 lemons, divided
3 tablespoons butter, divided
1 onion, finely chopped
½ pound sausage meat
2 tablespoons chopped parsley
Salt and pepper to taste
2 tablespoons oil
½ cup water

Cut the stems off the artichokes. Remove any discolored leaves and the choke, and make a well in the center for the stuffing. Carefully place the artichokes in boiling water that has half the lemon juice added. Simmer gently for 5 minutes; then remove the artichokes and let them drain upside down.

Melt 1 tablespoon of the butter in a skillet. Add the onions and sauté until they are soft. Add the sausage meat, parsley, salt and pepper and cook them together 6 to 8 minutes. Cool the mixture slightly, then divide it equally, and stuff each artichoke with a portion.

Melt the remaining butter in a Dutch oven. Add the oil and stir. Place the artichokes upright in the pan. Mix the remaining lemon juice with the ½ cup of water and add it to the pan. Cover and cook slowly for 35 to 45 minutes, until a leaf will readily come off the artichoke when pulled gently. Serve piping hot.

Note: Artichokes may be baked in the oven, if preferred, at a temperature of 375°F. The baking pan should be covered. Check occasionally to see if more water is needed, to keep the artichokes from sticking to bottom of pan.

Barley is one of many vegetables that taste more elegant when cooked in chicken stock rather than in water. Add the cooked barley to soup, use it in a casserole or a salad. For a dinner-table surprise, serve barley as a side dish, instead of pasta, rice or potatoes.

BARLEY IN CHICKEN STOCK

MAKES 6 SERVINGS

1 cup barley
2 tablespoons butter
1 small onion, sliced thin
1 cup sliced mushrooms
4 cups chicken stock
½ bay leaf
Pinch of nutmeg

Soak the barley in cold water to cover for about half an hour; drain it very well.

In a heavy saucepan, melt the butter; then add the sliced onion and sauté until it is just golden. Add the drained barley and the mushrooms. Sauté them for about 4 or 5 minutes, stirring occasionally. Stir in the chicken stock, bay leaf and nutmeg. Cover and let cook until the barley is tender, about 40 to 45 minutes. Drain off any remaining liquid. Serve hot.

BARLEY COOKED IN CLAM BROTH

MAKES 4 TO 6 SERVINGS

2 tablespoons olive oil
¼ cup finely chopped onions
1 cup barley
3 cups clam juice
Pinch of salt and pepper
½ bay leaf
1 tablespoon butter

Soak the barley in cold water to cover for about half an hour; drain it very well.

Heat the oil. Add the onions and sauté until golden. Add the barley and stir well, cooking over medium-low heat for about 5 minutes. Add the clam juice, salt, pepper and bay leaf, while stirring to mix. Bring to a simmer, cover and let cook 30 to 35 minutes, or until the barley is tender. Drain off any remaining liquid. Add the butter and stir to mix.

Boil all your green vegetables in an uncovered pan and they will remain bright-colored instead of turning a dull khaki shade. Cook until just barely tender; any longer and you might as well eat mushy canned vegetables. A grind of fresh nutmeg or a splash of fresh lemon juice, along with salt, pepper and butter, does wonders for the flavor of fresh green beans.

GREEN BEANS WITH SAUTÉED ONIONS

MAKES 4 SERVINGS

1 pound green beans
Boiling, salted water
2 tablespoons butter
1 onion, finely chopped
½ teaspoon salt
¼ teaspoon pepper

Trim the ends from the beans; then snap them in half or to desired lengths. Drop them into lightly salted, boiling water and cook them just until crisp-tender. Drain the beans well.

Melt the butter in a heavy pan and sauté the onion until it is golden. Add the beans, mix thoroughly, and season with salt and pepper. Serve promptly.

GREEN BEANS À LA CRÈME

MAKES 4 SERVINGS

1 pound green beans
Boiling, salted water
2 tablespoons butter
1 cup heavy cream
Salt and pepper to taste

Trim the ends from the beans; then snap them in half or to desired lengths. Drop them into lightly salted, boiling water and cook until they are just crisp-tender. Drain the beans very well.

Melt the butter in a heavy saucepan, add the beans and stir briefly. Pour the cream over the beans and simmer over medium heat until the sauce is slightly thickened. Season with salt and pepper to taste and serve.

Variation: Just before you add the cream, add ½ cup of sliced mushrooms.

WHOLE GREEN BEANS WITH TOMATOES

MAKES 4 SERVINGS

1 pound green beans
Boiling, salted water
2 tablespoons butter
3 tomatoes, peeled and cut into cubes
1 shallot, minced
Salt and pepper to taste
1 tablespoon chopped parsley

Trim the ends from the beans; then cook them in a small amount of boiling, lightly salted water until they are just crisp-tender. Drain the beans in a colander and run cold water over them to stop the cooking action. Drain well.

Melt the butter in a skillet. Add the tomatoes, shallot, salt and pepper. Stir to mix, then add the cooked beans, and bring all to a gentle simmer. Cook only 2 to 3 minutes in all. Serve the beans and tomatoes sprinkled with chopped parsley.

SPANISH GREEN BEANS

MAKES 4 SERVINGS

1 pound green beans
Boiling, salted water
1 cup canned tomatoes or 3 fresh, peeled tomatoes
3 tablespoons butter
2 tablespoons sliced almonds
¼ teaspoon marjoram
Salt and pepper to taste
2 teaspoons chopped parsley

Trim the ends from the beans and cook them whole in lightly salted, boiling water until they are just crisp-tender. Drain them immediately.

Chop the tomatoes into small pieces. Melt the butter in a heavy saucepan. Add the tomatoes, almonds and marjoram. Cook a few minutes, while stirring; then add the drained beans. Stir carefully to mix. Season with salt and pepper to taste; add parsley and serve promptly.

White beans are hearty, country fare but have little flavor. So you must create whatever seasoning you want, and cook the beans long and slowly so they will be tender and the flavors will be well-married. This recipe calls for carrots and cloves. Some other seasoning combinations that will please you are: parsley and chives; onion and bacon; or the Basque combination of green peppers, tomato and onion.

FLAGEOLETS

(White Beans)

MAKES 6 SERVINGS

1 pound white pea beans (Great Northern)
1 carrot, cut in chunks
4 whole cloves
2 tablespoons butter
¾ cup coarsely chopped onions
2 cloves garlic, minced
Pinch thyme
1 bay leaf
⅓ cup white wine
1 chicken bouillon cube
4 cups water
2 teaspoons salt
½ teaspoon pepper
1 sprig parsley

Cover the beans with cold water. Soak them overnight or for at least 6 hours. Drain and discard the water.

Place the beans in a cooking pot. Stud the carrot pieces with whole cloves and add them to the beans.

Melt the butter in a skillet. Add the onions and garlic and sauté 3 or 4 minutes, until they are golden. Add them to the beans, along with all the remaining ingredients. Bring to a boil. Skim any froth from the top of the pot and discard it. Reduce the heat and allow the beans to simmer gently for 1½ to 2 hours, or until they are tender. Drain the beans well and remove the carrots and bay leaf; serve with a pat of butter, as a hot vegetable. This dish is particularly good with roast lamb. Leftovers may be used for a salad, or served cold and dressed simply with a tablespoon or two of olive oil.

Tiny, firm, bright-green Brussels sprouts are like little corsages on the plate . . . *if* you do not overcook them. Please!

BRUSSELS SPROUTS WITH BACON

MAKES 4 TO 6 SERVINGS

1 pound Brussels sprouts
Boiling, salted water
2 slices bacon, diced
Salt and pepper to taste
½ cup heavy cream

Cook the sprouts in lightly salted, boiling water for about 15 minutes, or until they are tender. Drain them thoroughly. Put the bacon into a heavy saucepan and cook until it is just crisp. Add the drained sprouts, salt and pepper. Then add the cream and cook over low heat until the cream is reduced by half. Serve promptly.

BRUSSELS SPROUTS WITH CHEESE

MAKES 4 TO 6 SERVINGS

1 pound Brussels sprouts, cleaned and trimmed
Boiling, salted water
1 cup chicken broth
5 tablespoons grated Gouda cheese
3 tablespoons butter
⅛ teaspoon nutmeg

Cook the Brussels sprouts in boiling, lightly salted water for about 15 minutes, or until they are tender. Drain them very well and place them in a shallow, buttered baking dish. Pour the chicken broth over the sprouts and sprinkle them with grated cheese. Dot with butter and sprinkle nutmeg over the cheese. Place in a 350°F. oven and bake until the cheese is melted and golden brown, about 10 minutes. Serve promptly.

Bright, sprightly broccoli adds just the touch of gaiety a dinner menu often needs. Its distinctive flavor balances well with poultry, ham, or seafood.

BROCCOLI ORIENTAL

MAKES 6 SERVINGS

2 onions, quartered
Water to cover
1 teaspoon salt, divided
1 bunch broccoli
1 cup onion stock
4 tablespoons soy sauce
1 tablespoon dry mustard
¼ teaspoon powdered ginger
2 tablespoons cornstarch
¼ pound mushrooms, sliced

Put the onions and ½ teaspoon of salt in a saucepan. Barely cover the onions with water, bring to a boil, and cook until the onions are barely tender. Drain, reserving one cup of the water in which the onions were cooked. Set the onions aside.

Clean and separate the broccoli into stalks. Put the stalks into a saucepan, add the remaining ½ teaspoon of salt and a small amount of water. Bring to a boil and cook until the broccoli is just crisp-tender. Drain.

In a saucepan, mix the onion stock, soy sauce, mustard, ginger and cornstarch. Bring the liquid to a slow simmer and stir until it thickens to a sauce. Add the mushrooms and simmer another minute or two.

Place the broccoli on a large, warm serving platter. Arrange the reserved onion quarters on top of the broccoli and spoon the sauce over all the vegetables. Serve promptly.

You're in for an intoxicating surprise. Carrots cooked in Vichy water, or club soda as a substitute, are like the rich relatives of the poor carrots that get cooked in plain tap water.

CARROTS VICHY

MAKES 4 SERVINGS

1 pound carrots, peeled and sliced thin
1 bottle Vichy water (or club soda)
½ teaspoon salt
2 tablespoons butter
¼ teaspoon pepper
1 tablespoon chopped parsley

Put the carrots in a saucepan with Vichy water to cover. Add the salt and simmer until the carrots are tender. Drain them and add butter, pepper and parsley. Mix well and serve very hot.

The parsnip is a much undervalued and neglected vegetable, perhaps because people who try it boiled and plain stop right there. A parsnip is a sort of carrot, but sweeter and lighter in texture. By combining the two vegetables, and by adding the distinctive flavors of bacon and shallots, you elicit the most attractive characteristics of each. And you introduce parsnip-haters to "a new vegetable" in the bargain.

CARROTS AND PARSNIPS SUPRÊME

MAKES 4 TO 6 SERVINGS

½ pound carrots
½ pound parsnips
Boiling, salted water
1 tablespoon butter
2 shallots, minced
3 slices bacon, diced
Salt and pepper to taste
3 tablespoons chopped parsley

Peel the carrots and parsnips, and cut them into slanting slices. Put them into a saucepan of boiling, lightly salted water and cook until they are just crisp-tender. Drain.

Melt the butter in a skillet and sauté the finely chopped shallots until they are golden. Then add the bacon and cook for a few minutes. Stir in the drained carrots and parsnips. Add salt and pepper to taste; then toss the vegetables gently with the parsley. Serve promptly.

CAULIFLOWER AU GRATIN

1 head cauliflower
Boiling, salted water
4 tablespoons butter
4 tablespoons flour
3 cups milk
1 teaspoon chicken stock, fresh or made from a bouillon cube
½ cup grated Swiss cheese, divided

Wash the cauliflower and separate the flowerets. Place them in boiling, lightly salted water (just to cover) and cook about 15 minutes, or until the cauliflowerets are just barely tender enough to pierce with a fork. Drain, place them in a colander, and run cold water over them to stop the cooking action.

Melt the butter in a saucepan. Stir in the flour and mix well. Gradually add in the milk, while continuing to cook and stir until the sauce is thickened and smooth. Add the chicken stock or bouillon and about two-thirds of the grated cheese. Stir over low heat until the cheese is just melted.

Put the cauliflower into a shallow baking dish. Pour the sauce over it and sprinkle the top with the remaining grated cheese. Bake in a 350°F. oven for about 30 minutes.

Note: Broccoli may also be prepared in this manner.

One morning at my cooking school, I announced that we were going to prepare cauliflower as part of the lesson. Three students yawned and the rest of the class groaned. Then I told them that this would be cauliflower as they'd never tasted it before, because the recipe was my own invention — in which the vegetable is perked up with the crunch and flavor of chopped, sautéed pecans. After they sampled the results, the yawners and groaners turned into ebullient cauliflower enthusiasts. Chances are, the recipe will produce the same effect at your dinner table.

CAULIFLOWER WITH PECANS

MAKES 6 SERVINGS

1 head cauliflower
Boiling, salted water
2 tablespoons butter
½ cup coarsely chopped pecans
¼ cup fine, dry bread crumbs
Salt and pepper

Wash the cauliflower and separate the flowerets. Put them into boiling, lightly salted water and cook for about 20 minutes, or until they are tender. Drain them in a colander, then run cold water oven them to stop the cooking action. Leave them in the colander over the sink, to drain very well.

Melt the butter in a saucepan. Add the pecans and sauté them gently for about 3 minutes. Add the drained cauliflowerets and, stirring gently, reheat them thoroughly. Turn the cauliflower and pecans into a warmed serving dish. Sprinkle with bread crumbs, salt and pepper, and serve promptly.

CORN RELISH

1 cup sugar
1 ¼ cups cider vinegar
1 ¼ teaspoon salt
¾ teaspoon white pepper
1 teaspoon turmeric
1 teaspoon mustard seed
3 one-pound cans whole-kernel corn
1 green pepper, seeded and diced
1 onion, chopped
1 tomato, peeled and diced

In a large saucepan, combine the sugar, vinegar, salt, pepper, turmeric and mustard seed. Bring to a boil while stirring. Add all the remaining ingredients. Bring again to a boil, lower the heat and simmer for 10 minutes. Let the mixture cool; then put it in a bowl or jar and refrigerate it for 2 days before using. Corn relish will keep under refrigeration for 4 to 6 weeks.

ENDIVE CORDON BLEU

MAKES 4 SERVINGS

8 endive
Boiling, salted water
8 thin slices of boiled ham
8 thin slices Swiss cheese
3 tablespoons butter (approximately)
½ teaspoon salt
¼ teaspoon pepper

Drop the cleaned endive into boiling, lightly salted water and simmer the vegetables gently for 8 to 10 minutes. Drain them very well.

Meantime, place the ham slices on a large piece of waxed paper. Put a slice of cheese on each ham slice. Place one cooked endive on each cheese slice and dot it with about a teaspoonful of butter. Roll up the ham and cheese around each endive and place each roll in a buttered, shallow baking dish. Sprinkle with salt and pepper; melt the remaining butter and drizzle it over all. Bake in a 325°F. oven for about 20 minutes, until the rolls are thoroughly heated. Serve at once.

Escarole — like its relatives, endive and lettuce — is a jaunty member of the chicory family. It is firm, pale to very green in color, with slender, frilly-edged leaves. It is lively in salads and non-routine when braised and served as a hot vegetable. Braising is a wonderful way to serve endive, Boston and romaine lettuce, and celery, too.

ESCAROLE BRAISED IN CHICKEN STOCK

MAKES 3 OR 4 SERVINGS

2 tablespoons olive oil
1 clove garlic, halved
Large, outside leaves of 2 heads of escarole
1 cup chicken stock or bouillon

Heat the oil in a heavy pan. Add the garlic and escarole. Pour the stock over all. Cover the pan tightly and bring to a boil. Lower the heat and simmer until the escarole is just crisp-tender, about 15 to 20 minutes.

SAUTÉED MUSHROOMS

½ pound mushrooms
2 tablespoons butter
1 tablespoon chopped parsley
¼ cup dry white wine

1 tablespoon oil
Salt and pepper to taste
1 clove garlic, mashed

Wipe the mushrooms with a damp cloth and then slice them. Melt the butter in a skillet. Add the oil and when it is hot, add the mushrooms and sauté them quickly. Add the salt, pepper, parsley, wine and garlic. Mix thoroughly, then serve at once.

If you are lucky and have fresh peas, cook them in the manner prescribed for all green vegetables, but use very little water; they contain enough moisture of their own so that you needn't drown them. Sauté the drained peas according to this recipe. If you are unlucky and have only frozen peas, use this recipe to help make them palatable. (The same rule applies to frozen green beans, lima beans, carrots, potatoes — almost every vegetable.)

PEASANT PEAS

MAKES 3 OR 4 SERVINGS

1 tablespoon oil
1 tablespoon butter
1 onion, diced
3 slices bacon, diced
1 package (10 ounces) frozen peas, slightly defrosted

Put the oil and butter in a skillet. Add the diced onion and bacon and sauté until they are lightly browned. Add the peas. Stir and let the pan remain over heat just until the peas are thoroughly hot.

MASHED POTATOES

You should know how to make mashed potatoes that are fluffy, not gluey. To start, peel but do not cut your potatoes before cooking. Leave them whole, so they won't absorb water. Use enough water to cover the potatoes by at least an inch. Bring them to a boil, but never boil them rapidly; adjust the heat so you can see the water just bubbling. Do not overcook, or the potatoes will lose their firm texture. Drain them immediately, return them to the pan, and place over low heat, to evaporate the rest of the water. Introduce butter into the pan and mash the potatoes with a flat-bottomed potato masher, rather than with an egg beater or electric mixer. That way, they'll be mealy and fluffy, and not a purée. Before serving, add a small amount of warm milk or cream, just enough to blend, so the texture will be light. Salt and pepper to taste.

FARMER-STYLE LYONNAISE POTATOES

2 onions, peeled and quartered
4 tablespoons butter, melted
2 pounds potatoes, peeled and quartered
1/8 teaspoon thyme
1 teaspoon salt
1/4 teaspoon pepper

Place the onions in the bottom of a shallow baking pan. Pour the melted butter over the onions; then place the potatoes on top. Sprinkle with thyme, salt and pepper. Bake in a 375°F. oven for 30 minutes or until done, tossing once or twice during the baking time. Both the onions and potatoes should be lightly browned.

It's the caress of garlic that makes these potatoes for the passionate.

POMMES DE TERRE FONDUES

MAKES 4 SERVINGS

4 tablespoons oil
1 small onion, sliced
1½ pounds potatoes, peeled
2 cloves garlic, minced
½ teaspoon salt
¼ teaspoon pepper
1 tablespoon chopped parsley

Heat the oil in a large skillet. Add the onion slices and cook them gently until golden. Meantime, cut the potatoes into slices ¼-inch thick. Add them to the skillet and sauté until they are golden brown. Add the garlic, salt and pepper. Reduce the heat and cover the pan. Cook until the potatoes are tender. Sprinkle with parsley and serve promptly.

This is so good it may become your specialty from now on. The sauce is the common white sauce, made tangy with Swiss cheese. I prefer the imported Swiss to the domestic; it has more character and is slightly sharper in taste — though not as sharp as Cheddar.

POMMES DE TERRE AU GRATIN

(Potatoes in Cheese Sauce)

MAKES 6 SERVINGS

1½ pounds potatoes (about 8 to 10)
Boiling, salted water
4 tablespoons butter, divided
3 tablespoons flour
2 cups milk
½ cup grated Swiss cheese
Salt and pepper to taste

Peel the potatoes and cut them into ½-inch cubes. Cook them in lightly salted water until they are about half-done; then drain them promptly. While the potatoes are cooking, prepare the sauce.

Melt 3 tablespoons of the butter in a heavy saucepan. Stir in the flour with a whisk, making a smooth paste. Let the paste cook 2 or 3 minutes; then gradually stir in the milk. Continue cooking and stirring until the sauce is smooth and thickened. Add the grated cheese and stir until it is melted. Add salt and pepper to taste.

Put the drained potatoes into a large, shallow baking dish. Add the sauce and mix gently. Dot the top with the remaining butter. Bake in a 350°F. oven for 35 to 40 minutes, or until the top is golden brown.

FRANCONIA POTATOES

MAKES 6 TO 8 SERVINGS

5 tablespoons butter
3 tablespoons oil
3 to 4 pounds potatoes, peeled
1 teaspoon salt
½ teaspoon white pepper
2 tablespoons chopped parsley

Melt the butter in a large, shallow baking pan; then stir in the oil. Meantime, slice the potatoes lengthwise and dry the slices on paper toweling. Toss the potatoes in the butter and oil to coat them thoroughly. Sprinkle them with salt and pepper. Put the baking pan into a 375°F. oven for 45 minutes, basting the potatoes several times during cooking. Just before serving, sprinkle the potatoes with parsley.

OVEN-BROWNED POTATOES

MAKES 3 TO 4 SERVINGS

3 tablespoons butter
1 onion, sliced
1½ pounds potatoes
1 cup chicken stock
Salt and pepper to taste

Melt the butter in a small skillet. Add the onion slices and sauté them gently until golden. Meantime, cut the potatoes into thin slices and put them into a shallow baking pan. Add the onions, the chicken stock, salt and pepper. Bake in a 375°F. oven for about 30 minutes, or until the potatoes are tender.

Here's a masterful dish with no pretensions but huge appeal. Its gusto and zest is simple to achieve with just a few moments' preparation.

RATATOUILLE

MAKES 4 TO 6 SERVINGS

- *3 tablespoons oil*
- *1 onion, sliced*
- *2 cloves garlic, minced*
- *2 zucchini, unpeeled and sliced thin*
- *1 teaspoon salt*
- *½ teaspoon pepper*
- *1 teaspoon oregano*
- *1 small eggplant, peeled and cubed*
- *1 can (16 ounces) tomatoes, well-drained (or 6 peeled, fresh tomatoes)*

Heat the oil in a heavy saucepan. Add the onion slices and garlic and sauté for 3 or 4 minutes. Add the zucchini slices, salt, pepper and oregano. Cook gently for another few minutes. Add the eggplant and tomatoes; stir and let simmer until the eggplant is tender.

This may be served either hot or chilled.

Does Rice Pilaf sound too exotic or complicated? It's neither. It tastes simply delicious, and is deliciously simple to make. Partially cook the rice for about 15 minutes, cool it under tepid water from the tap to get rid of the starch, and refrigerate it, covered. Then when you need the rice, put it into a casserole with a tablespoon of water, seal the dish with foil and heat in a 350°F. oven for about 20 minutes. The speck of water steams the rice into a nice fluff.

RICE PILAF

MAKES 4 TO 6 SERVINGS

- *1 tablespoon butter*
- *½ cup chopped onions*
- *1 cup raw rice*
- *1 cup chicken stock*
- *1 cup beef stock*
- *⅛ teaspoon ginger*
- *2 tablespoons soy sauce*
- *1 bay leaf*

Melt the butter in a heavy Dutch oven or casserole. Add the onions and sauté until they are just golden and tender. Add the rice and brown it lightly, stirring with a wooden spoon. Stir in the chicken and beef stocks, the ginger, soy sauce and bay leaf. Cover the pan, place it in a 400°F. oven, and bake the rice for about 20 minutes. Test for doneness after the first 15 minutes of cooking time and allow more time if necessary. Remove the bay leaf before serving. Correct the seasoning if needed.

Soufflé, spinach or otherwise, has the glamor of opening night on Broadway. And sometimes the tension as well. This spinach soufflé is a little different. While it certainly is glamorous, there's never any suspense about the outcome. It's absolutely foolproof. What's more, most of the preparation can be done ahead of time. No wonder the critics rave!

SPINACH SOUFFLÉ

MAKES 6 TO 8 SERVINGS

- *1 pound fresh spinach*
- *7 tablespoons butter, divided*
- *3 shallots, finely chopped*
- *½ teaspoon salt*
- *¼ teaspoon pepper*
- *2 tablespoons lemon juice*
- *⅛ teaspoon nutmeg*
- *5 tablespoons flour*
- *1½ cups milk*
- *6 eggs, separated*
- *2 additional egg whites*
- *3 tablespoons grated Parmesan cheese*

Wash the spinach thoroughly and shake off most of the excess water. Melt a tablespoon of the butter in a heavy saucepan, one that is large enough to hold all the spinach. Sauté the shallots in the butter until they are golden and tender; then add the spinach. Quickly stir-cook until the spinach is just crisp-tender. Season it with salt, pepper, lemon juice and nutmeg; toss it gently but thoroughly. (If there is excess water, drain it off.) Set the spinach aside.

In another large saucepan, melt the remaining butter. Blend in the flour with a whisk, until the mixture is smooth and bubbly. Blend in the milk, continuing to stir while cooking, until the sauce thickens. Remove the sauce from the heat. Beat the egg yolks in a bowl. Stir a few tablespoons of the hot sauce into the beaten yolks; then pour this mixture back into the saucepan, stirring all the time. Add the spinach to this sauce and stir.

Beat all the egg whites until they are stiff; then fold them carefully and thoroughly into the spinach mixture. Butter a deep soufflé dish very thoroughly; then coat the sides and bottom with the grated cheese. Pour the soufflé mixture into the prepared dish. Bake in a 400°F. oven for 35 minutes.

Note: Cooked and chopped broccoli may be used instead of the spinach, for a broccoli soufflé.

STUFFED ACORN SQUASH

MAKES 4 SERVINGS

2 acorn squash
Small amount of water
2 tablespoons butter
1 tablespoon finely chopped onions
6 mushrooms, chopped
¼ cup dry white wine
1 chicken bouillon cube
1 tablespoon grated Romano cheese
¼ teaspoon dry mustard
Pinch curry powder
2 tablespoons water
1 cup bread croutons
4 teaspoons butter (additional)
4 tablespoons honey (optional)
Salt and pepper

Cut each squash in half (top to bottom) and remove the seeds. Cut a thin slice off each rounded, skin side to provide a flattened area. Place each half flesh-side down in a baking pan, with a small amount of water, and bake the squash in a 350°F. oven until about half-tender.

Meantime, melt 2 tablespoons of butter in a skillet. Add the onions and mushrooms, and sauté until they are tender but not browned. Stir in the wine, bouillon cube, cheese, dry mustard and curry. Stir until the mixture is smooth; then simmer for 10 minutes. Stir in the 2 tablespoons of water and again bring to the simmering point. Add the croutons and stir well. Remove the mixture from the heat.

When the squash is about half-done, remove it from the oven. Turn the halves over, sprinkle them with salt and pepper, and fill each half with one-quarter of the readied stuffing mixture. Top each filled squash half with a teaspoon of butter and a tablespoon of honey (if desired). Return the squash to the oven and bake the halves for another 20 minutes, or until they are tender and lightly browned.

The onion takes the blah out of summer squash. Using white wine instead of water gives it a Gallic élan.

PARSLIED SUMMER SQUASH

MAKES 4 TO 6 SERVINGS

3 tablespoons butter
1 onion, sliced thin
4 summer squash, sliced
¼ cup dry white wine
½ teaspoon salt
¼ teaspoon pepper
2 tablespoons chopped parsley

Melt the butter in a heavy saucepan. Add the onion slices and sauté gently until they are golden. Add the summer squash, mixing gently. Add the wine, salt and pepper. Cover the pan and simmer for 8 to 10 minutes, until the squash is barely tender. Sprinkle the vegetables with chopped parsley and serve promptly.

The older I grow, the harder it is to find good fresh tomatoes, except in my own garden. And believe me, there is no good tomato except one that is freshly picked. So, considering that you are apt to be stuck with tomatoes that are less than ideal, the following recipes will help you make the best of what you have.

Incidentally, if you can't obtain fresh — or raw — tomatoes just when you need them for a stew or casserole, use a good-quality canned tomato. You'll find that the pear-shaped, Italian tomatoes are meatier than others.

BAKED TOMATOES

MAKES 4 SERVINGS

- *4 tomatoes, cut in half*
- *½ cup bread crumbs*
- *3 tablespoons chopped parsley*
- *1 clove garlic, finely minced*
- *2 tablespoons olive oil*
- *Salt and pepper*

Place the halved tomatoes in a buttered baking dish, cut-side up. Mix all the remaining ingredients thoroughly; then put a tablespoonful of the mixture on top of each tomato half. Bake the tomatoes in a 375°F. oven for 20 minutes, or until they are tender. Sprinkle the tops with a little more chopped parsley just before serving, if desired.

TOMATOES STUFFED WITH EGGPLANT

MAKES 4 SERVINGS

- *4 large tomatoes*
- *¾ cup olive oil, divided*
- *1 onion, finely chopped*
- *2 cloves garlic, minced*
- *1 eggplant, peeled and diced*
- *12 green olives, chopped*
- *6 anchovy filets, minced*
- *¼ cup toasted almond slices*
- *2 tablespoons capers*
- *2 tablespoons wine vinegar*
- *½ teaspoon paprika*
- *1 teaspoon salt*
- *½ teaspoon pepper*
- *1 tablespoon grated Parmesan cheese*
- *1 tablespoon fine bread crumbs*

With a sharp knife, cut off the top of each tomato. Carefully scoop out the pulp, leaving a shell about ¼-inch thick. Heat ¼ cup of the olive oil in a skillet. Add the onions and garlic and sauté until they are golden and tender. Add the pulp from the tomatoes and the eggplant and cook gently another 3 or 4 minutes, or until just tender. Add all the remaining ingredients, except the cheese and bread crumbs. Mix very well; then use the mixture to stuff the prepared tomato shells. Sprinkle the tops with grated cheese and bread crumbs. Place the tomatoes in a buttered baking dish. Bake in a 375°F. oven for about 15 minutes. Serve promptly.

HEARTY STUFFED TOMATOES

MAKES 4 SERVINGS

4 large tomatoes
1 green pepper, quartered and seeded
1 small onion
4 precooked Italian sausages
Salt and pepper to taste
¼ teaspoon oregano
¼ teaspoon nutmeg
3 tablespoons fine, dry bread crumbs
1 egg
⅓ cup dry white wine

Cut a ¾-inch slice off the top of each tomato. Reserve these slices after removing the stem from each. Scoop out the center of each tomato, and drain off any excess juice. Reserve this pulp and juice for use at another time, in a soup or stew.

Put the green pepper, onion and sausages through a meat grinder. Place the ground mixture in a bowl and mix it with all the seasonings, the bread crumbs, egg and wine.

Divide this stuffing and fill each tomato shell with an equal part. Place the ¾-inch slice on top of each tomato and transfer the tomatoes to a buttered baking dish. Bake in a 375°F. oven for about 20 minutes, or until tender. Serve promptly.

TOMATO-PEPPER RELISH

½ cup sugar
2 cups cider vinegar
½ teaspoon cinnamon
12 tomatoes, peeled and sliced thin
4 green peppers, seeded and chopped
4 red peppers, seeded and chopped
2 onions, sliced thin

Combine the sugar, vinegar and cinnamon in a saucepan. Bring the mixture to a boil and stir until the sugar is completely dissolved. Add all the remaining ingredients. Return the mixture to a boil, lower the heat, and simmer, covered, for 1½ hours.

Zucchini squash requires seasoning that is both deft and bold. Don't be timid with salt; this vegetable accepts quite a lot. Remember that you can slice zucchini the long way as well as crosswise, for variety of appearance and ease of handling. Keep zucchini in mind as a raw vegetable, too, for salads or *crudités.*

ZUCCHINI SAUTÉ ITALIEN

MAKES 4 TO 6 SERVINGS

2 tablespoons butter
3 tablespoons oil
2 onions, sliced
3 cloves garlic, minced
1 pound zucchini, sliced
Salt and pepper to taste
2 tomatoes, cut in wedges
1 teaspoon oregano

Heat the butter and oil in a heavy saucepan. Add the onions and garlic, and sauté until the onions are golden and tender. Add the zucchini slices and mix gently with a wooden spoon. Sprinkle with salt and pepper. Cover the pan and cook over low heat for 3 or 4 minutes. Add the tomato wedges to the pan and sprinkle them with oregano. Cover and cook another 8 to 10 minutes, checking occasionally. The zucchini should be just crisp-tender, not overcooked, so the cooking time will depend upon the size and freshness of the vegetables.

ZUCCHINI SAUTÉ MONTE CARLO

MAKES 4 SERVINGS

1 pound zucchini
2 tablespoons oil
1 tablespoon butter
1 onion, sliced
2 tablespoons water
1 teaspoon salt
¼ teaspoon pepper
Pinch oregano
10 black olives
6 mushrooms, quartered

Wash and dry the zucchini; cut off the ends and discard them. Cut each zucchini into wedges. Cover the wedges with a damp towel, to keep them from drying out, while you prepare the other ingredients.

Heat the oil and butter in a skillet. Add the onion slices and sauté until they are golden and tender. Add the zucchini wedges, along with the water, salt, pepper and oregano. Mix gently with a wooden spoon. Add the olives and mushrooms, again mixing gently. Cover and simmer 8 to 10 minutes, until the zucchini is barely tender. Be careful not to overcook.

STUFFED ZUCCHINI PIÉMONT

MAKES 6 TO 8 SERVINGS

4 medium-sized zucchini
2 tablespoons butter
1 onion, chopped fine
2 cloves garlic, minced
½ pound sausage meat
½ teaspoon oregano
½ teaspoon basil
⅛ teaspoon monosodium glutamate
Salt and pepper to taste
1 pound spinach, washed and drained
12 mushrooms, cut up
2 tablespoons grated Parmesan cheese

Cut each zucchini squash in half lengthwise and scoop out the pulp, leaving a shell about ¼-inch thick. Chop the pulp and set it aside. Melt the butter in a heavy saucepan. Add the onions and garlic and sauté until the onions are golden and tender. Add the sausage meat, breaking it up into small pieces, and allow it to cook while stirring for 4 or 5 minutes. Add all the seasonings and the spinach, mixing well, and continue to cook until the spinach is soft. Then stir in the reserved zucchini pulp and the mushrooms. Stir well and cook for another few minutes. Remove the pan from the heat and divide this mixture equally among the zucchini shells. Sprinkle the tops with grated cheese. Place the stuffed zucchini in a lightly oiled, shallow baking pan in a single layer. Bake in a 350°F. oven for about 30 minutes, or until the zucchini shells are nicely tender.

ZUCCHINI À LA SUISSE

MAKES 4 SERVINGS

4 tablespoons olive oil
2 medium-sized zucchini, cut into wedges
½ teaspoon chopped shallots
1 clove garlic, finely minced
Salt and pepper to taste
⅛ teaspoon monosodium glutamate
¾ cup chicken stock or bouillon
½ package dry mushroom-soup mix
3 ounces Swiss cheese, cut in strips

Heat the oil in a heavy saucepan. Add the zucchini wedges and sauté them quickly. Add the shallots, garlic, salt, pepper and monosodium glutamate. Stir gently and cook 4 or 5 minutes. Add the chicken stock and soup mix, again stirring carefully. Let the mixture simmer 3 or 4 minutes without a cover, and stir occasionally. Then pour the mixture into a shallow casserole. Place the strips of cheese in a crisscross pattern on top. Bake in a 350°F. oven 5 to 10 minutes, until the cheese melts slightly and is lightly browned.

Mixed vegetables in sauce usually looks more like mishmash than macédoine. I like this composition because each flavorsome, colorful vegetable has its own separate place of honor in the casserole . . . and the pleasing flavors exalt one another.

VEGETABLE MACÉDOINE

MAKES 6 SERVINGS

4 carrots, peeled and sliced
Boiling, salted water
3 tablespoons butter, divided
1 onion, diced
3 small zucchini or summer squash, sliced
10 small mushrooms, quartered
2 teaspoons arrowroot
Cold water
1 cup hot water
1 chicken bouillon cube
½ teaspoon marjoram
¼ cup dry white wine
Fine, dry bread crumbs

Cook the carrots in boiling, lightly salted water for 10 to 12 minutes and drain them well. Melt a tablespoon of the butter in a skillet. Add the diced onion and sauté until it is golden. Add the slices of zucchini or summer squash and allow them to sauté lightly.

Cut the remaining butter into small pieces and place the pieces in the bottom of a large, flat baking dish. Arrange the drained carrot slices in a ring around the outer edges of the dish. Next place the sautéed squash-and-onion mixture in the dish, forming a concentric ring within the carrots.

Add the mushrooms to the now-emptied skillet and sauté them for 3 or 4 minutes; then pour the mushrooms and pan juices into the center of the other vegetable rings in the baking dish.

Dissolve the arrowroot in a small amount of cold water, in a large mixing bowl. Then add the hot water, bouillon cube and marjoram, and stir well. Add the white wine; then pour the mixture over the vegetables in the baking dish. Sprinkle lightly with bread crumbs. Bake in a 375°F. oven for 30 minutes, or until all vegetables are tender. Baste 3 or 4 times during the baking.

11
Sauces

I'VE SEEN usually placid people shatter into a thousand pieces at the mention of sauce-making. They think it is a difficult, complicated, mysterious process. Worse, they are so panicky they won't even try it.

It is true that good sauces are essential to a civilized cuisine, and that they indicate the caliber of a chef. They even tell you something about the cuisine and philosophy of a country. I've heard it said that England has 360 religions and one sauce, while France has one religion and 360 sauces.

It's true that a few sauces are tricky to make, until you get the feel of them. Hollandaise, béarnaise and mayonnaise (whipped to the proper texture by hand, if you please, not whirled in an uncontrollable blender) require a certain degree of sureness. But basically, sauce-making, like all cooking, is easy. It merely requires practice. Using a good stock and knowing how to cook your *roux* properly are the keys to success.

When I say "a good stock," I realize that it is not practical for you to spend hours preparing a stock every time you need a cupful or two. Here is how to conquer that problem. One: whenever you make a soup, cook a vegetable, or produce stock from some other dish, label and freeze what is left over, and you will always have a good stock ready for instant use. Use ice-cube trays for freezing, and you will be able to use small amounts at will. Use half-pint and pint-size plastic containers as well, to keep larger amounts handy. Two: As an alternative, for occasions when there is no homemade stock in your freezer, use a good, premium-quality beef or chicken base in either dry-cube or canned form.

Now for the *roux,* which is the thickening agent to which you add your stock and other ingredients, to create brown, white and other kinds of sauces. So you can get the feel of *roux*-making easily, without wasting good ingredients, here is a "dummy" recipe with which to practice.

Melt 2 tablespoons of Crisco, or whatever fat you don't mind throwing away. Gradually add the same amount of flour, 2 tablespoons, all the while stirring over very low heat. Use a whisk, for thorough blending. As you blend the fat and flour this way, observe how the consistency changes. As soon as you have a light *roux* — light in color and in consistency — take the pan off the stove and add a cup of hot water.

Introduce the water a half-cup at a time, stirring continuously until the *roux* begins to dissolve. Then put the pan back on low heat, and keep blending until you have the consistency you want. Notice that by killing the heat under your fat and flour (the *roux*), you have equalized the temperature of the *roux* and the introduced liquid. This is how to avoid having a lumpy sauce. Isn't that easy?

Beurre manié is another frequently used thickener for sauces. The words mean "kneaded butter." Here is how you make it. With your fingers, mix softened butter with flour and make little balls — like fat pearls. Use 2 parts flour to 1 part butter for a basic *beurre manié*. As a guide to the quantity you will need, remember that it takes 2 tablespoons of flour to thicken 1 cup of liquid. To make a sauce, you simply drop the kneaded-butter balls, a few at a time, into fairly hot liquid, and stir gently over low heat so the *beurre manié* (thickener) blends without lumping. Use a wooden spoon to stir; the butter melts quickly and what you need to do is dissolve the flour. You can also make *beurre manié* using equal parts of butter and flour, or any proportions that will give you the consistency you are looking for.

Roux and *beurre manié* have other uses besides as a base for sauces. So if you make too much of either, don't throw it away. Refrigerate it for thickening something else tomorrow. Say you are making a chicken soup and you want the stock to be a little thick and creamy. Take a couple of spoonfuls of *roux*, introduce it into the soup, and all of a sudden you will have a substantial, creamy soup.

A final hint: use unsalted butter when preparing sauces. Its superior melting qualities, and the control you'll have over seasoning will be extremely helpful.

CHICKEN STOCK

3 pounds chicken backs and necks
2 quarts water
1 carrot, cut up
1 stalk celery, cut up
1 bay leaf
1 large onion, quartered
2 cloves inserted in the onion pieces
¼ teaspoon thyme
Salt and pepper to taste

Wash the chicken backs and necks thoroughly in cold water. Put them into a large kettle or Dutch oven; then add all the remaining ingredients. Bring to a boil. Skim the scum off the top; then continue simmering, while covered, for about 2 hours, until the stock is good and rich. Strain it through a colander, discarding the vegetables and bones. Refrigerate. When the stock is completely chilled, remove the congealed fat from the top of the stock and discard. Use the stock as needed for specific recipes.

BROWN SAUCE

4 tablespoons butter, divided
2 shallots, finely chopped
2 cups dry red wine or beef stock
1 tablespoon chopped parsley
¼ teaspoon thyme
1 bay leaf
3 tablespoons flour

Heat 2 tablespoons of the butter in a heavy saucepan. Add the shallots and sauté gently until they are golden. Add the wine, parsley, thyme and bay leaf. Simmer gently for about 5 minutes, or until the wine is reduced by half. Set the pan aside to cool.

Put the 2 tablespoons of remaining butter into a heavy saucepan. Melt the butter, then stir in the flour to make a smooth paste; cook, while stirring, for 3 or 4 minutes. Remove pan from heat, strain the wine stock; then slowly add it to the butter-flour mixture, while stirring. Continue stirring and cook until the sauce is thickened and smooth.

Note: If preferred, 1 cup of beef bouillon may be substituted for half the wine.

SAUCE ROULADE

MAKES ABOUT 2 CUPS

2 tablespoons butter
¼ cup finely chopped onions
4 or 5 mushrooms, sliced
⅓ cup dry white wine
1 cup Brown Sauce (page 201)
1 tablespoon fines herbes
1 tablespoon chopped parsley

Melt the butter in a heavy saucepan. Add the onions and sauté them until golden. Add the mushrooms and continue cooking for 2 or 3 minutes. Add the wine, Brown Sauce, and *fines herbes.* Stir and cook over medium heat until the sauce is thoroughly hot. Add the parsley just before serving with Meat Loaf Roulade or other meat dishes.

MADEIRA SAUCE

4 tablespoons oil
3 onions, chopped
3 carrots, cut up
1 stalk celery, sliced
½ cup flour
1 quart hot water
Salt and pepper to taste
1 teaspoon thyme
2 bay leaves
2 sprigs parsley
1 teaspoon beef bouillon powder
1 tablespoon butter
¼ cup sliced mushrooms
¼ cup Madeira
2 or 3 tomatoes, quartered

Heat the oil in a Dutch oven. Sauté the onions, carrots and celery to a light golden color. Sprinkle flour over the vegetables and mix in well with a wooden spoon. Add the hot water while stirring; then add all of the seasonings and the bouillon powder. Lower the heat to keep the mixture simmering.

Melt the tablespoon of butter in a small skillet. Add the mushroom slices and sauté until they are tender, about 4 to 5 minutes. Add the sautéed mushrooms to the first mixture, along with the wine and tomatoes. Simmer over low heat for about an hour, adding a little more water if necessary to keep the consistency like cream.

When the sauce is well-flavored, at the end of about an hour's cooking time, strain it through a sieve or colander. Discard the vegetables.

MARINARA SAUCE

4 tablespoons olive oil
2 onions, chopped fine
2 cloves garlic, minced
2 large cans (29 ounces each) stewed tomatoes
3 anchovy filets, mashed
½ cup dry white wine
1 teaspoon salt
½ teaspoon oregano
½ teaspoon sugar

Heat the oil in a large pan. Add the onions and garlic and sauté until they are golden and tender. Add all the remaining ingredients. Stir them together very well. Bring the sauce to a boil; then lower the heat and allow to simmer gently, without a cover, for 30 to 40 minutes.

QUICK TOMATO SAUCE

1 tablespoon olive oil
1 large onion, chopped
¼ teaspoon oregano
¼ teaspoon basil
¼ teaspoon thyme
1 jar (16 ounces) prepared tomato sauce
1 can (8 ounces) tomatoes
½ cup dry red wine

Heat the oil in a heavy saucepan. Add the onions and sauté until golden and tender. Add all the remaining ingredients, stirring well. Let the sauce simmer gently for 20 to 30 minutes.

ESPAGNOLE SAUCE

1 large onion, diced
1 white turnip, diced
3 leeks, diced
3 carrots, diced
3 stalks celery, diced
4 shallots, diced
4 tablespoons bacon fat or oil
3 tablespoons flour
½ cup dry white wine
2 tablespoons tomato paste
2 bay leaves
½ teaspoon thyme
3 or 4 sprigs parsley
1 teaspoon salt
½ teaspoon pepper
2 quarts water
Veal, beef or chicken bones

Dice the onion, turnip, leeks, carrots, celery and shallots. Heat the bacon fat or oil in a large Dutch oven or kettle. Add the chopped vegetables and sauté them slowly over medium heat, stirring with a wooden spoon from time to time. Cook for 8 to 10 minutes; then stir in the flour and cook for another 3 or 4 minutes. Stir in the wine, tomato paste, bay leaves, thyme, parsley, salt and pepper. Mix very well; then stir in the water. Add the bones, making sure that the liquid covers the bones. Bring the mixture to a boil, lower the heat and allow the sauce to simmer gently for 3 to 4 hours. Strain through a colander. Chill; then remove all the fat from the top.

Note: Chilling is the easiest way to remove all excess fat, but if sauce is to be used immediately, allow it to stand for a few minutes and then carefully skim the fat from the top with a large spoon.

BASIC BROWN STOCK

3 tablespoons oil
4 pounds veal or beef bones
2 onions, quartered (unpeeled)
2 carrots, cut up (unpeeled)
1 celery stalk, cut up
Salt and pepper
1 can (4 ounces) tomato paste
1 bay leaf
¼ teaspoon thyme
2 whole cloves
1 quart hot water

Put the oil in a shallow roasting pan. Put in the bones, onions, carrots, and celery; sprinkle all with salt and pepper. Place the pan in a 450°F. oven and roast until the bones are very dark brown, about 45 minutes to 1 hour.

Add the tomato paste, bay leaf, thyme and cloves, and bake for another 10 minutes. Take the pan out of oven and transfer all the ingredients to a large pot. Add the water (this should be enough to cover the bones). Simmer uncovered for 4 to 5 hours, adding water as necessary to keep the bones covered. Skim off excess fat from the top from time to time. Strain the stock and refrigerate or freeze it until needed.

BORDELAISE SAUCE

1 tablespoon butter
1 tablespoon chopped shallots
½ cup Burgundy wine
1 cup Brown Sauce (page 201)
½ teaspoon fines herbes *(minced parsley, chives, chervil and tarragon)*
Salt and pepper to taste
3 tablespoons heavy cream
⅓ cup finely chopped parsley

Melt the butter in a small, heavy saucepan. Add the shallots and sauté gently until they are golden. Add the wine, Brown Sauce, *fines herbes,* salt and pepper. Let the sauce simmer very gently for about 5 minutes. Just before serving, stir in the heavy cream and parsley.

ORANGE LIQUEUR SAUCE

(Bigarade)

2 tablespoons fat (from roasting pan)
1 carrot, minced
1 stalk celery, minced
1 onion, minced
1 tomato, chopped fine
2 cups Brown Stock (page 204)
1 tablespoon butter
3 tablespoons sugar
⅓ cup cider vinegar
1 cup orange juice
1 teaspoon dry mustard
½ teaspoon cornstarch
1 teaspoon cold water
Rind of ½ orange, cut in strips
Rind of ½ lemon, cut in strips
3 tablespoons Grand Marnier
Thin slices of orange, or mandarin orange sections

Heat the fat in a saucepan. Add the minced carrot, celery, onion and tomato and sauté over medium heat for 10 minutes, stirring constantly. Pour in the Brown Stock, stirring the bottom of the pan well. When the mixture comes to a boil, lower the heat and allow the stock to simmer for 30 minutes. Strain, discard the vegetables, and set the stock aside.

Melt the butter in another pan. Add the sugar and cook, while stirring, until the mixture is brown. Add the vinegar and continue to cook until the mixture is reduced by half. Pour in the reserved stock and the orange juice; then add the mustard. Dissolve the cornstarch in the cold water and stir it into the mixture while it continues to simmer gently.

Blanch the orange and lemon peels in boiling water for 3 minutes. Drain and add them to the sauce. Stir in the Grand Marnier and simmer for 10 minutes. Just before serving, stir in the orange slices or sections. This sauce is excellent with roast duckling.

BÉCHAMEL SAUCE

MAKES ABOUT 5 CUPS

6 tablespoons butter
6 tablespoons flour
4 cups milk
Salt and pepper to taste
Pinch of nutmeg
½ cup heavy cream (optional)

Melt the butter in a heavy saucepan. Stir in the flour with a whisk, making a very smooth paste. Gradually stir in the milk, while continuing to stir. Cook over medium heat, stirring all the time, until the sauce is smooth and thickened. Let it bubble gently for 2 or 3 minutes; then stir in the salt and pepper and nutmeg. Add the cream, using just enough to bring the sauce to the consistency desired.

VELOUTÉ SAUCE

MAKES ABOUT 1½ CUPS

- 6 *tablespoons butter*
- ½ *cup flour*
- 2½ *cups hot chicken stock*
- 2 *egg yolks*
- ¾ *cup heavy cream*
- ½ *teaspoon salt*
- ¼ *teaspoon white pepper*
- 1 *tablespoon lemon juice*

In a heavy saucepan, melt the butter. Stir in the flour and cook, stirring constantly over low heat for about a minute. Remove the pan from the heat and let it cool a few minutes. With a whisk, beat in the hot chicken stock. When the butter, flour and stock are completely blended, return the pan to the heat and, continuing to stir, cook the sauce until it comes to a boil. Let it boil for 1 minute; then remove it from the heat.

Using a clean whisk, blend the egg yolks and heavy cream together in a bowl. Whisk in some of the hot sauce, 2 tablespoons at a time, until ½ cup has been added. Slowly pour the egg mixture back into the hot sauce remaining in the pan; keeping the pan off the heat, whisk the sauce until it is smooth and creamy. Bring the sauce to a boil over moderate heat, stirring constantly, and allow it to boil for 10 seconds. Remove the sauce from the heat and season it with salt, pepper, and lemon juice. Makes about 1½ cups of very thick sauce.

WHITE FISH SAUCE

2 tablespoons butter
2 tablespoons flour
1 cup bottled clam juice
½ cup heavy cream

Melt the butter in a heavy saucepan. Stir in the flour until the mixture is smooth. Stir in the clam juice with a whisk. Cook, while stirring, until the sauce is smooth and thickened. Stir in the cream very well. Remove from the heat.

OYSTER SAUCE

2 cups shucked oysters
2 cups beef stock
¼ cup butter
2 tablespoons chopped shallots
¼ cup flour
Juice of half a lemon
1 teaspoon anchovy paste
Few drops Tabasco sauce

Cook the oysters gently in beef stock for 5 minutes. Remove the oysters with a slotted spoon. Put them into a blender with 1 cup of the liquid, and blend them to a fine purée.

Melt the butter in a heavy saucepan. Add the shallots and sauté until golden. Stir in the flour and cook for 2 minutes. Stir in the remaining beef stock; cook and stir until the sauce is smooth and thickened. Add the oyster purée, the lemon juice, anchovy paste and Tabasco. Bring the sauce back to a simmer and cook it for another 3 or 4 minutes. Correct the seasoning, if necessary.

MORNAY SAUCE

4 tablespoons butter
4 tablespoons flour
3 cups warmed milk
½ teaspoon salt
¾ cup grated Swiss cheese

Melt the butter in a heavy saucepan. Blend in the flour with a whisk and cook over low heat for 2 or 3 minutes. Stir in the milk and continue stirring until the sauce comes to a boil and is smooth. Remove the pan from the heat; add the salt and cheese, and stir with a whisk until the cheese is melted.

BÉARNAISE SAUCE

5 shallots, chopped very fine
2 teaspoons tarragon
3 tablespoons wine vinegar
2 egg yolks
1 tablespoon hot water
½ pound butter, melted
2 sprigs parsley, chopped
½ teaspoon salt
¼ teaspoon ground pepper
Juice of half a lemon

Put the shallots, tarragon and vinegar into a small saucepan over medium heat. When the mixture begins to simmer, reduce the heat and allow it to simmer gently until the vinegar cooks off completely. Remove the pan from the heat.

Meantime, put the egg yolks and hot water in the top of a double boiler set over hot water, and beat the yolks continuously with a whisk, until they are very light in color and ribbony in texture.

Gradually add the melted butter to the beaten yolks, mixing well with a whisk all the time. The butter should be the same temperature as the yolks when you are combining them. Whisk for another few minutes after all the butter has been incorporated, making a nice, smooth sauce. Add shallot-and-tarragon mixture, the chopped parsley, salt, pepper and lemon juice. Stir to blend.

Béarnaise Sauce should be made about 20 minutes before serving, to allow the flavors to blend nicely.

HOLLANDAISE SAUCE

½ pound butter
2 egg yolks
1 teaspoon water
1 tablespoon lemon juice
Salt to taste
Pinch of white pepper

Melt the butter and set it aside. With a whisk, beat the egg yolks and water together very thoroughly in a bowl. Set the bowl into a pan of hot water and continue to whisk until the mixture is nice and foamy. Very slowly, add the melted butter, while continuing to whisk. When all butter is added and the mixture is nice and smooth, stir in the lemon juice, salt and pepper.

Important note for successful Hollandaise: The melted butter and egg yolks should be at just about the same temperature for successful and smooth blending. Do not have the butter bubbling hot when adding it to the eggs. Test the temperatures before you begin blending. Should the sauce separate, blend in a teaspoonful of hot water and stir until it is smooth again.

SAUCE MALTAISE

½ cup orange juice
1 cup Hollandaise Sauce (page 209)
⅓ cup finely minced orange peel

Place the orange juice in a heavy saucepan and, over moderate heat, reduce it by about half. Let the juice cool to a temperature that is comfortable to your touch. Very gently, stir the juice into the Hollandaise Sauce; then add the minced orange peel.

MAYONNAISE

2 egg yolks
½ teaspoon salt
¼ teaspoon pepper
1½ tablespoons wine vinegar
1 tablespoon Dijon mustard
1 cup corn oil
Juice of 1 lemon

Be sure all the ingredients are at room temperature. Put the egg yolks, salt, pepper, vinegar and mustard in a large bowl. Mix them rapidly with a whisk until the egg yolks are very pale in color. While continuing to stir, add the oil in a thin, steady stream until it is all absorbed into the egg mixture. Stir in the lemon juice.

SAUCE MIGNONETTE

¼ cup chopped shallots
1 cup wine vinegar
1 teaspoon coarsely ground pepper
2 teaspoons corn oil
½ teaspoon salt

Put the finely chopped shallots in a small bowl. Add the vinegar and let the mixture stand at room temperature for about 1 hour. Stir in the pepper, oil and salt. The sauce is then ready to serve with freshly opened oysters.

BEURRE NOIR

½ cup butter
2 tablespoons chopped parsley
3 tablespoons wine vinegar
1 teaspoon capers

Melt the butter in a heavy skillet over fairly high heat until it bubbles vigorously. Allow the butter to become a good brown color; then quickly stir in the parsley, vinegar and capers. Serve the sauce piping hot over fish or meat, as desired.

AVOCADO SAUCE

3 tablespoons butter
2 teaspoons chopped shallots
3½ tablespoons flour
1½ cups clam juice
¼ teaspoon white pepper
1 whole clove
¼ cup dry white wine
½ cup heavy cream, divided
Juice of half a lemon
1 ripe avocado, peeled, stoned, and cubed

Melt the butter in a heavy skillet. Add the shallots and cook them for a few minutes. Stir in the flour until the mixture is smooth. Let it cook for a minute or two; then gradually stir in the clam juice with a whisk, to make a very smooth sauce. Add the pepper and clove. Continue cooking, while stirring, until the mixture thickens. Stir in the wine, half the cream, and the lemon juice. Pour this sauce into a blender with the cut-up avocado. Add the remaining cream and blend until very smooth. Return the mixture to the pan and keep it warm over a very low heat until serving time. Do not allow the sauce to boil. Remove the clove before serving. Use Avocado Sauce with any seafood dish.

PLUM BRANDY SAUCE

¼ cup plum chutney
¼ cup chili sauce
¼ cup plum preserves
½ cup apricot preserves
1½ ounces brandy or applejack
2 tablespoons honey
1 tablespoon soy sauce
½ cup brown sugar
½ cup cider vinegar
½ cup applesauce
¼ teaspoon cinnamon
¼ teaspoon nutmeg
¼ teaspoon cloves
Juice of half a lemon

Combine all the ingredients in a saucepan. Blend well while heating slowly. Bring the mixture just to a boil; lower the heat and let the sauce simmer gently for 4 or 5 minutes. Serve the sauce on roast pork or ribs.

Note: This sauce may be kept indefinitely if the applesauce is omitted in the first preparation and stirred in just before serving.

SAUCE CASSIS

2 ounces cognac
½ cup currant jelly
Dash of cayenne pepper
2 ounces crème de cassis liqueur
1 tablespoon grated orange rind

Combine all the ingredients in a small saucepan. Heat them gently over a low flame, just until the jelly is melted and all the ingredients are nicely blended. Serve warm, with pork or ham.

12
Salads

I AM RATHER a purist when it comes to salad. Perhaps that is because I am French and was brought up on customs that are different from yours. In Europe, the salad is always served after the entrée. Here, it is usually served either before or with the main course. To me, that makes no sense. When it's served first, it kills, rather than sharpens, your appetite. Worse, when you eat a cold salad together with a hot entrée — an insanity of itself — you cannot savor your good bottle of wine, because the acid in the salad dressing makes the wine taste harsh. Ah, but if you *follow* your lunch or dinner entrée with a small, light salad, then you will have appetite for your meal, palate for your wine, and no guilt feelings if you can't manage to finish those couple of leaves of lettuce. Then, after the salad, you can have a bit of mellow cheese to take the sharpness out of your mouth, and with the cheese you'll be able to finish any wine that is left in the bottle.

There is another difference between European salads and American, and that is the ingredients. In France *salade* means lettuce, period. And we use just one flavorful kind at a time: Bibb, Boston, romaine, escarole, chicory, endive. We like to have a different lettuce every day in the week, if a garden supply is handy. Iceberg lettuce, however, is one thing I abhor. In my opinion, it is good only for sandwiches. In a salad, you might as well eat notebook paper. I suppose it is popular in this country because it keeps longer than other kinds of lettuce and the supermarkets can bag and sell it more profitably.

Here's an economy hint. Don't discard lettuce that you can't use for a salad because you are going away for the weekend or because you've changed your menu. The lettuce will be superb if it is lightly sautéed in butter, then simmered in stock or broth until just wilted. Season it with salt and pepper.

Watercress, to me, is an exceedingly virtuous green. Its vivid color gives joy, its crisp stems and leaves have snap, and its taste has character. I can't imagine why it's regarded as a garnish only, a decoration to be seen but not eaten. This stimulating recipe should change some minds.

WATERCRESS SALAD

MAKES 4 SERVINGS

4 bunches watercress
2 tablespoons wine vinegar
1 teaspoon salt
½ teaspoon pepper
1 tablespoon Dijon mustard
4 tablespoons oil
4 hard-cooked eggs

Wash the watercress thoroughly, and dry it. Wrap it loosely in a towel and place it in the refrigerator to chill.

Prepare the dressing in a small bowl. Start with the vinegar; then add the salt, pepper and mustard. Mix very well; then add the oil and beat. Peel the eggs and chop them coarsely. Arrange the watercress in a glass salad bowl; spread the chopped eggs on the cress, then pour dressing over all. Serve promptly.

I like to prepare spinach, either for eating it raw or for cooking it, by stripping the entire stem from each leaf. Then there's nothing tough to encounter.

SPINACH SALAD

MAKES 4 TO 6 SERVINGS

4 slices bacon
2 hard-cooked eggs
2 tablespoons finely chopped onions
½ clove garlic, finely minced
1 teaspoon salt
½ teaspoon pepper
2 tablespoons wine vinegar
4 tablespoons olive oil
½ pound fresh spinach, washed and dried

Cook the bacon. Drain it on paper toweling, crumble it into a small bowl, and set it aside. Peel the eggs, chop them coarsely, and place them in a large bowl. Add the onions, garlic, salt, pepper, vinegar and olive oil. Add the spinach and toss lightly but thoroughly. Just before serving, sprinkle the crumbled bacon over the top of the salad.

MOLDED SPINACH-SESAME SALAD

MAKES 4 TO 6 SERVINGS

- 2 *tablespoons oil, divided*
- 1 *clove garlic, minced*
- ¼ *teaspoon salt*
- 1 *pound spinach, washed*
- 4 *tablespoons sesame seeds*
- ⅛ *teaspoon monosodium glutamate*
- ¼ *cup soy sauce*
- ¼ *cup sake*

Heat 1 tablespoon of the oil in a large skillet. Add the garlic and sauté until it is golden and tender. Add the salt and spinach, and simmer over medium heat for about 5 minutes, or until the spinach is just crisp-tender. (No added water is needed, as enough will cling to the leaves after washing.)

In a small skillet, heat the remaining oil. Add the sesame seeds and sauté until they are well-browned, stirring occasionally. Drain the cooked spinach of any remaining liquid, and then combine the spinach with the sesame seeds and the remaining ingredients. Pack the mixture into small custard cups and refrigerate until thoroughly chilled. Unmold to serve.

GREEN BEAN SALAD

2 pounds green beans
Boiling, salted water
1 tablespoon wine vinegar
2 tablespoons olive oil
1 tablespoon Dijon mustard
1 teaspoon salt
½ teaspoon pepper
Pinch of saffron
1 small onion, finely minced
1 slice bacon, cooked and crumbled

Trim the ends from the green beans and cut them into about 2-inch lengths. Cook them quickly in lightly salted water until they are just barely crisp-tender. Drain them and then plunge them into cold water. Drain them thoroughly. Mix all the remaining ingredients very thoroughly in a small bowl. Pour the dressing over the beans and chill.

The Europeans have always known that the success of potato salad depends on adding the seasonings while the potatoes are still warm and accepting of flavors. Be careful to cook your potatoes only until they're just barely done. Otherwise they'll fall apart in a most ungracious way.

EUROPEAN POTATO SALAD

MAKES 6 SERVINGS

3 to 4 pounds potatoes
¾ cup chicken broth
2 tablespoons wine vinegar
1 tablespoon Dijon mustard
1 teaspoon salt
½ teaspoon pepper
1 tablespoon chopped chives
4 tablespoons oil

Cook the potatoes unpeeled. When they are done, drain and allow them to cool just enough to handle. Remove the skins and slice the potatoes into a bowl. Pour the chicken broth over the potato slices and toss slightly.

In a small bowl, mix the vinegar, mustard, salt, pepper, chives and oil. Blend the mixture very well, then pour it over the potatoes and toss them very lightly to mix.

Note: A half clove of finely minced garlic may be added, if desired, along with a few slices of crisply cooked, crumbled bacon.

SWISS POTATO SALAD WITH PEARS

MAKES 4 SERVINGS

5 medium-sized potatoes
2 pears, medium-ripe
¼ cup white wine vinegar
½ cup oil
Salt and pepper to taste
½ teaspoon sugar
1 tablespoon prepared mustard
½ cup rich chicken or beef broth
2 tablespoons chopped chives
6 slices bacon

Boil the potatoes in their jackets until they are just tender. Cool, peel and then slice the potatoes into a bowl. Peel the pears and cut them into thin slices; add them to the same bowl.

In a separate, small bowl, mix the vinegar, oil, salt, pepper, sugar, mustard, broth and chives. Pour this over the potatoes and pears. Chill.

Cook the bacon until it is crisp. Remove it to paper toweling to drain thoroughly. Crumble and sprinkle the bacon over the salad just before serving.

BEET, MUSHROOM, AND ENDIVE SALAD

MAKES 4 TO 6 SERVINGS

4 or 5 cooked beets
12 mushrooms
Juice of 2 lemons
6 endive
1 teaspoon salt
½ teaspoon pepper
1 tablespoon chopped chives
½ teaspoon Dijon mustard
2 tablespoons wine vinegar
5 tablespoons olive oil

Peel and slice the beets and set them aside. Clean the mushrooms, trim the stems, and then slice the mushrooms into a bowl. Sprinkle them well with the lemon juice.

Cut the endive leaves in half and arrange them on a platter. Place the beet slices around the edge of the platter; then pile the mushroom slices in the center. Mix all the remaining ingredients in a small bowl and pour the dressing over the vegetables.

MEDITERRANEAN SALAD

MAKES 4 TO 6 SERVINGS

- ½ *cup olive oil*
- 1 *onion, finely chopped*
- 2 *cloves garlic, minced*
- 12 *mushrooms, sliced*
- 5 *tomatoes, peeled and chopped*
- 1 *small eggplant, peeled and cubed*
- 1 *teaspoon salt*
- ½ *teaspoon oregano*
- ½ *teaspoon basil*
- *Juice of 2 lemons*
- 12 *anchovy filets*
- 12 *black olives*
- 12 *green olives*
- 2 *hard-cooked eggs*

Heat the olive oil in a large skillet. Add the onions and garlic and sauté gently until they are limp and light golden in color. Add the mushrooms, tomatoes, eggplant, salt, oregano and basil. Stir carefully and cook just until the vegetables are crisp-tender, about 6 to 8 minutes.

Remove the vegetables from the heat and transfer them to a bowl. Add the lemon juice and allow the salad to cool; then refrigerate.

Arrange the salad in a shallow glass bowl or on any desired serving dish. Place the anchovy filets and olives on top. Cut the eggs into quarters and place them around the edges.

GREEK FENNEL SALAD

4 fennel (about 1 pound)
4 tablespoons olive oil
2 or 3 fresh tomatoes, peeled and quartered
½ teaspoon thyme
1 bay leaf
Juice of 1 lemon
2 cups dry white wine
¼ teaspoon coriander
Salt and pepper to taste

Wash the fennel in cold water. Dry it thoroughly, then cut it into about four pieces each. Heat the oil gently in a heavy pan. Place the fennel, tomatoes and all the remaining ingredients in the pan. Cook gently for 25 to 30 minutes. Let the salad cool; then refrigerate it. Serve very cold.

This is a refreshing departure from the ubiquitous cucumber and tomato arrangement.

ZUCCHINI AND TOMATO SALAD

MAKES 6 SERVINGS

4 small zucchini
4 tomatoes, sliced
3 tablespoons lemon juice
4 tablespoons olive oil
1 tablespoon vinegar
1 clove garlic, finely minced
1 teaspoon salt
½ teaspoon pepper
½ teaspoon marjoram

Wash and dry the zucchini. Slice them and arrange the slices alternately with the tomato slices on a glass plate. Thoroughly mix all the remaining ingredients in a bowl. Pour the dressing over the zucchini and tomato slices and serve promptly.

SHRIMP AND CRABMEAT SALAD TOURLAVILLE

MAKES 6 SERVINGS

1 pound shrimp, cooked and peeled
½ pound crabmeat, cooked
1 hard-cooked egg, chopped
1 cup finely chopped celery
4 radishes, sliced
1 carrot, grated
Juice of 1 lemon
1 cup mayonnaise
1 tablespoon prepared mustard
1 tablespoon ketchup
½ tablespoon chili sauce
¼ teaspoon salt
¼ teaspoon mace
¼ teaspoon summer savory

If the shrimp are large, cut them into pieces. Put them into a bowl with the picked-over crabmeat, the egg, celery, radishes and grated carrot. Mix gently.

In another bowl, thoroughly mix all the remaining ingredients. Put both bowls into the refrigerator to chill thoroughly. Just before serving, pour the dressing over the salad ingredients and toss very lightly but thoroughly. Serve on shredded lettuce.

SALAD DRESSINGS

How you dress a salad is most important. I don't happen to believe in either prepared salad dressing or in so-called Russian, Thousand Island and French dressings. They are heavy — oppressive, in fact — and do nothing but conceal the flavors of your delicious lettuce and garden vegetables. A good salad dressing is merely oil and acid (wine vinegar or lemon juice) seasoned so it is compatible with the rest of your menu. Common sense tells you what is and what isn't compatible. Just think of what a knockout blow to your senses it would be to follow a delicate lemon chicken with a spicy dressing laden with garlic. Or how impossible it would be to appreciate a vaporously light lemon dressing after dining on spaghetti and meat balls.

Also, please don't have your lettuce swimming in dressing. Toss your lettuce at the last moment, with just enough dressing to glisten the leaves. I prefer that my salad greens be presented in a large bowl — large enough so there is tossing space. I pour a minimum of dressing onto the greens at the instant of serving, toss the salad at the table, and serve it *toute de suite*. I also prefer that the salad bowl be glass or porcelain; most wood salad bowls are made of cheap wood that becomes glucky, smelly and unhygienic from lingering oils.

As for seasoning the dressing, I advise you to put everything together ahead of time, so the seasonings will have time to marinate. Probably you will be using dried herbs rather than fresh ones. If so, you can't expect them to give you the full flavor that fresh herbs do when sprinkled into your dressing, or onto your salad, at serving time. The way to get the most from dried herbs, salt, pepper and other seasonings is to begin with your wine vinegar or lemon and add the seasonings to this. The reason is that, while herbs and seasonings do not melt well in oil, they will expand in the acetic liquids and release their flavors. Even though you use only a smidgeon of vinegar or lemon in proportion to oil, it will be enough to capture the flavors. Give the marriage of herbs and liquid 2 or 3 hours; then add your oil. Mix the dressing together and store it in a covered jar until you are ready to use it. I must caution you, though, that any more than a whisper of onion or garlic will make your dressing become overpowering if you let it marinate ahead of time. So it is better to add those ingredients later.

Now a little information about oils. Good olive oil is very rich, and quite expensive. It's best to buy a good imported, commercial olive oil; the offbeat local ones are usually not refined properly, are heavy, and become rancid quickly. France and Italy produce some excellent olive oils; the Greek oils tend to be heavy. For pure green salads that I'm not going to doctor with spicy herbs, I like to use a peanut or corn oil. Best of all is walnut oil; unfortunately, it's very expensive.

VINAIGRETTE SALAD DRESSING

1 tablespoon wine vinegar
2 tablespoons corn oil
½ teaspoon salt
¼ teaspoon pepper
Pinch of marjoram
½ tablespoon chopped parsley

Mix the vinegar and oil in a bowl, or in a bottle with a cover. Add the remaining ingredients and mix everything together very well. This will dress a salad to serve 4 persons, or the recipe can be doubled and the leftover dressing can be kept in a covered bottle in the refrigerator.

SALAD DRESSING AUX FINES HERBES

⅓ cup red wine vinegar
1 teaspoon tarragon
½ teaspoon basil
½ teaspoon oregano
¼ teaspoon monosodium glutamate
1 egg yolk
Salt and pepper to taste
1 tablespoon chopped chives
1 clove garlic, minced fine
⅔ cup corn oil

Put the vinegar into a bowl. Add all the remaining ingredients, except the oil. Blend together very well with a whisk. Mix in the oil and blend again. Then set the dressing aside for about an hour, for the flavors to blend well.

SALAD DRESSING À LA MOUTARDE

⅓ cup vinegar
⅔ cup oil
1 tablespoon Dijon mustard
¼ cup finely chopped onions
1 tablespoon lemon juice
1 tablespoon capers
Salt and pepper to taste

Put the vinegar into a small bowl. Beat in the oil; then add all the remaining ingredients. Mix very well.

DILLED SALAD DRESSING

2 tablespoons red wine vinegar
1 teaspoon salt
½ teaspoon pepper
1 teaspoon dill weed
½ teaspoon tarragon
1 small onion, finely minced
4 or 5 tablespoons corn oil

Put the vinegar into a small bowl. Add all the remaining ingredients, except the oil. Mix thoroughly with a whisk and chill. Just before serving, mix in the oil.

BLUE CHEESE SALAD DRESSING

⅓ cup wine vinegar
⅔ cup mayonnaise
¼ cup corn oil
1 clove garlic, minced
¼ teaspoon monosodium glutamate
1 teaspoon dry mustard
¾ cup crumbled bleu cheese
Salt and pepper

Mix together thoroughly the vinegar, mayonnaise, oil, garlic, monosodium glutamate and dry mustard. Stir in the cheese; then add salt and pepper to taste.

SALAD DRESSING DIABLO

⅓ cup wine vinegar
⅔ cup olive oil
2 tablespoons finely chopped anchovies
2 cloves garlic, finely minced
2 teaspoons chopped chives
1 teaspoon Worcestershire sauce
½ teaspoon Tabasco sauce
1 teaspoon dry mustard
Salt and pepper to taste

Put the vinegar into a bowl. Add all the remaining ingredients and mix very well with a whisk.

13
Desserts

IF IT WERE up to me I would have only fruits for dessert. Maybe I feel that way because when I was a kid I loved desserts so much and, as my family was not a wealthy one, could have so few that I took a job as an apprentice in a pastry shop. After only one month's work among the mounds of cloying, treacly concoctions, my lust vanished. Since that wanton experience, sweet desserts have had no appeal for me whatsoever. Now, when I do have occasion to choose something ambrosial, I prefer enchantments that are light and simple, like Crème Caramel (page 241). Still, to me fruit is the very best finishing touch for any meal.

That's me. You and your guests are entitled to more voluptuous desserts. So I will give you some marvelous recipes that I learned in Paris. Good French *pâtissiers* use only the very best butter, eggs, cream and chocolate. These pastry chefs work with candied fruits and flowers, spend time, and use their artistry to create exquisite masterpieces — always. The results are such wondrous delights that the pastry shops ought to be in every tourist guidebook along with the Louvre and the Eiffel Tower.

When you are planning the dessert for your menu, be aware of the texture of the entire meal. Be careful not to mix a spicy, heavy entrée with a feathery, cloudlike dessert. Or vice versa. The effect will be that of an elephant in a porcelain shop! Co-ordinate your foods, the way you co-ordinate the colors and textures of your costumes.

FRUIT SALAD

MAKES 4 TO 6 SERVINGS

½ cup apricot nectar
2 ounces kirsch
1 Anjou pear
1 Bartlett pear
1 Delicious apple
2 oranges
½ cup seedless white grapes
½ cup Tokay grapes
1 banana
Strawberries, raspberries or blueberries

Combine the apricot nectar and kirsch in a bowl. Peel, core and slice the pears and apple. Put them into the bowl, making sure the fruit is covered with the liquid. Peel and section the oranges so no bitter rind or white pulp remains. Add the orange sections and the grapes to the fruit in the bowl, cover with plastic film, and chill. Just before serving, peel and slice the banana, and add it, along with the berries, to the bowl of fruit. Stir carefully to mix. The number of servings depends on the total amount of fruit used.

Note: Without the addition of banana slices and berries, the fruit salad will keep well in the refrigerator for 3 or 4 days.

Crème Pâtissière is the cream that goes into French open-face tarts. (These tarts look so beautiful that, when I do them on television, I am always showered with compliments.) The cream, however, is also a versatile and delightful accompaniment to various fruit dishes.

The pastry shell is sweet and flaky, and light as a sigh. Th fruits are never seasoned with cinnamon or cloves, as they are in America; we use vanilla, sometimes a little nutmeg for a spice, and perhaps a liqueur. You can use canned fruit as effectively as fresh, when you want to eliminate the time-consuming business of poaching. I like to present a French tart with a lace paper doily under it, on a plate, so it looks like a Valentine.

CRÈME PÂTISSIÈRE

MAKES 2 CUPS

1 quart milk
8 egg yolks
1 cup sugar
1 teaspoon vanilla
1 cup flour

In a saucepan, scald the milk and keep it hot over medium-low heat. In a large bowl, beat the egg yolks until they are very light in color. Gradually add the sugar and then the vanilla, while continuing to beat. When the mixture is very light, beat in the flour.

Very slowly, pour the mixture into the hot milk, beating continuously with a whisk until the cream is smooth and thick. Remove it from the heat and pour it into a large glass dish. Let the cream cool to room temperature, stirring it occasionally to prevent the formation of a crust. Cover and refrigerate until needed.

HONEY-GLAZED BAKED APPLES WITH APPLEJACK CREAM

MAKES 6 SERVINGS

6 baking apples, peeled and cored
1 cup dry white wine
6 tablespoons honey
¾ cup applesauce
¼ cup applejack, divided
1 cup Crème Pâtissière
½ cup heavy cream, whipped
Dash of vanilla or Grand Marnier
⅛ teaspoon ground cloves

Put the apples in a baking dish; pour in the wine. Put 1 tablespoon of honey on top of each apple; then bake at 350°F. until the apples are tender, about 30 minutes. Cool and chill.

Mix the applesauce with 1 tablespoon of the applejack. Fill the center cavities of the apples with the applesauce mix. Mix the Crème Pâtissière with the whipped cream, vanilla or Grand Marnier, and the remaining applejack. Pour this cream sauce over the apples. Sprinkle the tops lightly with ground cloves and serve.

FRESH STRAWBERRY CRÈME

MAKES 6 SERVINGS

- *1 quart fresh strawberries*
- *2 tablespoons superfine sugar, divided*
- *½ ounce kirsch*
- *1 cup heavy cream*
- *2 cups Crème Pâtissière (page 233)*
- *½ teaspoon vanilla*

Wash and hull the strawberries. Reserve 6 large, perfect berries for garnishing. Cut the remaining berries into quarters and mash them lightly with a fork in a bowl. Stir in 1 tablespoon of the sugar and the kirsch, mixing gently.

Whip the cream. Stir in the remaining tablespoon of sugar. Fold the whipped cream gently but thoroughly into the Crème Pâtissière, adding the vanilla. Fold in the mashed strawberries. Chill until serving time.

Serve in sherbet glasses or large wine glasses, topping each serving with a whole strawberry.

POACHED PEARS WITH CRÈME PÂTISSIÈRE

MAKES 6 SERVINGS

- *6 firm, ripe pears*
- *2 cups water*
- *1½ cups sugar*
- *1 teaspoon vanilla*
- *2 ounces kirsch, divided*
- *1 cup heavy cream*
- *3 tablespoons superfine sugar*
- *1 cup Crème Pâtissière (page 233)*

Peel the pears, leaving them whole with the stems intact. Remove the cores by cutting through the bottom of each pear. In a heavy saucepan, over medium heat, make a syrup of the water and sugar; then add the vanilla and 1 ounce of kirsch. When the sugar is entirely dissolved and the mixture is boiling, carefully place the pears in the syrup. Lower the heat and let the pears simmer until just tender, about 10 minutes. Do not overcook. Remove the pears with a slotted spoon to a dish and allow to cool.

Whip the cream with the superfine sugar, and fold the whipped cream into the Crème Pâtissière, adding the remaining ounce of kirsch. Chill for use.

When the pears are cooled, carefully fill them, through the cored bottoms, with the chilled cream. Place them in a serving dish and spoon additional cream over the tops.

This dough is used to make the famous French tarts, and it is one that you don't have to treat like a Christmas-tree ornament. Handle it as much as you need to; it's spunky enough to take it without turning nasty on you. Devote your attention, instead, to the care of your rolling pin. *Never* wash or scrape it, or the wood will swell or warp, and dough will cling to it. A wipe with a clean damp cloth is ample hygiene for a rolling pin.

SWEET DOUGH

2 cups flour
½ cup sugar
¼ teaspoon salt
¾ cup butter
2 eggs
¼ teaspoon vanilla
2 ounces almond paste (optional)
Parchment paper
Dried beans

Mix the flour, sugar and salt in a bowl. Cut in the butter very well. Add the eggs, vanilla and almond paste (if used). Knead the dough well to make it very smooth. Let the dough rest for about an hour in a cool place; then roll it out and fit it into a 10-inch pie plate.

Prick the dough all over very well with a fork. Fit a piece of parchment paper over the dough and fill the pie plate with a layer of dried beans. (This is to keep the crust flat during baking.) Bake in a 400°F. oven for 8 to 10 minutes, or until the crust is golden brown. Remove the beans and the paper and let the crust cool. It may then be used for Tarte aux Fruits (page 236).

TARTE AUX FRUITS

1 pie crust (Sweet Dough, page 235)
2 cups Crème Pâtissière (page 233)
1 small can apricots, drained
1 small can sliced pineapple, drained
1 small can pears, drained
1 jar apricot preserves

Fill the baked crust about three-quarters full with Crème Pâtissière. (The *crème* may be flavored with a liqueur, if desired, by adding an ounce or two of kirsch or Grand Marnier.)

Arrange the well-drained fruit on the *crème* in an attractive design. Heat the apricot preserves in a small saucepan and strain them into a bowl. Brush this glaze over the fruit. Refrigerate the *tarte* until serving time.

Note: If using strawberries, cherries, or other dark fruit, glaze with warmed currant jelly.

TARTE AUX POMMES NORMANDE

(Normandy Apple Pie)

MAKES 8 TO 10 SERVINGS

2 tablespoons plain gelatin
½ cup cold water
4 cups applesauce
⅓ cup sugar
2 tablespoons applejack, brandy or cognac
1 teaspoon vanilla
Sweet Dough (page 235)
1 jar apricot preserves
4 apples, preferably red Delicious
2 or 3 tablespoons sugar
Juice of half a lemon
2 tablespoons butter

In a small saucepan, soften the gelatin in the cold water for about 5 minutes. Put the applesauce in another saucepan with the sugar, liquor and vanilla. Put the applesauce pan over low heat and cook, stirring occasionally, until the mixture is nicely thickened. Put the small saucepan with the gelatin over heat just long enough to melt the gelatin; then stir the gelatin into the applesauce mixture. Set aside.

Roll out the sweet dough and fit it into a 10-inch pie plate, allowing enough pastry around the edge to make a collar about ½ inch above the edge. Prick the shell all over with a fork, cover with parchment paper, fill with dried beans, and bake in a 375°F. oven 10 minutes, until the crust is a light golden color.

Put the apricot preserves into a saucepan and heat slowly until the jam is liquid. Press it through a sieve into a bowl, discarding the skin and reserving the purée for glazing the pie after the baking is complete.

When the pie shell is done, remove it from the oven and pour in the applesauce mixture. Peel and slice the apples. Arrange them over the applesauce and sprinkle with 2 or 3 tablespoons of sugar, depending upon the sweetness of the apples. Sprinkle with lemon juice and dot with butter. Return the pie to the oven and bake at 375°F. for 25 to 30 minutes, until the apples are soft and done. Remove from the oven and, while pie is still warm, brush the top with the apricot purée. Cool and then chill for 4 hours before serving. May be topped with whipped cream or ice cream.

BRIOCHE ORDINAIRE

1 yeast cake
½ cup warm milk (not hot)
3 to 3½ cups flour
5 eggs
2½ teaspoons salt
5 teaspoons sugar
¾ pound butter, at room temperature
½ cup water

TOPPING FOR ROLLS:
1 egg
1 teaspoon sugar

Dissolve the yeast cake in the warm milk. Put the flour on a large mixing board and make a well in the center. Beat the eggs in a bowl, adding the salt and the milk-yeast mixture. Gradually pour this into the center of the flour, and work the flour into the liquid to make a dough. Add the sugar and butter while continuing to mix the dough with your hands. When all the ingredients are blended together, the dough should be nice and smooth, and should easily form into a ball.

Put the dough in a floured bowl and cover it with a damp towel. Refrigerate it overnight; then use as directed for Jambon en Croûte, page 117.

Note: If it is to be used the same day, put the dough in the freezer for about an hour, or until the dough is good and firm.

Any leftover dough may be made into rolls by pinching off pieces and forming them into balls. Put the balls in greased muffin tins. Mix 1 egg with 1 teaspoon of sugar and brush the tops of the balls with this mix. Cover the tins with a towel and let the dough rise in a warm place until the balls are doubled in volume. Bake in a 375°F. oven for 15 to 20 minutes.

APPLE STRUDEL

DOUGH:

2 cups flour
½ teaspoon salt
1 whole egg, large
2 tablespoons melted butter
6 to 8 tablespoons water

STUFFING:

4 red apples
1 teaspoon vanilla
½ cup white raisins
¼ cup chopped walnuts
Rind of 1 lemon, grated
¾ cup sugar
¼ cup melted butter
3 tablespoons powdered sugar

First prepare the dough. Sift the flour onto a board. Add the salt, mix, and then make a well in the center. Now combine the egg, butter, and 6 tablespoons of water, and pour this into the well. Begin to mix the liquid with the flour, working from the center outward, until the dough is smooth. If the dough seems to be too hard and inelastic, use the last 2 tablespoons of water, but only if needed.

Roll the dough out into a large rectangle and roll it so it is as thin as possible. Place it on a large, floured cloth towel, and brush it with the 2 tablespoons of melted butter. Cover the dough and let it stand for 30 minutes.

Peel, core and cut the apples into thin slices. Place the slices in a bowl with the vanilla, raisins, walnuts, lemon rind and sugar. Toss the ingredients and let them stand for about 15 minutes; then spread this apple mixture over the dough and sprinkle half of the melted butter over it.

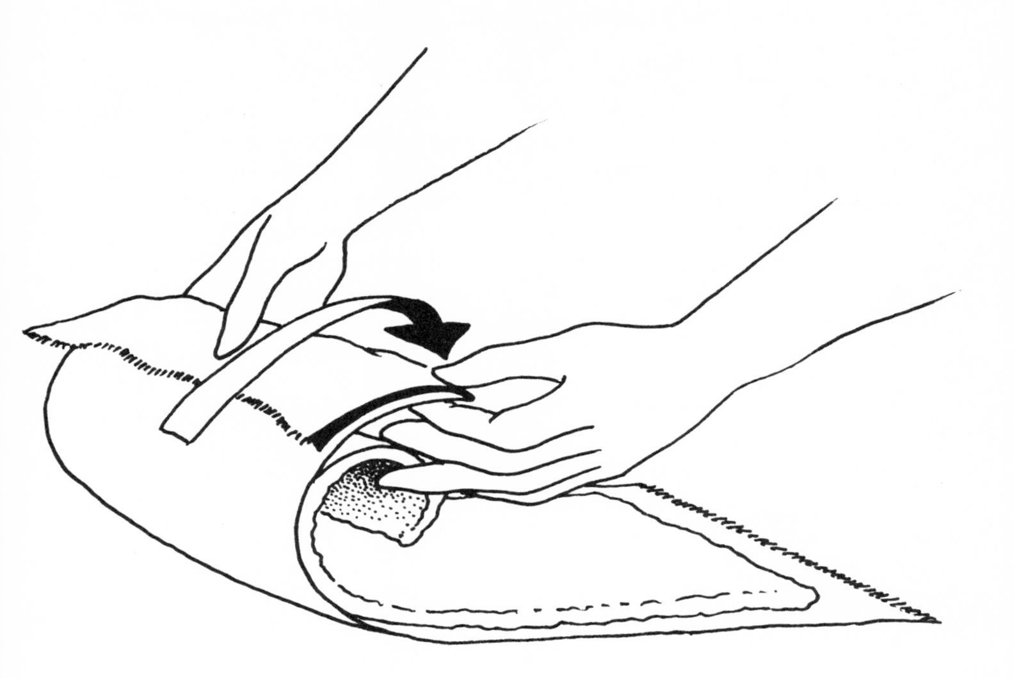

Roll the dough up into a cylinder, using the cloth towel to lift the dough as you roll it. Place the roll, seam-side down, in a lightly buttered baking sheet. Prick the dough with a fork to allow some of the steam to come out, and brush the top of the dough with the remaining butter. Bake in a preheated 350°F. oven for about 45 minutes. Cool the strudel and sprinkle it with the 3 tablespoons of powdered sugar.

This banana-studded, citrus-confettied sauce is as rich and smooth as satin. Give it the flourish of a fast, dazzling flame, making sure everybody's watching as you do, and spoon it onto mounds of vanilla ice cream. Hearts will melt.

BANANA FLAMBÉ

MAKES 6 TO 8 SERVINGS

4 tablespoons butter
½ cup honey
Juice of half a lemon
Juice of half an orange
½ teaspoon grated lemon rind
½ teaspoon grated orange rind
2 bananas, peeled and quartered
2 ounces rum
1 ounce crème de banane
6 to 8 scoops of vanilla ice cream

Melt the butter in a heavy saucepan over medium heat. Add the honey and blend it into a smooth sauce. Add the lemon and orange juices and the rinds. Heat thoroughly. Add the bananas and heat only until warm. Then turn the heat very high and let the pan get hot. Remove from the heat. Add the rum and *crème de banane.* Place the pan back on the heat, tip it toward the flame and let the contents catch fire for a few seconds. Spoon the banana flambé over scoops of vanilla ice cream placed in individual, glass serving dishes.

This is a glamorous dessert — the kind that looks as if you'd slaved over it for hours, and had attended the chef's school in Lausanne for many years. In fact, it's a very simple dessert to construct; even the gorgeous coverlet of meringue whips up in moments and takes only three ingredients.

PINEAPPLE MARTINIQUE

MAKES 4 TO 6 SERVINGS

1 whole, ripe pineapple, halved lengthwise
4 bananas, peeled and sliced
2 tablespoons butter
1 tablespoon honey
¼ cup dark rum or brandy
¼ cup Cointreau
4 egg whites
Pinch cream of tartar
4 tablespoons sugar
1 pint vanilla ice cream
4 tablespoons brown sugar

Scoop out a large cavity in each pineapple half. Chop up the fruit from the centers. Sauté this with the banana in the butter and honey. Pour the rum and the Cointreau over the fruit, heat and flambé. Set aside.

To make the meringue, beat the egg whites with the cream of tartar and the sugar until the whites are very stiff. Then put half the ice cream into each pineapple shell. Pour the flambéed banana-pineapple mixture over the ice cream. Pile the meringue over all, making sure the fruit is sealed to the edges. Sprinkle with brown sugar. Bake in a 450°F. oven for 6 to 8 minutes, or until the meringue is lightly browned.

This is a creamy custard and an elegant classic. It has the finesse required for your most discriminating party guests, and is soothing enough to tame the wildest of your tribe at the family dinner table. I tell you, the French think of everything!

CRÈME CARAMEL

MAKES 6 SERVINGS

½ *cup water*
¾ *cup sugar*
2 *cups milk*
2 *teaspoons vanilla (or a 2-inch piece vanilla bean)*
¼ *cup sugar, additional*
4 *eggs, well-beaten*

Put the water in a heavy saucepan and stir in the ¾ cup of sugar. Bring the water to a boil, stirring until the sugar is completely dissolved. Lower the heat and allow the syrup to simmer for about 20 minutes. Watch carefully toward the end of the simmering time, when the syrup begins to color. When it is about the color of maple syrup, remove the syrup from the heat. Pour a small amount of the syrup into each of 6 heavy custard cups, turning each cup until it is nicely coated.

Scald the milk (heat but do not boil), with the vanilla bean, if you are using one. Remove the pan from the heat and remove the bean from the milk. Mix the additional ¼ cup of sugar into the milk; then slowly pour this mixture into a bowl containing the well-beaten eggs. Mix quickly. If you are using extract instead of a bean, add the vanilla. Pour this custard mixture through a strainer and into the caramel-coated custard cups, dividing it equally.

Place the cups in a large, shallow baking pan. Pour enough hot water into the baking pan to come about three-quarters of the way up the outside of the cups. Bake in a 325°F. oven for 1 hour, or until a silver knife inserted in center of the custard comes out clean. Cool the cups on a rack; then chill the custard thoroughly before serving. To serve, run a silver knife around the edge of each cup, to loosen the contents; invert the cup over a glass serving dish and unmold the custard.

My friend Pat Linden, who helped me write this book, has a lust for chocolate that is nonpareil. I am positive that she would commit mayhem if her daily, unbridled indulgence of her fondness for chocolate were denied her. In obeisance to Pat and to all the irrepressible chocolate junkies of the world, I present you with instructions for the sweet, velvety, whipped-cloud perfection called Chocolate Mousse.

MOUSSE AU CHOCOLAT

MAKES 4 TO 6 SERVINGS

6 ounces semi-sweet chocolate
2 tablespoons water
½ teaspoon powdered, instant coffee
4 eggs, separated
Pinch cream of tartar
½ cup heavy cream
2 teaspoons vanilla
1 teaspoon rum

Combine the chocolate and water in the top of a double boiler. Place over hot water and heat until the chocolate is melted and the mixture is smooth when stirred. Stir in the instant coffee and blend well. Set aside and keep warm.

Beat the egg yolks very well until they are light in color and ribbony in texture. Fold them into the warm chocolate; then refrigerate the mixture until it is set.

Whip the egg whites with a pinch of cream of tartar just until soft peaks form. Stir about 2 tablespoons of the beaten egg whites into the chocolate mixture and blend well. Carefully fold in the remaining egg whites. Whip the heavy cream and fold in the vanilla and rum. Then fold this into the chocolate mixture.

Spoon the mousse into dessert cups or wine goblets. Chill for at least 5 hours; then serve it topped with a garnish of whipped cream, and a few curls of chocolate, if desired.

Instructions have frequently been given by *haute cuisine* chefs that egg whites must be whisked in a copper bowl, to achieve their fullest possible volume. I think some of those chefs are still taking their instructions from the nineteenth century, before we had more convenient devices at hand and when we still had a bevy of servants within elbow's reach to do the cleaning and scrubbing that we now must do ourselves.

While it may be true that a copper bowl makes eggs stand up better because of the chemical reaction that takes place, we have replaced expensive copper bowls with more practical china ones, and we can also replace the acidic reaction of the copper. Home

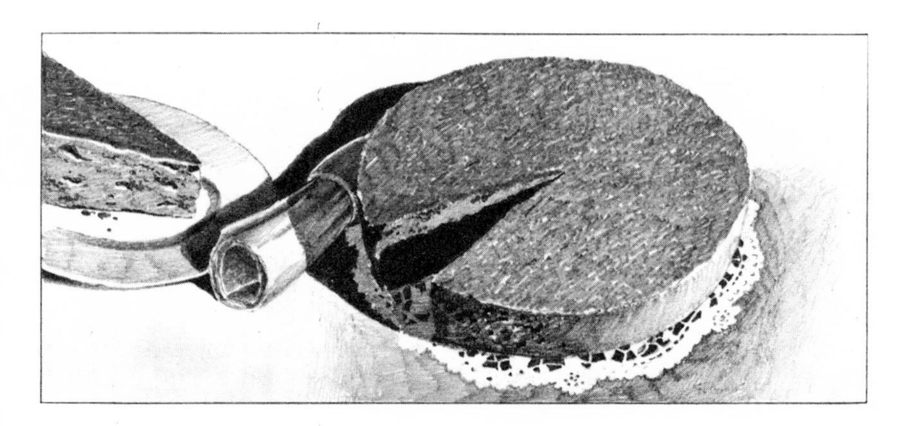

economists tell you to use a pinch of cream of tartar, which is basically a form of salt. It works just fine. But cream of tartar isn't always sitting there ready for you to grab. So when you haven't any, just use a pinch of salt instead. Either way, you will have puffed-up egg whites, and with no trouble at all.

OEUFS À LA NEIGE

(Eggs in the Snow)

MAKES 6 SERVINGS

- 5 *egg whites*
- ½ *cup sugar*
- 2½ *cups milk*
- ½ *cup water*
- 6 *tablespoons sugar, additional*
- 2 *tablespoons flour*
- 2 *egg yolks, well-beaten*
- 1 *teaspoon vanilla*

Beat the egg whites to soft peaks. Add the ½ cup sugar gradually and continue beating to form very stiff peaks.

Combine the milk and water with the additional sugar in a large, shallow pan and bring the mixture to a gentle simmer. With two spoons, form snowballs out of the beaten egg whites. Carefully lower each ball into the simmering milk and poach them for about 2 minutes. Turn each snowball and cook for another minute; then remove them with a slotted spoon and drain on paper toweling.

Place the flour in a bowl and add about ¼ cup of the hot poaching liquid. Beat with a whisk until the mixture is smooth. Stir in another ¼ cup of the liquid; then add the beaten egg yolks, stirring constantly. Return this mixture to the poaching liquid remaining in the pan and cook, stirring constantly, until the custard thickens. Add the vanilla. Let the custard cool; then chill it. Spoon the chilled custard into individual dishes, float the snowballs on top of the custard, and serve.

All the magic of Europe is baked into a Génoise. This very moist, opulent sponge cake weds happily with a variety of fillings and toppings. Mocha is just one of the many fillings you can use.

MOCHA GÉNOISE

1 tablespoon butter
1 tablespoon flour
BATTER:
¼ pound sweet butter
2 cups flour
1 teaspoon baking powder
8 large eggs, at room temperature
1 cup sugar
1 teaspoon vanilla

Prepare an 8-inch springform pan (or use two round layer pans, each 8 by 1½ inches) by coating it thoroughly with a tablespoon of butter and then sprinkling it with a tablespoon of flour. Set the pan, or pans, aside.

Melt the sweet butter and cool it slightly. Sift the flour with the baking powder and set it aside. Break the eggs into a large bowl and beat them very thoroughly. Then gradually add the sugar, while continuing to beat. Continue beating (an electric mixer at high speed is best) until the mixture holds soft peaks, like a meringue, when the beaters are withdrawn.

Carefully fold half of the sifted flour into the beaten egg mixture; then fold in the cooled butter and finally the remaining flour. Fold in the vanilla.

Pour the batter into the prepared pan or pans. For a springform pan, bake in a 350°F. oven for 30 to 35 minutes, until the cake shrinks slightly from the sides of the pan and is springy to the touch. If you are using layer pans, bake at 350°F. for 20 to 25 minutes. Remove the side from the springform pan and cool the cake on a rack. Or invert the layer-cake pans on a rack and allow them to cool until the cake layers can easily be removed.

When the cake is thoroughly cool, slice it carefully into 3 layers with a serrated knife. For the layer cakes, split each one in half. Prepare the filling.

FILLING:

4 eggs
14 ounces confectioners' sugar (a 1-pound package minus ½ cup)
1 pound soft butter
1 tablespoon powdered, instant coffee
1 tablespoon cocoa

In a large bowl, beat the eggs very well. Add the sugar and continue beating until the eggs are frothy and pale yellow in color. In another bowl, work the butter to a very smooth, soft paste with an electric beater. Slowly add the egg mixture to the butter, to make a smooth cream. Stir in coffee powder and cocoa. Spread this mocha cream between the cooled cake layers. Glaze with fondant.

GLAZE:

½ pound fondant (or ½ pound confectioners' sugar, 2 egg whites, and 1 tablespoon lemon juice)
1 tablespoon coffee powder
Brandy or coffee liqueur

Fondant may be purchased in many bakeries, in specialty food stores, or in the gourmet section of supermarkets. If you cannot find it, it can be made at home by stirring together vigorously ½ pound confectioners' sugar and 2 egg whites until the mixture is the consistency of cream. Add 1 tablespoon of lemon juice, the powdered coffee and brandy, and proceed according to glazing directions that follow.

If using purchased fondant, first melt it slowly over low heat. Combine the coffee powder with a little water and a little brandy; stir this into the fondant. Use the flavored fondant to glaze the Génoise, letting the glaze dribble down the sides of the cake. Decorate, if desired, with candied fruits or flowers or toasted almond slices.

MERINGUE NUT TORTE

1½ cups blanched almonds
1 cup skinned hazelnuts
1½ cups sugar
8 egg whites
Pinch cream of tartar

Spread all the nuts out on a cookie sheet or a jelly-roll pan. Bake them in a 450°F. oven for 20 minutes, checking during the last 5 to 10 minutes to be sure the nuts are not getting too brown. Remove them from the oven and cool. Lower the oven heat to 250°F.

When the nuts are completely cool, put a cupful into a blender and blend to the consistency of coarse cracker crumbs. Transfer them to a bowl, and continue blending until all the nuts are done. Mix the sugar into the nut crumbs. Set aside.

Beat the egg whites with the cream of tartar until they are stiff. Gradually and carefully fold in the nut-sugar mixture. Spray a baking sheet with a non-stick food spray. Spread the meringue on the sheet in strips, so that you have 4 bands, each measuring about 11 inches long and 4 inches wide. Bake in a 250°F. oven for about 40 minutes, or until the tops are crusty. Invert the baking sheet onto waxed paper and carefully remove each meringue strip. Cool them on racks.

When you are ready to assemble the cake, put one strip of the meringue onto a serving platter. Spread it with chocolate Butter Cream (page 248), and add a second layer of meringue. Spread this

with liqueur-flavored Butter Cream; top with another meringue layer and spread that layer also with liqueured cream. Add the final meringue layer. Put the remaining chocolate cream on the top of the final layer and around the sides of the entire cake. Decorate the finished torte with almond halves or maraschino cherries — as you wish. Chill at least 2 hours before serving.

BUTTER CREAM

1 cup sugar
⅓ cup water
Pinch cream of tartar
8 egg yolks
1 pound sweet butter, softened
1½ tablespoons kirsch
3 teaspoons or more cocoa

Combine the sugar, water and cream of tartar in a saucepan. Stir and bring it to a boil over medium heat. Cook until the mixture reaches 240°F. on a candy thermometer, or until a small amount forms a soft ball when dropped into cold water.

While the syrup is cooking, beat the egg yolks until they are very light. When the syrup is ready, cool it slightly; then beat it into the egg yolks, allowing a thin stream to flow while beating. Add the butter, and beat until very light and smooth. Refrigerate until needed.

When you are ready to use the butter cream, divide it so that there is about one-third in one bowl and two-thirds in a second bowl. Flavor the smaller amount with 1½ tablespoons kirsch. Flavor the larger amount with 3 teaspoons cocoa, or more, to your taste. Use as filling for Meringue Nut Torte (page 247).

This dessert tastes maddeningly marvelous, and the recipe is almost too simple to be true. But the result has great style and is quite different from routine cheesecakes. Here are some insights that will ensure success.

When melting chocolate, do *not* stir continually or it will become hard rather than smooth. Melt the chocolate over water, in a double boiler, and leave it there until ready to use, so it will remain melted.

Be sure the raisins are thoroughly presoaked in the brandy.

The batter will look frighteningly thin as you pour it into the pan. Don't worry; it gets itself together in the baking.

Fill the springform only to about an inch of the rim, to leave room for rising. The cake will settle down again later.

To unmold, release the sides of springform. With a long spatula, gently and slowly separate the cake from bottom of pan. Center a paper doily over the bottom of the cake, and the cake plate over that. Then invert.

CHOCOLATE RUM CHEESECAKE

CRUST:

18 vanilla cookie wafers

¼ cup butter, melted

Grated rind of 1 lemon

FILLING:

1½ pounds cream cheese, at room temperature

1 cup sugar

3 eggs

10 ounces semisweet chocolate bits, melted

¼ cup raisins, soaked in rum

1 ounce dark rum

1 teaspoon vanilla

2 cups sour cream

To make the crust, crush the vanilla wafers into fine crumbs. Put them into a bowl. Add the melted butter and grated lemon rind. Mix thoroughly; then press the crust into the bottom of a 9-inch springform pan. Refrigerate.

Put the cream cheese into a bowl. Beat with an electric mixer until smooth. Add the sugar gradually and again beat well. Add the eggs, one at a time, mixing well after each addition. Beat in the melted and cooled chocolate. Using a wooden spoon, stir in the raisins, the rum, vanilla and sour cream. Mix very well. Pour the mixture into the prepared springform pan. Bake in a 350°F. oven for 1 hour and 10 minutes. Allow the cake to cool to room temperature; then remove the outer rim of the springform. Refrigerate the cake for at least 2 hours before serving.

SCHWARZWALD TORTE

(Black Forest Cherry Torte)

8 eggs, separated
1 whole egg
1 tablespoon water
1 cup sugar
¾ cup fine, dry bread crumbs
⅓ cup unsweetened cocoa
½ cup flour
½ cup slivered almonds, chopped
1 jar commercial filling for cherry pie
1 teaspoon kirsch
1 pint heavy cream
2 teaspoons vanilla
2 or 3 tablespoons sugar, additional
Finely shaved, bitter chocolate
Maraschino cherries

Lightly grease and flour a 9-inch, round cake pan and set it aside. With a whisk, beat the 8 egg yolks, the whole egg, and the water together thoroughly. Beat in the sugar; then add the bread crumbs and mix well. Mix together the cocoa and flour and stir it into the egg and crumb mixture. Stir the chopped almonds into this batter.

Beat the 8 egg whites with an electric beater until they are stiff but not dry. Stir a few tablespoons of the egg whites into the batter; then fold in the remaining beaten whites, carefully and very thoroughly. Pour the mixture into the prepared cake pan and bake in a 350°F. oven for 25 to 30 minutes, until the cake tests done. Turn it out onto a rack and allow it to cool completely.

While the cake is baking, mix the cherry filling together with the kirsch, and put this in the refrigerator to chill.

When the cake is completely cooled, cut it into 3 layers. To make even layers, use a sharp knife and first go completely around the cake, cutting into the edge only about an inch. Using this cut as a guide, cut all the way through.

Whip the heavy cream with the vanilla and the additional sugar until it forms soft peaks. Put one layer of the cake onto a flat plate. Put the prepared pie filling onto this layer, keeping the filling an inch away from the edges of the cake. Place the second layer of the cake on top of the cherry filling. Sprinkle with a little kirsch, then spread this layer with some of the whipped cream. Place the remaining cake layer on top; frost the sides and top with the remaining cream. Sprinkle shaved chocolate over the top and sides and decorate with maraschino cherries.

A pouf of air, scented with orange-laced liqueur, the soufflé is, to many, the *ne plus ultra* of desserts. This *is* a luxurious dish, though relatively inexpensive. It's romantic, too, and like any romance you want to turn out well, it requires gentling. Don't try to rush this recipe; wait until the last possible minute to fold in the egg whites, or they will become watery.

A trick to make the soufflé soar readily is to butter the inside of the mold. The butter will melt with the dusting of sugar you'll apply, and help to move things along. The butter-and-sugar trick also means you don't have to construct a collar around the mold, a step I find rather a nuisance.

After you have placed the soufflé in the oven, gently and tenderly close the oven door and allow your masterpiece to bake and rise until it peaks about 2 inches above the rim of the mold. When it is done, bear your triumph to the table instantly, for the golden crown will soon descend. Mate the soufflé with cups of piping hot chocolate, for the ultimate experience.

SOUFFLÉ AU GRAND MARNIER

3 tablespoons butter
3 tablespoons flour
5 egg yolks
¾ cup milk, hot
¼ cup sugar
2 tablespoons Grand Marnier
Pinch cream of tartar
5 egg whites

Melt the 3 tablespoons of butter in a heavy saucepan. Add the flour, mixing well until smooth. Stir in the egg yolks. Add the hot milk gradually, stirring until very smooth. Stir in the sugar. Cook over medium heat, stirring continuously, until the custard is thickened. Remove the pan from the heat and beat the custard well for another minute or two. Stir in the Grand Marnier. Set the custard aside while you prepare a 1½-quart earthenware soufflé dish by buttering it very well; coat the dish with some sugar and shake out the excess.

Add a pinch of cream of tartar to the egg whites and beat them until they are stiff but not dry. Take about 3 tablespoons of the whites and stir this into the custard mixture. Add the remaining egg whites, folding them in gently and carefully.

Pour the mixture into the prepared soufflé dish, put in a 375°F. oven and bake for 25 to 30 minutes, or until the top is nicely browned.

Serve the soufflé promptly as is, or with fresh strawberries or sliced peaches that have been marinated in kirsch.

FROZEN BANANA DAIQUIRI SOUFFLÉ

MAKES 4 TO 8 SERVINGS

4 egg whites
2 cups heavy cream
1 teaspoon vanilla
3 tablespoons superfine sugar
3 large bananas
2 ounces dark rum or crème de cacao, or a combination of both
2 cups Crème Pâtissière (page 233)

Beat the egg whites until they are stiff but not dry and set them aside. Whip the cream with the vanilla and sugar until soft peaks form and set aside. Peel the bananas, cut them into chunks, and put them in a blender with the liqueur. Process until very smooth; this should make 2 cups of banana purée.

Combine the purée with the Crème Pâtissière; then fold in the beaten egg whites very thoroughly. Fold in the whipped cream; then put the mixture into 2 large or 4 small soufflé dishes. Place in the freezer until firm.

CRÊPES

1 cup flour
2 eggs
2 tablespoons melted butter or oil
1 cup milk
3 teaspoons sugar (for dessert crêpes)
½ teaspoon salt
½ teaspoon vanilla
¼ cup beer

Put the flour, eggs and butter into a bowl and blend them together. Then add the milk gradually, beating it in well with a whisk and making sure the mixture is very smooth each time. Add the sugar, salt, vanilla and beer to the mixture. The consistency of the batter should be that of light cream. If it is too thick, add a little more beer or milk. Pour the mixture through a sieve, pressing through as much as possible. Let the mixture rest for at least an hour before making the crêpes.

With a piece of paper toweling, put a fine film of oil in a crêpe pan. Get the pan very hot. Put about 2 ounces of batter into the hot pan. Turn the pan about to coat it completely. When the batter is nicely browned, turn the crêpe quickly to brown the other side. The crêpe may seem hard when done, but it will soften as it stands.

Wipe out the pan with a towel that has oil on it. Pour in more batter and continue until all the crêpes are cooked. Stack them up as they are finished, grouping them by fives or sixes, with waxed paper in between.

It is recommended that you make crêpes on the day they are to

be served. If made in the afternoon for evening use, keep them from drying out by covering them with a clean, damp towel and refrigerate them until they are needed.

This recipe will make about a dozen crêpes. If they are to be filled with seafood, chicken, or meat mixtures and used for a main dish, omit the sugar and vanilla. Add instead a pinch of nutmeg. For dessert fillings, see the following two recipes.

VANILLA-ALMOND SAUCE FOR CRÊPES

1 cup sugar
½ cup water
¼ cup boiling water
1 pint vanilla ice cream
½ cup slivered almonds

Combine the sugar with the ½ cup of water and bring this to a boil while stirring. Continue cooking until the syrup is a light brown. Add the boiling water a little at a time, stirring constantly.

Put a small scoop of ice cream in each crêpe and roll the crêpes up neatly. Put them into individual serving dishes. Pour some syrup over each top, sprinkle with slivered almonds, and serve at once.

GRAND MARNIER SAUCE FOR CRÊPES

1 cup sugar
½ cup orange juice
½ cup water
¼ cup boiling water
Juice of 1 lemon
2 ounces Grand Marnier
1 pint vanilla ice cream
1 orange, sectioned

Combine the sugar with the orange juice and the ½ cup of water. Bring this to a boil while stirring constantly; let the syrup cook until lightly browned, stirring occasionally. Add the boiling water a little at a time; then add the lemon juice and the orange liqueur.

Scoop ice cream into the crêpes; then roll and place them in serving dishes. Spoon the sauce over the crêpes and top them with orange sections. Serve at once.

14
Wine and Cheese

WINE

HAS IT OCCURRED to you to wonder why nearly every Frenchman, from Premier to peasant, is able to quickly and unerringly choose the wine that's just right for his meal every day of the week, while most Americans — rich, poor, and medium — make a big, bewildered fuss over the subject? The reason is that, in France, we are brought up with wine as you are brought up with milk; it is a fact of everyday life. Naturally, we are accustomed to drinking the modest wines of our country — not the great, rare and expensive treasures; and we enjoy their nuances with little ado. Here, wine-drinking is a relatively new experience and quite another story. For one thing, until quite recently, you've had to rely on imports; California wine-making and the widespread distribution of these products are relatively new developments. For another, the American public has been trained to trust advertising and publicity more than its own common sense. The inexperience is not your fault, but it has resulted in a lack of confidence, confusion, and a great deal of twaddle. Let me try to make it simple for you.

The wines to drink with meals:

Harmony is all you need look for; pleasure is what you're after. It stands to reason that a full-flavored, robust wine will overpower and detract from a dish that has fragile flavor. And that a light, delicate wine will taste as insipid as water with a spicy, tangy meal. So choose the wine that suits the dish. And, if the dish has been concocted with a wine, choose the same type of wine to drink. It needn't be the identical wine, mind you; merely the same type.

For example, a French red Burgundy wine tastes delicious with Boeuf Bourguignon, and so does a California Zinfandel, because they're the same general type. Coq au Vin, which is made with red wine, partners naturally with a similar red wine for drinking. The adage, "White meat with white wine; red meat with red," is merely a guideline. Use your own mind and palate, according to the occasion. Fish is as nice with a light red wine — a Bordeaux or rosé — as it is with a white wine. You may find that a sauce or side dish will dictate the choice.

When you are neither fearful nor self-conscious, you can relax and enjoy yourself. With your own experience to guide you, you'll quickly agree that a red wine with an acidic food, such as vinegar or tomatoes, sets up an unpleasant metallic taste in your mouth. So you'll avoid serving such wine with salad dressings of vinegar, or with tomato dishes — not because the "connoisseurs" tell you to, but because your own common sense says so.

The general types of wine:

There are scores of medium-priced wines that you'll love. Save the fifty-dollar rarities for rare occasions, and shun the cheap "bargains" as you would frozen TV dinners. The latter are shoddy, raw-tasting and a terrible punishment for the palate. The following list gives the regions and the types of wines they produce, whose names you'll use most frequently when you want to put your best glass forward.

RED BORDEAUX, also called claret. These vary in taste from fairly light and soft to fruity and complex. The Bordeaux region includes the district of Médoc, which produces the wines of Margaux, St. Julien, St. Estèphe, and Pauillac; the district of St. Émilion; the district of Pomerol; and the district of Graves. The Médocs are lighter-bodied than the wines of St. Émilion and Pomerol.

WHITE BORDEAUX The dry to medium-dry white Bordeaux wines come from the district of Graves. The district of Sauternes, which includes the wine of Barsac, produces exceedingly sweet white Bordeaux; you would drink them with a sweet dessert.

RED BURGUNDY wines vary from mellow to authoritative, from robust to earthy. In the lighter group are the Beaujolais wines, which include Fleurie and Moulin-à-Vent. Also delicate are the wines of Côte de Beaune, which includes Pommard and Montrachet. More robust are the Côtes de Nuits wines and the Côtes du Rhône wines, the latter of which includes Hermitage.

WHITE BURGUNDY wines include Pouilly-Fuissé, a dry and fruity wine from Mâcon; Meursault, a dry white from the Côte de Beaune; and the famous dry and light Chablis, from the north of Burgundy.

THE LOIRE VALLEY produces the dry white wines of Pouilly-Fumé and Sancerre, the dry to sweet wines of Vouvray, and the rosé wine of Anjou.

GERMAN WINES are better alone than with foods, they range in taste from dry *(natur)* to very sweet and include Riesling, Moselle, Sylvaner, and Gewürztraminer.

ITALIAN WINES include the reds: Chianti, Barolo, Valpolicella, Bardolino; and the whites: Soave, Verdicchio, Orvieto.

California wines:

The California vintners produce some excellent wines, but not in mass quantities; that is, those that are produced in mass quantities are good, but not superb, table wines. However, a well-made Cabernet Sauvignon, or other California varietal wine (a varietal contains at least 55 per cent of the grape it's named for), can be as good as a very good red Bordeaux from France. An admirable wine is an admirable wine wherever it comes from and deserves your sampling. And junk is junk, no matter the label. Take it from me, the *vin ordinaire* of my country is a very pitiful beverage, not nearly as pleasing as your well-made everyday California wines.

If you're accustomed to the types of French wines but not to those of California, this table may help you in your selections.

CALIFORNIA		FRANCE
Cabernet Sauvignon	is like	Red Bordeaux
Sauvignon Blanc	is like	White Bordeaux
Pinot Noir	is like	Red Burgundy
Pinot Blanc	is like	White Burgundy
Zinfandel	is like	Red Burgundy
Gamay Beaujolais	is like	Beaujolais
Chardonnay, or Chardonnay Blanc	is like	White Burgundy
Chenin Blanc	is like	White Loire

Champagne:

For my taste, champagne isn't a very good wine to drink with a meal because the bubbles make it too filling. But if you do go hog-wild for some royal occasion and serve a champagne dinner, serve a good French *brut* or California champagne, and plan the menu so you will have champagne from the appetizer through dessert. Another luscious way to celebrate is to serve champagne with dessert only.

As for which champagne, I must tell you — not because I am a Frenchman, but because it is fact — that by law the only champagne there is comes from the Champagne region of France. However, California "champagne" can be very good, even though it is an utterly different wine from the French one. Given the choice between an expensive California or a cheap French champagne, I'd buy the California.

Cooking with wine:

I find that I'm using wines in cooking more and more, because modern meats and vegetables have become vapid. The way we're growing foods now, quickly and with chemicals, many of them lack the flavor I once knew. It's become impossible to duplicate the meals and recipes of my childhood unless I *add* something that will help put back the vanished taste. Wine, I find, is the pleasing, agreeable addition.

There is nothing complicated about cooking with wine. Here are the only two keys you need: Always use a wine that is not extravagantly priced, but that is good enough to drink by itself. Incorporate the wine while the food is cooking, so the flavors will marry. If you add wine after the dish is cooked, the acid gives a bitter taste.

CHEESE

If you're going to eat cheese, eat cheese. Good, honest cheese, not that weird processed and pasteurized stuff that's like waxed paper or doctored-up car wax. One clue to buying real cheese is where it comes from. The glorious cheeses are from France, Italy, and Holland, for those are the cheese countries. The American contribution to the world's great cheeses is Cheddar.

In cooking, cheese serves as a binder and a flavor booster. The most frequently used cheeses are Swiss, Parmesan and Romano. Some American dishes are made with Cheddar, for its sharp taste.

In a meal, cheese comes after the salad and before the dessert. Personally, I could have a meal just of cheese, but that's because I come from Europe, where there is such an incredible variety of exalted cheeses that have been lovingly, even secretively, processed, nurtured and aged.

Think how useful cheese is. There you are — the entrée is finished and the salad is cleared away — with a little wine left in the bottle and a last piece of bread. What better way to enjoy those last tantalizing sips of wine? And what better accompaniment for the cheese than the wine?

As the centuries have proven, the most satisfactory way to serve after-dinner cheese is to have a small assortment — say a Swiss, a Camembert and a bleu — on a tray or platter. Each guest can then select the one he prefers. Of course, you will have taken the cheeses from the refrigerator an hour or two ahead of time, so they can attain room temperature. You can't really taste anything that's ice-cold. After the cheese, if those riches haven't done you in, thirty or forty relaxing minutes later, you can have your sweet dessert and coffee.

Cheese trays at cocktail parties are something else. Serve as many or as few as you wish. Since no dinner is to follow, the rich cheese won't steal appetites away and ruin your culinary efforts.

15 Culinary Clues

GOOD THINGS TO KNOW

Avocados:

When using only one-half of an avocado, leave the pit in the other half and wrap it in plastic wrap to prevent contact with air. The acid in the pit will keep the avocado green.

When making Guacamole or another dip with avocado, leave the pit in the dip until you're ready to serve it. The pit will keep the dip's vivid color.

Bread:

French toast, bread pudding and poultry stuffing are best made with bread that's slightly stale.

To make bread crumbs easily, use the blender. Store extra bread crumbs in containers in the freezer.

Butter:

Sweet, unsalted butter is preferable to salted butter, because you can control the amount of salt you want to taste, if any. It also burns more slowly than salted butter, when heated.

A combination of butter and oil for heating reduces the hazards of burning and splattering.

I never use margarine because I dislike the flavor.

Cheese:

Grate dried-out cheese in the blender and store in the freezer.

Make Parmesan bread to go with soup or salad by sprinkling grated Parmesan cheese over buttered bread slices and then toasting them in the oven until they are crisp.

Citrus fruits:

Select oranges, lemons and grapefruits by hefting them in your hand. If they feel heavy for their size, they will be juicy.

When grating the rind, grate some extra and store it in small plastic bags in the freezer.

Eggs:

Cover extra egg whites and store them in the refrigerator for later use. Store the yolks in a dish of cold water.

Fat:

"Lard" is pork fat that's been rendered and clarified.

The drippings from bacon are superb for frying potatoes or for rubbing down their skins before baking.

Garlic:

To dice or chop garlic, sprinkle it with salt to hold the bits together. To crush garlic easily, smash it with the flat side of a heavy-bladed knife.

Garlic salt:

This product contains a lot of salt and not much garlic. Be sensible when you use it.

Lemons:

To get the most juice from lemons, let them stand in hot water a few minutes before cutting them. When you need only a few drops, just puncture a hole in the lemon and squeeze it; that way you won't dry out a whole lemon for a mere drizzle.

Here is Dr. Bernard's magic potion: If you burn your hand, quickly apply a slice of lemon to take the ouch away.

Milk:

Soak pans and plates that have contained milk, eggs, or cheese immediately in cold, not hot, water to reduce sticking.

MSG (Monosodium Glutamate):

This "Chinese medicine" improves the flavor of foods, but use it with reserve. The slightest pinch is usually more than enough. If you go overboard, you will get a headache.

Oils:

Olive oil is discussed in the chapter on salad dressings. Corn oil has a lovely color and stands up to a good deal of heat. Peanut oil is very flavorful. Vegetable oil made with soybeans has a flavor that I find strange.

Corn, peanut and soy oils are interchangeable, depending on the flavor you want. Olive oil is good in salad dressings that are made with spicy herbs, and in heavy, spicy dishes. Olive oil and one of the other oils, mixed half and half, is an excellent and efficient preparation. Olive oil and butter, mixed half and half, is good for sautéing or frying.

Onions:

What makes you weep is the volatile oil that sprays upward as a vapor when you cut the onion. Peel onions under cold, running water to reduce the effect of the spray.

Paprika:

If you use paprika for sautéing meat, be careful, because it burns quickly and will give you a flavor other than the one you're looking for.

Parsley:

To keep parsley or watercress a week or two in the refrigerator, wash it, stand it with the stems in a glass of water, and cover the whole thing with a plastic bag secured by an elastic band.

Pasta:

A drop or two of oil in the boiling water will help keep pasta strands separate while cooking.

Use leftover pasta in the next day's soup; use fresh-cooked pasta to stretch out yesterday's leftovers *en casserole.*

Precooking:

A great many foods can be partially cooked the day before, then cooked to completion at mealtime, and still be crunchy, pretty and flavorful. Professional chefs do this all the time, but with care; the final cooking must be done very gently.

Salt:

The best salt for cooking is sea salt. Iodized table salt is less "salty" than sea salt, and requires somewhat more lavish use. Coarse salt is used when preparing large quantities of food.

To help remove the smell of fish or onion, rub your fingertips with salt and rinse them under cold water.

To correct an overly salty soup or stew, add a lump of raw potato and simmer.

Sour cream:

When there isn't any sour cream in the house and you *must* have some, stir a little lemon juice into fresh cream and let it stand a few minutes to "sour."

Spices:

Avoid buying fancy, expensive spices that you use once and never again.

Vinegars:

Wine vinegar has a nice flavor, is abundant, and is excellent for salad dressings. My second choice is cider vinegar, for mundane things. White vinegar is used for pickling.

Water:

Boiling water is an art and requires practice. It is important to know just the right degree of boiling: too low a simmer will not cook properly, nor will a savagely fomented surf.

Whipped cream:

You can whip cream ahead of time, place it in mounds on a sheet of waxed paper and freeze it; then transfer the mounds to plastic containers for continued freezing.

MEASURING BY METRICS

For a long time the United States used a system of measurements different from the most of the world's. As a result, thousands of cookbooks remain anomalous, and hundreds of thousands of cooks have to think with two heads. If the now nearly universal metric system is still awkward for you, here is a simple explanation to get you over the hump.

In Europe, solid ingredients are listed by weight, according to the standard unit of a gram. The U.S. system has been to list these ingredients by volume, in arbitrary terms such as a teaspoon and cup, or by quantity, such as 2 eggs. To illustrate how the metric method of measuring solid ingredients by weight standardizes, simplifies, and makes measuring more exact, consider the problem of measuring ¼ cup of butter. It is messy and imprecise to cram butter into a cup, measure it accurately, and remove it for use. Measurement by weighing the butter atop a metric scale, however, until the scale shows 64.5 grams is easy and foolproof.

In the metric system, liquid ingredients are listed by a standard unit of capacity — 1 liter, which can be divided into 10 deciliters or 100 centiliters. A liter equals 1.0567 liquid quarts or 33.8 fluid ounces; a deciliter equals 3.38 ounces; a centiliter equals .338 ounces.

Cooking with metrics means using exact measure. But it won't change your way of cooking a whit. Just as now, you'll be free to use more-or-less amounts of ingredients, guided by your own taste and guesswork. Cooking will *not* have an added worry! The only time exact measure is ever important is when you're baking, so you can learn to use metrics for that. And I advise you not to discard your old equipment; you'll need it to follow old recipes. As a bridge from old to new, you may find it helpful to use measuring cups, scales and other devices that show both former U.S. and metric measurements. This conversion table will also be useful in the interim until you can do things in your head.

Remember that what you'll actually be using will be liters and grams presented in round figures — rather than as translations from cups and pounds, which aren't real comparisons. You'll find conversion tables quite useful when you want to translate a metric recipe back into grandma's equivalents.

METRIC CONVERSION TABLE

1. Liquid Measures

Former U.S.	*Metric*
1 cup = 8 fluid ounces	2.37 deciliters
1 tablespoon = ½ fluid ounce	1.5 centiliters
1 teaspoon = 1/6 fluid ounce	0.5 centiliters
1 pint = 16 fluid ounces	4.73 deciliters
1 quart =32 fluid ounces	9.46 deciliters

2. Solid Measures

Former U.S.	*Metric*
1 pound (16 ounces)	453 grams
2.2 pounds	1000 grams (1 kilogram)
3 ½ ounces	100 grams

OVEN TEMPERATURE EQUIVALENTS

Farenheit	**Celsius or Centigrade**
225°F.	105°C. (cool)
275°F.	135°C. (very slow)
325°F.	160°C. (slow)
375°F.	190°C. (moderate)
450°F.	230°C. (hot)
500°F.	260°C. (very hot)

OTHER EQUIVALENTS

1 cup heavy cream whips to double its volume, yields 2 cups
1 pound peas in the pod yields 1 cup shelled (average)
3 bread slices, ½-inch thick, yields 2 cups bread crumbs
¼ pound cheese yields 1 cup grated cheese
1 pound shelled nuts yields 4 cups chopped nuts
1 cup uncooked macaroni doubles in cooking, yields 2 cups
1 cup uncooked rice triples in cooking, yields 3 cups
1 pound unpared apples yields 3 cups pared, sliced apples (average)
1 good-sized onion yields about ½ cup diced onions
3 small onions yield about ½ cup diced onions

Index